"This insightful book presents the belief that sacraments and liturgy are based on the most fundamental experiences of human life, and that they derive their true meaning from a broad-based 'sacramentality' of human life. Everyone in academic and pastoral circles teaching or studying sacraments will find this a must book."

Thomas Simons
Modern Liturgy

"Cooke's *Sacraments & Sacramentality* is delightful. It takes friendship as its point of departure, not baptism or eucharist, as is customary. Using what is the stuff of everyday life for most Christians, Cooke has opened up new vistas of theological understanding and religious appreciation."

Commonweal

"Human symbol-borne self-transcendence provides the context for this comprehensive treatment of the sacraments. The compassionately and beautifully written book is a clear pool of profound personal wisdom, yet it is well grounded theologically, even though the theology comes through effortlessly...."

The Living Light

"The book abounds in fresh ideas. The pastoral details of sacraments are seen with clarity and beauty as the reader looks at sacraments through Cooke's wide-focus lens. This book is eminently useful for Christian adults. All teachers and pastoral personnel will find it a valued resource and a stimulus to rethink Christian rituals. The book attractively presents magnificent ideas capable of provoking the reader to think and act as a Christian in the modern world."

Robert Y. O'Brien
Religious Education

"Each book by Bernard Cooke seems to be even better than the last, and this one is no exception. It is a splendid book for which religious educators, clergy, and searching adult Christians generally have been waiting. Those in educational and pastoral ministries will be especially appreciative of the synthesis of continuity and creativity in this volume. There is nothing like it in existence."

Monika K. Hellwig
wn University

D1113244

"Bernard Cooke's volume is a bold, thorough, step-by-step approach that takes people where they are and leads them through their human experiences to the experiences of encounter with God. A book for the times, insightful, wide-ranging, it should go a long way in positioning the sacraments in a context congenial to the mind of post-Vatican II. It is, I think, destined to be a standard for a long time."

William J. Bausch
Pastor and Author, *A New Look at the Sacraments*

"A unique feature is Cooke's innovative re-ordering of the sacraments, making friendship the basic sacrament for understanding the meaning of sacramentality, and therefore the paradigmatic sacrament.

"I have found that this book helps students develop a sensitivity to the sacramentality of all of life that is lived in the caring and compassionate lifestyle of Jesus; it enables them to discover implications of the sacraments beyond the liturgical ceremonies themselves."

Joseph Martos
Horizons

"This is a view of the sacramentality of divine and human interaction of a kind we have not had but have needed. I welcome the discussion of symbolic behavior in the forms it takes in the Catholic communion. The richness of the book is its rootedness in the mysteries of redemption, the church, and human life and love."

Gerard S. Sloyan
Author, *Jesus in Focus*

"This book is a positive attempt to move the notion of sacrament away from being something passive to the sacramental reality at the very heart of human consciousness. Cooke unusually but very refreshingly presents friendship as the basic sacrament, because, he says, it is the sacrament of human friendship and it is love of another person that enables us most fully to touch and know God."

Jim Caffrey
The Furrow

SACRAMENTS
&
SACRAMENTALITY

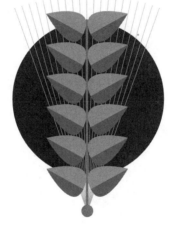

XXIII
TWENTY-THIRD PUBLICATIONS
Mystic, CT 06355

Revised edition 1994

Thirteenth printing 1999

Twenty-Third Publications
185 Willow Street
P.O. Box 180
Mystic, CT 06355
(860) 536-2611
(800) 321-0411

ISBN 0-89622-588-7
Library of Congress Catalog Card Number 93-61190

PREFACE TO
SECOND EDITION

In the years since *Sacraments & Sacramentality* was first published, a number of excellent books on Christian sacraments have appeared, books that incorporate many of the newer orientations of sacramental theology, but none of which suggest a further shift in the course of development. So, why, then, this revision of the first edition?

First, in several instances the changes in this new edition deal with the reinforcement of emerging emphases. Above all, in a number of places I have introduced small changes in the text in order to underline the role of *divine presence* both in sacramental ritual and in the broader contexts of life that bear Christian sacramentality. This represents my growing awareness that with our increasing use of sociological and psychological models to understand "grace" it is necessary not to lose sight of the *divine* activity that lies at the heart of all growth in Christian personhood.

A second element of modification has to do with the treatment of Christian marriage. In the earlier volume I had suggested that it, rather than baptism, was the initial sacramental exposure of a child born into a Christian family. Readers seemed to find this suggestion appealing, but not a few of the unmarried objected to giving marriage a paradigm role when I went on to treat human friendship as revelatory of God's loving and transforming presence to women and men. This objection has merit: It is the reality of human relationships, above all that of true friendship, that is the basic experience of humans which reveals the God known by Jesus as "Abba" to be a loving God—and Christian marriages, though obviously a distinctive form of friendship, function sacramentally insofar as they are relations of mature love.

The lengthiest addition to the text deals with the theological explanations of Christ's presence in eucharistic celebration. Using the earlier edition in classroom teaching of sacraments or in treating the same material in numerous public lectures on eucharist, I was always questioned about the meaning of "transubstantiation." Apparently my earlier avoidance of the term because it is so widely misunderstood was not a good strategy; so without focusing simply on the understanding of that term, I present in this revision a not too technical explanation of eucharistic presence of the risen Christ. I hope that will contribute to people's awareness of Christ being with and for them when they gather in his name for eucharistic liturgies.

For a time I played with the idea of a much lengthier revision, one that would treat at greater length the various sacramental liturgies. However, I rejected this approach because I did not want to distract from the main purpose of this book: to draw attention to the *basic sacramentality of Christian life* that grounds the meaning and effectiveness of the liturgical rituals. Understanding, appreciating, and living out this sacramentality is, I believe, the most important element in the development of Christian spirituality.

CONTENTS

SACRAMENTS & SACRAMENTALITY

INTRODUCTION

C hange generally upsets people, and the changes that have happened in the church during the past few decades have disturbed or at least perplexed many Catholics. For the most part, people have understood the Second Vatican Council as a step forward, as proposing for Christianity a more realistic approach to modern life, and as bringing in "a breath of fresh air." But they are not really certain what the council did; they do not understand the nature of the changes implied in the council's documents, nor why such changes should be made; they have little notion of what, if any, new roles they are meant to play as a result of the council.

Nowhere is this uncertainty more apparent than in Christian sacraments. If there is anything that appears basic and essential to "being a Catholic," it is some participation in sacramental liturgy—children are to be baptized and later confirmed, the sick and dying should be anointed, sins need to be forgiven, and Catholics should share in eucharist, "attending Mass" on a regular basis. It used to be that people understood what was expected of them at such sacramental occasions; they were to be there, attending with reverence and, it was hoped, some understanding of the religious ritual being performed by the pastor. Now the rituals themselves are being altered, some pastors are urging people to take a more active role, and some prominent sacramental practices such as "confession" seem almost to have disappeared.

Since I often give talks or teach classes on the sacraments, I am asked, and with increasing frequency, what it is that is happening. Sometimes the question is fairly anguished: "Is there any future for sacraments?" "Are the sacraments on the way out?" More often the questioner believes that somehow or other it is all going to work out for the better, but he or she would like to understand better what is occurring, so that they can appreciate it, share in it, and even be part of fostering it.

What both groups of people need to be told, and in many instances fortunately are being told, is that a basic shift is taking place in the sacramental life of the church, that this shift is very positive, and that it is a key element in Christianity's coming to greater religious maturity. One way of describing this shift is to say that Christian sacraments are finally coming into their own. This new appreciation flows from a major development of sacramental theology, a development that must be shared on the level of popular understanding if sacraments are to become—as they should—a central element of Christian people's lives.

That is the purpose of this present book: to share this theological knowledge. It is written with no illusions that it will supply exactly what is needed at this moment. No one book can do that. Happily, a number of excellent books that deal with various facets of this need have appeared recently; a selective bibliography in the present book will mention these.

What this book hopes to do is to show that "sacrament" is not something limited to certain formally religious actions. "Sacrament" includes much more than liturgical rituals; as a matter of fact, it touches everything in our life that is distinctively human. Moreover, this book is written with the conviction that sacramental rituals themselves can never be revitalized until "sacrament" is understood and lived in this broader sense. Nor, for that matter, can people thoroughly understand what it means to be Christian if they do not understand the fundamental sacramentality of their human and Christian lives.

I hope this book will be part of the process of Catholics and other Christians regaining a more down-to-earth understanding and appreciation of the significance, that is, the sacramentality, of their lives. So, while its purpose is certainly that of making sacramental liturgies better understood, this book is about a broader topic: the sacramentality of Christians and their everyday lives.

I trust that my attempt to avoid technical language and esoteric discussion will be successful, and readers will come to understand better the reality of sacraments. Still, the topic being discussed and this book's approach to that topic will demand reflective reading; the reader's own human and religious experience will be the constant reference point to which the book will appeal; this will require reflection upon that experience. That Christian sacraments deserve such careful reflection I am convinced; that the same can be said for this particular explanation of sacraments remains to be seen.

For the opportunity to offer this book as part of the ministry to Christian sacraments, I am deeply grateful to my friends at Twenty-Third Publications who suggested it be written and faithfully guided it through publication.

PART ONE

THE SACRAMENTALITY
OF HUMAN EXPERIENCE

1   SACRAMENTS ARE FOR HUMANS

S acrament" is certainly one of the most basic notions in Christianity. It is taken for granted by millions. It is rejected or at least is suspect by other millions. For the most part it is understood very inadequately. Yet, what is involved in sacrament is what is most basic to our very being as humans; it is tragic that this aspect of sacraments has been largely overlooked.

Historical Understandings of Sacrament

For centuries now, the principal meaning of "sacrament" for most Christians has focused on certain ritual actions (baptism, eucharist, etc.), actions that are considered specially "religious." During long periods of our Western history, particularly in the Middle Ages, these liturgical actions were what structured people's lives and experiences. The calendar was really the sequence of the celebrations of Christian liturgical feasts. Rich in symbolism, these sacramental actions were lived by people and relatively little formal explanation was provided. As a matter of fact, much of the explanation that was given (through sermons, for example) was inadequate or even false; thus, the living out of sacraments was frustrated, and sacramental liturgies were deprived of their intended effectiveness.

Surprisingly, it took many centuries for anything like a systematic explanation, and therefore a "definition," of sacraments to emerge in Christian thought. Perhaps the reason was that ultimately sacraments cannot be defined. This was already suggested by one of the earliest words applied to these liturgical celebrations: the Greek word *mysterion.* The celebration of sacraments was the celebration of those ultimate "mysteries" that had been revealed in the life and death and resurrection of Jesus of Nazareth. These mysteries embraced all the deepest mystery of human life, of the created universe, and even of God. Sacramental liturgies brought men and women into a world beyond the purely human, into the realm of the sacred, into contact with divine power and, it was hoped, divine mercy and grace.

Yet, somewhat instinctively, Christians seem always to have retained the notion that there was something fundamentally human about sacraments. While these mystery celebrations were intended to worship and acknowledge God, they were also meant to benefit the humans who performed them. This insight was crystallized in the centuries-old adage, "Sacraments exist for people" *(Sacramenta pro populo).* Even though this principle was often more voiced than observed, it still expressed the realization that Christians were meant to benefit from sacraments, that such benefit was the principal reason for sacramental liturgy.

For the past thousand years or so, this understanding has taken the form of belief that salvation came to people through sacraments; sacraments "give grace." They overcome human sinfulness; they give men, women, and children the moral strength to lead good lives and so reach their destiny; they bring people closer to God.

At the time of the Protestant Reformation, many of the Reformation churches decried any magical understanding of this grace-giving and rightly stressed the link of sacraments with the preaching of the word of God. After all, sacraments are the place where the word of God is communicated to Christians and where their faith is nurtured; it is in faith that they come to God. But this does not in any way deny the grace-giving that takes place in sacramental liturgy; rather, it draws attention to one important aspect of this grace-giving. It draws attention to the fact that sacraments are intended to better humans as human, and that sacraments are, therefore, to be performed humanly.

To many people in the Catholic tradition, this Reformation view sounded like a repudiation of sacraments. And in a large segment of the Reformation there was some rejection, or at least down-grading, of sacraments. So, to safeguard belief in the intrinsic effectiveness of sacraments, Catholic teaching for the past four hundred years has stressed the objective power of sanctification possessed by sacraments. The expression that summarized this teaching was that sacraments work *ex opere operato.*

Unfortunately, this Latin phrase often conveyed to popular understanding the (less than accurate) notion that sacraments worked automatically—one only had to receive a sacrament in order to get grace. Catholic teaching always insisted that the attitude and openness of those "receiving sacraments" influenced the extent to which sacraments could give grace. Yet, this acknowledgment of the need for human input during sacramental actions was overshadowed by the idea of sacraments being channels through which people received necessary spiritual power. At times, the popular understanding of sacramental effectiveness came close to the magical. The action of God in sacraments was seen as mysterious and hidden, as completely unexplainable and spiritual—an understanding of "mystery" that was the very reverse of the New Testament understanding where "mystery" means what God has revealed in Jesus as the Christ.

In a special way this mysterious power was seen to be the privileged possession of the ordained. It was they who by the "laying on of hands" had the ability to perform the sacred actions of changing bread and wine into Christ's body and blood; it was they who were empowered to forgive sins and thus act as people's saviors. So, the ritual activity for the non-ordained came to be viewed as one of *receiving* grace, of being brought into saving contact with God through those who had the "power of orders."

In implicit fashion, one of the two principal elements of sacraments to which this book hopes to draw attention, namely, the saving presence of God, was recognized and honored over the centuries. Even though the common imagery of God's location was that of divine dwelling "up in heaven," and though formal theological reflection developed a "down from above" approach to the granting of grace through sacramental liturgies, there was always something of an assumed awareness that participation in sacramental worship meant an entry into sacred space where one was more in contact with God.

For that reason, underlying much of the sixteenth-century debate about the mode of Christ's eucharistic presence was the assumption that in one way or another *Christ was present* as the community celebration recalled the mystery of his death and resurrection. At the same time, the bitter polemic regarding the character of eucharist points to the lack of explicit connection in people's thinking between the external symbolism and God's saving presence, and between that presence and the causing of "grace."

Present Changes in Understanding

In the last few decades all this has begun to change drastically. As part of the vast social change in the world, people expect religion itself to be much more down to earth, not only giving promise of a better life in the hereafter but being a force for the betterment of the human condition in history. Influenced by the revolutionary shift in our ability today to deal with the forces of nature and society and to begin shaping our environment rather than simply trying to protect ourselves from it, Christians have begun to ask how religion is meant to be part of this new human endeavor. How are people meant to enter into the shaping of their own destiny? Perhaps "grace" is something to be lived creatively instead of something passively received.

At the same time and for a variety of reasons, there has been a noticeable increase in attention to the presence of God in people's lives. This is more than an awareness of the creative power of God sustaining the whole of the universe and especially humans in existence; it is an awakening to the *personal* dimension of Christian faith, to the fact that the great grace given humans is God's self-gift in friendship.

All of this has touched the way in which people think about sacraments. It has begun to change their attitude toward sacraments and their expectations of what gain comes to them from sacraments. How can participation in sacramental liturgies have any real effect on a person? What real difference do sacraments make in people's lives? Or—to limit the scope of expectation—what difference do sacraments make in the whole business of being truly Christian, in the intimacy of one's relationship to God? Even granting that sacraments might have more effect if there were more careful and creative celebrations of these liturgies, do sacraments have any intrinsic power to make either individuals or human society as a whole more truly human?

In responding to such questions, traditional Christian thought, particularly the Catholic tradition, can draw from a rich heritage. For centuries, there has been a recognition, often quite vaguely formulated, that sacraments have some special relationship to the fundamental process of humans being human. Medieval theologians like Thomas Aquinas talked about the way in which the sequence of sacraments (from baptism to last anointing) parallels the stages of a person's life. And in historical periods and cultural situations (such as the Middle Ages in western Europe) in which people's lives were lived out in a thoroughly Christianized context, sacramental activities did accompany the entire course of a person's life. All this was summarized in the theological saying we quoted earlier, "Sacraments exist for people" (Sacramenta pro populo).

Transformation of Our Humanity

It is this basic insight that, in a somewhat new and religiously revolutionary way, Christian thinkers today are drawing upon in order to discover just how sacraments are meant to be a key element in the process of Christians helping to make human life a more truly human and fulfilling reality. What we might suggest, then, as a tentative understanding of Christian sacrament is this: Sacraments are specially significant realities that are meant to transform the reality of "the human" by somehow bringing persons into closer contact with the saving action of Jesus Christ.

If we are to speak of "transforming the human," this raises the questions: What do we mean by "human"? What do we see as the past and present reality attached to this term? What do we see as the possibilities for the future that are contained in this notion?

There are, of course, many points of view in response to these questions. Among them, Christianity's understanding is distinctive; Christian faith believes that Jesus of Nazareth, in his life, death, and resurrection, introduced a very new and decisive element into the vision and the reality of what it means to be human. This is the faith point of view that we will explore, trying to see what its implications are for those of us who share Christian faith. Many others, obviously, will not grant these fundamental presuppositions; at the very least, however, they will be able to see the consistency of Christian belief.

What we are becoming more aware of is that Christianity, while it clearly involves certain rituals that unite the faithful and nourish

their community, is not meant to be a "religion"—at least in the ordinary understanding of that term. Instead, what Jesus began was
a *new way of life*. Christianity is not a part of people's lives; they are
not meant to "have a religion" in the way that they have a profession and certain recreational activities and a particular political
allegiance. Christians' faith is meant to embrace and transform all
aspects of their being and activity. What it means to be human,
what it means to grow as a human, what it means for people to
share life as humans—these have been changed forever by what
happened in Jesus' life and death and continues to happen in the
mystery of his resurrection.

If Christian sacraments are to be transformative, that is, if
Christians are to perform sacraments more effectively, they must
become involved in these actions with a higher level of awareness.
On this point the *Constitution on the Sacred Liturgy* from Vatican II
leaves no room for doubt: ". . . Christ's faithful, when present at
this mystery of faith, should not be there as strangers or silent
spectators. On the contrary, through a proper appreciation of the
rites and prayers they should participate knowingly, devoutly, and
actively."

All this demands a greater awareness of just what it means to be
human. Instead of living at a low level of consciousness, people
must give more direct attention to many things they now take for
granted. To put it bluntly, using the language Saint Paul used centuries ago, we Christians must wake up; we must find out what is
really going on.

What Does Human Mean?

One thing that is absolutely basic to being human is our ability to be
conscious, to be aware of what is going on within us and around
us. This human awareness is more than a perception of what
touches us from outside—many levels of animal life possess this.
We are aware that as self-identifiable knowers we have this perception of "the world." When we reflect on this aspect of our human existing, it is truly a mysterious and wondrous reality.
Though we are confined bodily to the relatively insignificant portion of space that we occupy at any given moment, our range of
conscious existing extends far beyond that. In our knowing we are
able to move far beyond our immediate surroundings. We can
know about things that escape immediate observation (such as the
microbes we can see with a microscope or the subatomic structures

of matter that we cannot directly see); we can think about things (like mathematical formulations) that our own minds have created as abstract ideas and that have no existence outside our thought; we can know about things that happened long ago, and dream about a future yet unrealized.

Because we are knowers, we can extend the range of our human existing in almost infinite fashion; without ceasing we can enrich the world of conscious existence we move in. We can quite literally bring the richness of the universe that surrounds us into ourselves; and we can even add to the wonder and beauty of that world by our own creative imagining—by our music and art and poetry.

Reaching Out to People

By far the most important part of our "going out" to the world around us is our reaching out to people, to men and women and children who share with us this capacity for consciousness. We are not only able to know that these people are there; we are able to touch them in friendship and concern and shared interests. We are able to form human community with them. We are able, that is, to love.

Self-interest we can have (and do); we can and do depend upon others to provide for our needs. But there is something else, human friendship, that has always defied clear explanation or definition. Throughout history, women and men have tried, not too successfully, to grasp the essence of this experience that is such a fundamental, important, and rewarding part of human life. We still do not know exactly how to explain friendship; we do know that it is precious.

Because of this capacity for affective existing, we humans are able to be for one another, to exist together, to share consciousness with and learn from one another. Paradoxically, because of the capacity to love, we can possess one another as friends without limiting anyone's freedom or personal distinctiveness. Of course, this ability can often be used in wrong ways. Many people are incapable of loving maturely; no one of us loves with complete maturity. In greater or lesser degree we try to possess others in ways that exploit them; we use them for our own selfish goals; we wish to cling to others, often with little regard for the other person's good. But when we do things like this, we recognize that this is a poor expression of our power to love; such actions do not really deserve the name "love."

In our better moments we recognize that human love and friendship are a gift and treasure without compare, that no material riches can outweigh it or compensate for it if it does not exist in our lives. With friends, our lives have meaning; without some persons who truly care for us and whom we in turn love, our human existence is drab and lonely and oppressive and shallow. From a religious point of view the very essence of human sin (as we will see later in greater detail) is the deliberate refusal to love. And it is a sin not because there is some abstract "law of God" that says we should love one another, but because denial of love destroys our own personhood and destroys the shared life of human community upon which we all depend in order to be human.

Free to Be

Linked to our ability to know and to love is our human freedom. Clearly, whatever freedom we have is limited by the particular situation in space and time in which we find ourselves. Yet, we do have the power in the most important matters to shape our future and ourselves. We are not able to become Napoleon or Julius Caesar—or for that matter, any prominent person of today—but each of us is able to establish a unique identity as the person we are; we are truly able to decide who and what we wish to be.

No one else can be the person I am; in the last analysis, no one can keep me from being me. While I cannot effectively decide to achieve things that lie beyond my abilities—for example, to become the world's leading sculptor or Olympic athlete—I can decide to be a good and loving and honest person. I can decide to make life happier for those around me. I can decide to be concerned for others and to be of help to them. I can decide to live alert and interested and continually growing in my awareness of the world around me. Yes, there are obstacles to all this; sometimes there are formidable barriers that stand in the way of my becoming the person I wish to be. Ultimately, though, the human person has the ability to surmount these barriers, or perhaps it would be more accurate to say that together, helping one another, we have the capability of overcoming or even removing these barriers.

To live this way—alert, aware, concerned, and loving and open to others, free and self-determining—does not come easily. It is a challenge, a task to be undertaken, a price we have to pay for being truly human. Actually, our Christian faith tells us that this goal would be beyond us if it were not for the personal help of God.

The "contrariness" that is linked with many of the obstacles we face is part of the mystery of evil. There is a power, evil, that is a strange but quite apparent force in our human lives. This force invades the experience of each of us in various ways; it obstructs our attempts together to shape a genuinely human society. It takes the form of dishonesty and infidelity to one another. It takes the form of injustice and exploitation and war. Its power is ultimately so great that only the countering power of divine love is able to overcome it.

Summary

So far, we have been trying to see more clearly what it means to be human, so that we can understand how this humanness is transformed in sacrament. We have done this by reflecting on our ability to be personally conscious of our world, on the ability to reach out to others in friendship, on the power we have to determine freely our own identity and destiny. Another way of coming to a deeper understanding about what it means to be human is to reflect on one's own experience; this we will do in the next chapter. This kind of personal reflection is not just background for understanding sacraments; we will see that it is an integral element in doing sacraments intelligently. Unless one lives reflectively, or at least is trying to become more self-aware, one is incapable of celebrating sacraments in anything but the most superficial fashion. Sacraments are moments of reflection, shared with one another in celebration, that bring together and deepen all our other reflections about life. They are key experiences that provide new insight into our other experiences and so deepen them. The next chapter will lead us into a clearer appreciation of what our experience as humans is and can become.

Questions for Reflection and Discussion

1. What does it mean to say that "sacraments are for people"?
2. What is distinctive about being human?
3. What does it mean to live free?
4. What obstacles stand in the way of our being truly human and free?
5. Why discuss the meaning of "human" in a book about sacraments?

2   TO EXPERIENCE IS TO LIVE HUMANLY

Why concentrate on examining our human experience? From one point of view, the fact that we experience is immediately obvious. No one has to tell me that I am experiencing something. Even if I do not use that term or spend time talking about it, I am inescapably involved in that sequence of states of awareness that make up what we call our human experience. So why pay so much attention to it? The reason for looking at it more closely is precisely because it is so constant and inescapable, because for practical purposes the actual human life of each of us is the sum total of our experiences. I am what I experience.

Experience is not, however, a neutral reality, a given over which we have no control. Whatever might happen to me in a given instance, my experience can be more or less superficial and shallow (or the opposite) depending on the extent to which I am really aware of what is going on. I can just wander from one happening to another without discovering, or wishing to discover, what is going on under the surface, without knowing what forces are at work in my life shaping my development and my future. I can simply put up with or, in some instances, enjoy what is happening, without any attempt to shape the happening by my own insights and values.

To live and experience in such a shallow way is, of course, a "cop-out." I am refusing to accept my humanness; I am living quite irresponsibly. That does not mean that my life should be a tense process of living always on the sharp edge of awareness and decision; that would be enough to drive a person to mental collapse. But we are meant to have a basic control over our life experience. Even in those situations where we have little say about the outside influences that touch our lives and our experience, we retain the power and the responsibility to decide how we will react to those influences. It is up to us to determine how those influences will be allowed to shape the experience of being the particular person each of us is. If, for example, someone criticizes me, I can listen carefully and then intelligently agree or disagree—and perhaps learn something about myself—or I can become defensive and refuse to hear what the person is saying. In the first case, the experience can be that of being helped by a friend; in the second case, the experience may well be that of being personally attacked.

Perhaps part of the reason why many men and women feel so little responsibility for their own experience is that they think of experience simply as something that happens to them. On any given day, their job brings with it opportunities and demands over which they have no control; they can't decide who will be working with them since the activities they share with these people will be decided by others; events in the world at large will have a more or less immediate effect on them, perhaps even determining whether or not they will continue to have their job. And all this is something that happens to them, something that is unavoidable and this is their experience for that day. Most of such experience is routine, very little of it is memorable. Most of it seems to make little difference, but when we think about it, we realize that for each of these people that is what is meant for them that day to be the person each is.

Experience a Given?

We are not as passive, however, as purely receptive in all this as it might appear. Modern studies in philosophy and psychology have highlighted the extent to which each of us builds his or her own world, the world as perceived by us. We are not simply the recipients of stimuli from outside; we sort out and interpret these incoming stimuli. Actually, we have no uninterpreted experiences. We "read" in a particular way whatever happens to us. Each of us fashions his or her particular "world," a reality-as-perceived that may be quite similar to the individual "worlds" of other people, if one is fairly objective about things and fairly honest and open to reality. Ultimately, though, it is distinctive and unrepeatable. No one sees things through my eyes, for no one else experiences things as I do.

Two persons, for example, can have quite parallel exposure to outside influences. They can work side by side on an assembly line doing the same kind of task; they can be neighbors in the same section of town; they can send their children to the same school; they can attend the same church, etc. But one of these persons can go through all this with an optimistic and contented attitude, seeing in these various situations many opportunities for enjoyment and growth and help to others. The other person can view it all in a discontented or blasé fashion, feeling imposed upon by things he or she cannot control, resenting many of the people he or she must deal with. While similar on the outside, the inner worlds of these two persons are quite different. One has built a world in which happiness and personal fulfillment are present; the other has created a world of discontent and frustration. What it means to be human is quite different for these two individuals; what they can and will contribute to other people's human experience is also quite different.

Creating Our Personhood

That sequence of experiences that we call our "life history" is not just a process of creating our particular "world." More radically, it is the process of creating our own person. In the course of all the many experiences through which we pass, we gradually discover who we are. By talking and working and suffering and relating to others in particular ways we come to know ourselves as beings who do those things: communicate and work and suffer and relate to others. Apart from what we have experienced ourselves—and that, of course, includes what we have learned about ourselves from what others have told us about ourselves—we have no way of discovering who and what we are. In a very true sense, each of us as a person is the result of the experiences we have had.

However, our continuing life experience is not only a discovery of our self-identity. We also decide who we wish to be. Obviously, there are limits to such deciding. There is a particular and fairly narrow set of possibilities from which I can pick in deciding who and what I will strive to become. Not to respect this limitation, to try to become someone or something beyond my capabilities is to live with fantasy and to invite disappointment. But within my particular range of possibilities, I do decide in any particular situation how I wish to experience, what I wish to concentrate on and bring to the forefront of my awareness, what I wish to accept as something I identify with, and what I wish to dissociate myself from, whether I wish to deal openly or cynically with others, whether I wish truly to listen to others, or whether I wish to dismiss them out of prejudice or stereotyping.

Naturally, we do not often, if ever, explicitly and formally go through this process of deciding how we wish to experience, and therefore become one kind of person or another. But go through it somehow we do; and it is critically important for each of us to reflect occasionally on her or his experience, to challenge the manner in which one's "world" and selfhood are being shaped. This process we have just described has been called by many names: "becoming mature," "growing up," "achieving holiness," "striving to reach one's destiny," "salvation," etc.

Meaning

We have, then, indicated the extent to which subjective influences enter into our human experiences. Each of us is exposed to an outside world that is objectively there, but no two of us perceive that world in exactly the same way; each makes a personal "world" that bears more or less (we hope more) resemblance to what is actually there. In this process, one of the most important factors is the meaning we attach to various things or to the experience as a whole. So, in preparing to understand Christian sacraments, we might profitably take a closer look at the role of meaning in our lives.

People need to be saved from the apparent meaninglessness of their lives. To a large extent this means unmasking and negating the ideologies, that is, the explanations of "reality" that are propagandized by those in power to reinforce their power—which tell people that they are "little" and unimportant. Such ideologies become immensely influential when, as is often the case, they are unquestioningly taken over by cultures as explanations of the way things actually are. Recently, as a result of the critical, historical, and social analyses by some feminist scholars, we have become aware of the extent to which such ideologies have damaged most women's self-estimation. Nor is this something of the past alone; it says something about the common evaluation today of women's household labors when the phrase "working women" refers to those women who have a job outside the home. What is particularly true of women is true also of all the marginalized people of the world; they are considered "ordinary" and therefore unimportant; and all too often they accept this judgment and think of themselves as unimportant.

It is not accidental that one of the key symbols that has functioned in our world during the past few centuries is the image of "the machine." The ideal of things functioning as they should, with precision and effectiveness and endurance, is that of the carefully constructed and well-oiled machine. We apply the image to basketball teams, to successful political parties, obviously to prosperous manufacturing enterprises, and even to the human person as a cog in that manufacturing process. Our society is product-oriented; we judge people's worth in terms of what they produce; we identify that with achievement and we reward them accordingly. But that leaves human freedom and human dignity out of the picture. Machines do not act freely and they do not have meaning apart from their productive efficiency; and parts of a machine do not have meaning except insofar as they function within the machine.

Meaning seems to have vanished from much of our life today. Any number of twentieth-century thinkers have drawn attention to this threat. Perhaps it has been the experience of two world wars and the danger of a third, or the collapse of so much in human society that had seemed solid and lasting. Whatever the cause, there is little doubt that life in recent years has become more and more meaningless for millions of people. For a large portion of the human race there seems to be no permanent significance in anything they do; they seem to have no importance as people. As far as they can see, they could simply disappear from the scene and nothing would be changed; no one would miss them for more than a short time; history would record neither their life nor their death; no achievement of theirs would live on or have any effect on people. So, what sense does it all make?

But the problem of finding meaning in human experience is not all that new. Humans have always faced the need to make some sense out of the flow of happenings that made up their days and years. To a considerable extent, this is what initiation rites of various kinds were all about. This is what took place as parents guided their children through infancy and childhood. This is, or should be, a principal aim of the formal education we provide for young people. As young persons come to awareness and move toward adult life, those who are older and, we hope, wiser guide them in discovering the meaning of the various occurrences and situations that make up their lives.

The meaning of our experiences is often ambiguous. When, for instance, a person gives a gift, does that mean that the giver is expressing friendship, or offering a bribe that will require future repayment? Or if a student is given a failing mark on an essay, does that mean that the student is slow, or that the student did not work hard enough on the essay, or that the teacher is incompetent, or that the class material is beyond the capacity of an ordinary student of that age, or that the teacher graded the essay with a prejudiced view of the student? For the student involved, for his or her parents, for the teacher, the "objective" fact of the failure is seen differently, and so for each of these persons the failure is, or can be, a quite different "reality."

The Intrinsic Meaning of Experience

When we look at it carefully, we see that the meaning of any experience and the meaning of the things that enter into that experience are intrinsic to the experience itself. Not all experiences are that full of meaning, but some are. And it is these particularly meaningful happenings that have impact on people's lives, on the way they view themselves and their relationships to one another, on the decisions they make, and therefore on the things they actually do, and eventually on the human society they build together.

The aspect of meaning that is most important to a person is the meaning that person attaches to himself or herself. Do I as this particular person have any meaning? What meaning do I attribute to myself? What meaning do I have for others? Suppose that I grow up in a loving and supportive family. In that case, there are persons around me who, in one way or another, are saying, "You mean a great deal to me." To some extent that will come to mean that they need me, just as I need them. But most basically it will mean that for them I am someone, a person who is dear to them and without whom their lives would be somewhat empty. What I mean for them is that life is worthwhile, that there is someone with whom joys and sorrows can be shared, that being together makes life more truly human.

If, on the other hand, I have grown up in a broken home, in a situation where I was unwanted and rejected, it is clear that I have quite a different meaning for those around me, and consequently a very different meaning for myself. Should life be good to me, I may later make some friends who let me know that for them I am important and wanted. But unless this happens, I may continue throughout life with a very negative notion of myself, finding little or no meaning in what happens to me or in what I do.

Often the meaning contained in a given experience is not recognized that explicitly. Quite often it is felt rather than clearly understood; it has its effect on the emotional level rather than on the level of clear perception. Sometimes the meaning of an experience only gradually crystallizes for me. At times the meaning of an experience is single and straightforward; at other times it is ambiguous. When a mother feeds her child, the meaning experienced by the child (perhaps only instinctively by an infant) is that of being cared for, of personal security, etc. When a local candidate for political office invites me to lunch, the meaning is much less clear.

The Role of Key Experiences

So, not all experiences are equally meaningful. Some psychologists and educators have drawn attention to this rather evident fact, and have pointed to the special role of "key experiences." These key or "peak" happenings have more meaning, at least more meaning as experiences. From the meaning attached to these key experiences, a person then finds meaning in the rest of life and establishes a meaning for himself or herself.

There are two kinds of key experiences: 1) There are the striking, out-of-the-ordinary, one-time occurrences—surviving a very serious auto accident, making a scientific discovery, being in a war and working with its victims—that challenge and change the meaning of everything that we thought we understood. 2) There are the more ordinary but basically important experiences that we all share—births and deaths and pain and worry and achievement and friendship—whose meaning affects the meaning of everything else.

Perhaps by looking a bit more closely at two of these latter, more universal experiences we can better appreciate their complex meaning and the impact they have on the meaning of a particular person's life. Let us look at work and death. Work, taken in a broad sense, is certainly one of the most common experiences in human life. Whether it is a parent caring for the home and children, or a man or woman in a factory job, or a lawyer arguing a case in court, or a research scientist in a laboratory, humans with rare exceptions are engaged in some form of work. Yet, "work" can mean very different things for different people.

Even if two individuals are engaged in what is externally the same kind of work—bus drivers—they can view the work in very different ways. For one person the daily routine of bus driving is a constant battle with impolite car drivers, inconsiderate and complaining passengers, unpleasant working conditions, over-demanding bosses, etc. For the other person the daily routine is quite enjoyable—greeting one's regular passengers and coming to know their interests and life stories, watching the seasonal changes in the familiar but evolving territory of the bus route, being able to help strangers find their way in town.

Social analysts have pointed out the extent to which the attitude toward work is a major factor in human life today. Because of the routine and monotony that came with industrial development and increased with technology, work often gives no outlet for a woman or a man's imagination or creative skills. Often, a person is only doing what a complicated machine could do better. The only meaning that the work has is in terms of the marketability of the product; labor is totally product-oriented; the work has no human meaning, at least as far as the worker is concerned. Such an experience of work has proved to be deeply dehumanizing for a large segment of the work force. Some persons seem able to insulate themselves from this depersonalizing effect, but even in these cases the experience of work does not contribute to their life-meaning, except insofar as it provides the financial means for then doing something else more truly human.

As a result of this situation, which unfortunately has applications far beyond what we ordinarily consider industrial work, many humans do not have the experience of personally achieving something by their labor. Their work experience is one of earning money. Personal pride in work well done, a sense of reasonably discharging a role for the good of their fellow humans—these are elements of a healthy discovery of self-meaning that today's work situation rather seldom provides. As a result, a large portion of most people's daily experience is deprived of the human meaning it might and should have.

The Experience of Death

Death is another experience that is not only common but universal. Studies have made explicit the extent to which an individual's or a society's view of death colors their insight into the entire meaning of human existence. It is not difficult to see why this is so. If death is believed to be the end of everything for a man or woman, if one simply ceases to be at the moment of physical death, the years of one's life are viewed quite differently than if one believes that the person does not go out of existence with death, but instead passes into another and more ultimate situation of life.

There are strong indications that the fear of death is at the root of a human's entire structure of fears; in one way or another all the other evils that we fear share in the ultimate evil of death. So, if there is nothing done to change the completely negative meaning of death, there is nothing to prevent the fear of death from being part of all our experience. However, if the meaning of death can be altered, if, for example, it is seen to be not the end of human existence and awareness, but rather the passage into the fulfillment of all that life here was meant to be, then death is not viewed as something to be feared—to be risked, yes—but not ultimately feared by one who has this altered understanding of death's meaning. And if the meaning of death is altered, the meaning of every other experience is radically altered.

We could go on, detailing the effect that comes from key experiences, but the idea is clear. The fundamental thread of experience, from birth through growth to death, has one or other meaning dependent upon one's "philosophy of life"; this meaning influences and forms part of the meaning of every experience we have. All the individual happenings of our days are seen as part of this continuing life history; and the meaning of the history as a whole determines in large part the meaning we attach to any incident in it.

Extraordinary experiences of major importance to a person act somewhat differently as interpreters of life's meaning. Often, because they break into one's daily routine unexpectedly and with unaccustomed meaning, they challenge all the meanings that we thought explained ourselves. Or perhaps they open up vistas of possibility and expectation we never dreamed of. Or they reveal depths of significance in some aspects of our lives that we previously considered rather unimportant and meaningless. Or, especially if they are moments of great tragedy, they bring into question the very existence of any meaning for human life.

Years ago, I had the opportunity to meet and converse with one of the crew of the plane that dropped the atom bomb on Hiroshima. To put it mildly, that happening changed his whole perspective on human life. While his participation in that event was not accidental, none of the crew could have foreseen the awesome catastrophe they were the immediate agents of. Not only was the meaning of this particular action, or of the entire war against Japan, brought into question by the immensity of this killing, the whole meaning of modern humanity was challenged. Could human historical existence make any sense if humans, basically good human beings, were capable of this kind of mass carnage? Needless to say, there must have been at least as much deep questioning among the survivors of Hiroshima.

Somewhat parallel to this instance is the profound effect on the lives of millions of people of the Holocaust, the genocide of millions of Jewish men, women, and children under the Nazi regime in Germany (1930s to 1945). What is particularly instructive about this example is the extent to which a happening of this magnitude can affect not only those directly involved in it (though, obviously, the effect is more intense in their lives), but many others also who in one way or another relate to it or identify with the people directly involved. Jews around the world still resonate profoundly with the whole episode, and they question what it means for them as humans, as Jewish, as believers in the God of Israel. Millions of us who are not Jewish are increasingly facing the question that the Holocaust raises for us: How could such a thing happen in a country whose culture and human progress were as advanced as any in the world and whose Christian traditions were centuries old?

Peak experiences need not be tragic. Many are experiences of success in some endeavor, or encounters with truly great human beings, or experiences of unusual beauty. Even though most of us are not inclined toward scaling the Himalaya Mountains, we can imagine what the experience must be for those who climb a peak such as Everest or Annapurna. Or, again, we can imagine the experience of a talented young pianist performing for the first time with a world-class symphony orchestra.

For many men of my generation the great experience that gave special meaning to their lives was involvement in World War II; it was the great crusade against evil (Hitler in Europe, Tojo in Japan) that was waged for freedom, for our country, we even said "for civilization." Young men from small-town America were exposed to foreign lands and peoples; they had a sense of achievement beyond the expectations of their humdrum lives, and for the sake of the goal they shared they ran the ultimate risk of death. For many of these men nothing since has measured up to the significance of that key experience.

For most of us, the "peaks" are perhaps a bit lower, but they do have special impact on the understanding we have of ourselves and our lives. It may be the recognition given a young student for achievement in school; it may be the experience of a winning team in some sport; it may be the birth of a child; it may be the experience of being chosen to lead one's fellows. For some people there may be a peak experience of God, a sharp awareness of God's reality and loving presence, a genuine conversion experience. This might come in a quiet moment of prayer; it might come unexpectedly in the midst of intense activity; but it leaves the person undeniably aware of closeness to the divine. Beyond our own peak experiences—and we generally have only a few in our lives—we can and do share vicariously in the peak experiences of others: in our reading of literature and history, in movies and plays, in conversations and celebrations.

Friendship as a Peak Experience

For most of us, probably one of the most basic and influential key experiences is friendship. It might be good, then, to take a somewhat closer look at human love and at the way in which it gives meaning to people's lives. It does so, in somewhat distinctive fashion, between parents and children, among siblings, with lovers, and among good friends; but there is a similarity in the way these different situations of loving make human life and each human person significant.

1. A true friendship tells me that I am important, at least to my friend. Things that in themselves may be quite insignificant prove to be of genuine interest to this friend. His or her appreciation of my activity, interest in my ideas and point of view, concern about my well-being are all indications that I do have a real importance for this person. Should something happen to me—a sickness or losing my job or suffering some failure—this is of real concern to my

friend. And should I die, or even just move to another part of the world, I will be genuinely missed by this other person. So, in the process of gradually discovering my own identity, this friendship can give me the assurance that I am not unimportant as a human person.

2. A real friendship can let me know that I am good, and therefore that I can and should love myself. So many people have a lurking worry about their own value. Not only are they insecure about people's acceptance of them, but they have a self-depreciating judgment that if others did not like them they would be quite justified. On the other hand, if someone genuinely loves me for myself, this is the most unmistakable judgment about my goodness; this other person has obviously seen something lovable (that is, good) in me. And if I can accept this person's friendship and with it his or her view of my value, I will have a basis for the self-esteem so critical to my own healthy self-image.

As a friendship grows over some length of time and the friend's judgment of my goodness persists, I can gradually run the risk of letting this person know who I really am. I can take off the masks behind which I ordinarily hide my deepest attitudes, views, and values, the masks that present to the outside world a self that is somewhat different from the self I know in my inmost heart. And—wondrous discovery—even when I do this and my friend comes to know me as I really am, there is still acceptance of me as a friend. As a matter of fact, the revelation of my true self to this other person deepens the relationship and binds this person to me in even deeper friendship.

3. Even if I am not that conscious of it, the friendship gives me a quiet sense of accomplishment. In many little ways, and sometimes in more important ways, I am able to be of help to this friend. I can really make her or his life happier; I can be a personal support to my friend as my friend is for me; I can be a source of human enrichment for this person. Instinctively we are aware that gaining and retaining friends is a major achievement in one's life. People who have amassed no riches, who have gained no renown, who have exercised in their lives no power, rightfully take pride in the fact that they won a wide circle of friends. One thing about this, if one accepts Christian faith in a future life, these bonds of human friendship are the only "riches" that will be carried beyond the grave.

4. Friendships let us know that we are not alone in our human

adventure. Without friends we plod along in a life of loneliness. Perhaps there are persons, psychological "loners," who can survive and even prefer this kind of lonely existence. But for the vast majority of us, life and life's achievements are rather empty if there is no one with whom we can share our hopes and fears and achievements and failures and interests. Life experienced as a sharing in real human community has quite a different meaning than life lived in isolation and loneliness. If my life is to be meaningful, it has to have meaning for someone.

The meaning given a person's life by another's love and friendship is seen most clearly, and is experienced most deeply, when two people "fall in love." For many people, this experience brings a truly human meaning to their lives for the first time; for all those it happens to, it gives life quite a new meaning. One can truly say that scarcely anything in life can be as meaningful as this kind of deep and special love. There is real insight (if one does not become sentimental about it) in the phrase of the popular song, "Lovers are very special people." It is their love for one another that has given a special meaning to their lives, for it is truly a new life, a shared life, that grows out of their love.

But what is more strikingly true of those deeply in love with another is realized in various ways and degrees in every genuine friendship. And, as we will see later in much more detail, for those who in faith accept as a reality the love of God for them as individuals, this divine love can and does have a major effect on the meaning they see in their lives. No person can be considered other than ultimately important if he or she is the object of God's interest, concern, and personal love. To the extent that this divine love can be accepted into one's life and appreciated for what it is, it has a transforming (that is, saving) effect. This means that God's love for humans is the ultimate humanizing influence in their experience.

Summary

Having taken a closer look in the previous chapter at what is distinctive about being human, we saw in this chapter that being human is equivalent to experience. The sequence of experiences that make up our life history is what it means for us to be human.

However, what we actually experience in any happening depends upon the meaning we perceive in that happening. This perceived meaning is partially discovered in the event and partially imposed on it by our interpretation, for we inevitably interpret whatever happens to us.

Among the experiences each of us has, some key experiences carry more meaning than others and therefore influence the meaning we give all our experiences. Some of these key experiences are extraordinary, such as a serious accident; others, like work or death or friendship, are part of each person's life. We will see how these latter give us special entry into the interpretation of life that is intrinsic to Christian sacraments. But first we must look more closely at the process of interpreting experience, since this is what sacraments are meant to do.

Questions for Reflection and Discussion

1. Explain: I am what I experience.

2. Is it true to say that each person makes the world that he or she experiences? Why?

3. How do we know what our experiences of life mean?

4. What is meant by a "key experience"?

5. Explain how the experience of death influences our interpretation of life.

3   INTERPRETING EXPERIENCE

I n our attempt to grasp more adequately the basic sacramentality of our human lives, we have seen, so far, the central importance of whatever meaning is contained in our personal experience. Underlying much of what we have talked about is the fact that our experience is always an interpreted experience. Even if we are mature people who have learned to be quite objective about ourselves and about what is happening around us, we inevitably see things from our particular point of view. This individual interpretation is so much a part of the experience itself that we usually are not even conscious of it, but the interpretation makes the experience to be what it is for us.

Suppose, for example, that I am walking at night along a dimly-lit street and suddenly a group of six young men cross over from the other side of the street and come in my direction. There is no doubt that they intend to encounter me, and at that moment the experience for me can well be one of apprehension. As far as I can judge, they intend to stop me, and I cannot but wonder whether these are the same men who, according to newspaper reports, have been terrorizing this neighborhood in recent weeks. So for me, at least temporarily, the experience is an unpleasant one; it involves a good deal of concern, even fear for my safety. I see it as a moment of dangerous confrontation, and I have visions of myself as the latest victim of roving gangs.

But, as the group comes closer, I recognize them as students of mine who are coming over to say hello, perhaps to invite me to the party they are going to. Suddenly my interpretation of the situation changes drastically; I no longer see them as a menace. I feel assured rather than threatened, and my inclination is to go toward them rather than run in the opposite direction. The changed interpretation has made my personal experience entirely different.

Or suppose that someone invites me to lunch. Basically, the situation is quite neutral; this person wishes to eat lunch with me. However, I can interpret the invitation in one of several ways. I can see it as simply a gesture of friendship, or I can suspect that this person has a hidden agenda—to solicit my support in his political campaign—or I can see it as an attempt by this person to say "I'm sorry" for some earlier affront, or I can suspect that the person is in some personal trouble and needs someone to talk to. Whichever way I interpret it, the experience of being invited and of accepting the invitation is quite specific.

Individual and Social Interpretation

There is no completely uninterpreted experience in our lives; we always "read" a particular happening in a particular way. Although there is increased awareness of this in our own day, this insight is really not all that new. For centuries people have been aware that the same group of "facts" can be seen quite differently by different people; the existence of political differences is one example of this. Exchange of views on any current event, the editorializing in newspapers or television newscasts, arguments about economics or world events or religion—such instances make it clear that all is not perfectly clear and that the realities of life can be viewed quite differently by different people. One indication that we quite commonly recognize this element of interpretation is the popular joking description of the distinction between an optimist and a pessimist. Both look at the same half-filled glass of water; the optimist says that it is half full and the pessimist says that it is half empty. Again, the very use of the word "opinion" reflects our awareness that people see the same happenings in different ways.

So, modern thought cannot claim to have for the first time discovered that human experience involves interpretation. But thinkers today have drawn our attention to the extent and nature of this phenomenon. We have learned that interpretation is not just a matter of an individual seeing things from a particular perspective. Interpretation is more basically a social process. Cultures and languages are themselves systems of interpretation. Even human perceptions as "objective" as controlled scientific experimentation are regulated by an accepted way of imaging and thinking about the physical universe. When we write histories, we are not simply narrating the raw happenings that occurred; we are telling a story about what happened, that is, our explanation, our understanding of what happened, our version of what took place.

These modern analyses of the process of interpretation have helped us be a bit more cautious about our ability to know reality as it actually is. They have helped free us from the illusion that our way of seeing things is the only true way. We are not reduced to complete subjectivity in our human knowledge; if we were, we would abandon all education, all scientific research, all serious conversation. But we are forced to be more humble about the extent to which we understand our world or even ourselves. And, of course, we are learning to be more humble about the extent to which we can know God.

This is having a major and unsettling impact on official Catholic teaching. For centuries we had made excessive claims about the *absolute* truth of dogmas, that is, statements of belief that were solemnly defined by church councils or on two modern occasions by popes. Now we realize that although these statements are not false, they cannot express the fullness of truth in a way that is beyond change. Only God is absolute. All human statements, all human understandings are conditioned by the times and culture in which they occur; simply because they are human they are all somewhat relative. Realizing this, we have now accepted the fact that our faith understandings and our expressions of those understandings are in a process of unending growth. We are a pilgrim people on the way to the ultimate insight into the mystery of God that will mark our existence in the life beyond death.

Models of Thinking

One particular instance of this deepened awareness of the subjective element in our experience is the recent study of the way in which our understanding of reality is structured by "models" and "myths." Models are basic patterns or mental structures that we have devised as ways of understanding and explaining how things happen. For example, we use a planetary model (that is, planets circulating around a sun) in our attempt to understand the nature and operation of atomic matter; we talk about electrons moving around a nucleus, though we have not directly seen this happen. We do have a certain body of evidence from scientific research, and for the moment this planetary model gives us the most consistent arrangement of this evidence. But some of the evidence from research does not fit a simple application of this model, and it is altogether possible that at some later date we will not only refine this model (which we are constantly doing) but move to a quite different one. However, to envisage a more adequate model will require some genius who can creatively imagine some pattern that makes better sense out of the evidence we have.

One simple model used by all of us in the Western world is the interpretation of time as a line. We take it for granted that a person experiences past, present, and future as sequential points on the line we call "time." Yet, for most humans in the past and probably still for many humans today, a circle rather than a line is the basic model used to interpret the sequence of experiences. This basic model, whether line or circle, has a constant effect on the way in which people experience life, on the meaning they attach to it, on the attitude they take toward human activity and its ability to shape the future, and on the decisions they make about individual and social life.

Myths as Narrative Models

Connected with these models of thought are narrative explanations about what is happening, explanations that are interrelated stories about what has happened and what is now happening in human existence. We are more and more using the word "myth" to name such stories, stories that are grounded in reality but which in their actual form are a somewhat imaginative recreating of reality. Not too long ago, we thought that only ancient peoples, in a rather primitive and unsophisticated period of human history (before the advent of modern science), used myths to interpret their experience. Now we have learned that a certain amount of myth-making is intrinsic to all human experience.

We have stories about our individual selves (our life history) that may or may not bear much resemblance to ourselves and our achievements. We have stories about our ethnic or political groupings. We have stories about the founding of our nation, stories about the neighborhood we live in. Even if these stories are not conscious distortions, they always represent one particular point of view from which happenings have been interpreted. More often than not, these stories are subtle justifications for social situations that we wish to validate and sustain. Sociologists call this process "legitimation." And we have one "master myth," the basic story into which all the other stories fit or at least are meant to fit; this is the story that explains what human life as a whole is all about.

Each of us is born into a particular family, nation, culture, language, etc.; and each of us immediately begins a process of being introduced into the particular mythology of those groups. As we start to experience human life, particularly in the earlier stages of our life, people gradually explain what is happening around us. Inevitably, the explanation, that is, the models for arranging our impressions and the stories describing what is going on, is the one that these people have inherited and by which they now live. As we grow into adulthood, the process of more formal education continues this task of helping us learn to interpret experience more accurately, or at least interpret according to the accepted patterns of our culture and social group. Perhaps we learn to question some aspects of this cultural wisdom we are given; perhaps we are able to share in the "re-mythologizing" that gradually leads a group to a more accurate interpretation of reality. But to a very great extent we will always function within that context of interpretation that is reflected in our language, in our cultural institutions, and in the processes and structures of our society.

Needed: A Hermeneutic of Experience

How accurate, then, is this mythology in which we have been raised and by which we live? How adequate, or perhaps misleading, are the models according to which we have been educated to view reality? What we need is what we might call a "hermeneutic of experience," a set of principles, insights, and critical judgments that equips us to interpret our experience in a more accurate and more profound way. Simply put, we need to develop the capacity to see experience as it is and so be able to tell it as it is. Though it may be a bit artificial, we will continue to use the term "hermeneutic of experience" throughout this book, because it helps name a process that is at the very heart of Christian sacraments.

There has been growing awareness of the extent to which we humans, for the most part without even being conscious of it, in-

terpret the experiences that come to us. And along with this increased awareness has come the desire to discover the manner in
which this process of interpretation occurs. All the various dis-
ciplines of knowledge—social sciences, history, physical science,
psychology, etc.—have been examining their procedures to see
how various elements of interpretation color their understanding
of "data." The study of these various interpretations that enter all
our knowing goes by the name of "hermeneutics." Rather than go
into any sophisticated discussion of hermeneutics, let us look at
two instances of thought today benefiting from such reflection.

1. One area of human life where much attention has been given
to the process of interpretation is psychology. We must be careful
not to think that men and women had no insight into the complex
functioning of human consciousness prior to Freud and psycho-
analysis. Actually, there are some amazingly insightful studies of
human psychology that come from the ancient world and the medieval period in both East and West. But there is no question that
the past century or so has seen greatly increased interest in and examination of humans' inner life.

The practice of psychology is geared primarily to therapy, to
healing psychological disorders that people might have, or to helping avoid such disorders by nurturing healthy elements of psychological life, fostering mental health, etc. But if one looks carefully at
what goes on in such study and therapy, one will see that it is
largely a matter of helping people discover how they are interpreting what happens to them. Though a neurotic person's friends
and acquaintances might be very loving and concerned, very accepting and uncritical, the neurosis drives him to interpret all the
gestures of friendship and concern with suspicion. People (he
thinks) are secretly criticizing him, people think he is really worth-
less, people who congratulate him on successes are really in-
sincere. What the therapist must do is help him discover the extent
to which he is unjustifiably interpreting what happens, to discover
if possible the root of this sick misinterpretation, and so become
more able to experience things in a relatively objective fashion.
Psychological therapy is basically a process of helping a person develop a genuine hermeneutic of his or her states of awareness and
emotional response.

2. We are also increasingly aware of the superficial way we often interpret things that are going on in our human society: economic happenings such as a recession, political campaigns and

elections, or the social upheaval that occurs as disadvantaged groups begin to struggle for equality. Careful work in the social sciences, which has helped us discover or at least clarify some of the forces at work in human society, has made us aware of the extent to which our "understanding" of societal happenings has been colored by prejudice, false information, fears, etc. This has made it possible for us to know the humans around us with greater balance and honesty. As a result, our hermeneutic can bear closer relationship to reality.

All of us need to develop, as humans, a more adequate hermeneutic of experience, the ability to encounter openly whatever comes into our lives—people, happenings, personal pain or joy—and to "read" the encounter with insight and accuracy, so that the experience we have correlates with what is actually occurring. As we mentioned earlier, the entire process of education, beginning with the earliest instructions given an infant by its parents, is one of developing in a person the capacity to understand what is really going on within one's consciousness and in the outside world. If we continue to grow as persons, this process of acquiring a more adequate hermeneutic of experience never ends. We are constantly learning more about ourselves and about what surrounds us; we are consequently correcting somewhat the interpretations we earlier placed on things. All human progress, at least that which touches what is most personal in us—our consciousness, emotional responses, personal relationships, freedom, and decisiveness—requires an advance in the capacity to interpret and to experience more deeply and more accurately.

It would be a mistake, though, to think of this development of a more accurate hermeneutic of experience in formally cognitive terms alone. Much of our interpretation of what happens around and to us does not come through clear understandings we already have. Rather, it comes at the level of emotional response, our "gut reactions." What this implies is that the education of the whole person must take serious account of the aesthetic aspect of our hermeneutic of experience. What must happen—through exposure to art, music, literature, dance, and whatever is truly beautiful—is that a person's sensitivities to the ugly or the beautiful, to the refinement or coarsening of one's personhood become more developed and mature. This element of education becomes particularly significant in an age of television.

Interpreting the Word of God

All this applies to our Christian faith, to the experience of living religiously, to the impact of our Christianity on the rest of our lives. Trying to understand just exactly how it does apply, many Christian theologians today have focused their attention on the word of God. For many centuries we were accustomed to use the term "word of God" almost exclusively for the Bible, which told us about God, about the meaning and demands of our human life, about our final destiny. And although Catholics and Protestants might argue about the extent to which the Bible by itself sufficed as a guide to life, all agreed that it was the word of God.

More recently we have become aware, largely as a result of technical biblical studies, that the basic experience of life that each of us has is the first and fundamental word that God speaks to us. Nothing tells me more immediately and realistically "what God thinks of me" than the actuality of who and what I am. Nothing gives me a clearer indication, at least so it seems, about God's attitude toward me, the divine concern or lack of it, God's favor or "wrath" than what actually happens to me in my daily life. If my experience is a series of disasters, suffering, failure, oppression, and if my life has no prospect of success or meaning or happiness as I struggle against starvation and disease and utter poverty, then it is rather difficult, to put it mildly, to interpret all this as a sign that a loving God is personally concerned about me. And if anyone tells me that that is the case, I find it practically impossible to hear what that person is saying to me.

Religion as Hermeneutic

Religiously, the manner in which each of us interprets her or his personal experience is the springboard for thinking about the divine. If we look at the various religions, we see that they are all intended to interpret, at a new level of understanding, what people think is happening to them. Because they are talking about the transcendent, the ultimate (God), religions are talking about the all-embracing story, that is, the myth into which all other personal or societal myths are meant to fit and find their final meaning. Religion is meant to supply a hermeneutic of human experience, as a matter of fact to be the hermeneutic that leads us to discover the ultimate meaning of being human, of being that particular human each of us is.

We have a common-sense appreciation of all this, of the way our daily experience can act as word of God. Sometimes, after a series of minor disasters, we remark half jokingly, "I think someone up there is trying to tell me something." We don't take "the message" seriously as a divine revelation, but we recognize the basic fact that there is a meaning, a significance that is always imbedded in our ordinary experience of life. Perhaps one reason we do not take "the message" seriously is that it is not all that clear; our lives need interpretation if we are to grasp their meaning accurately.

If our daily human experience is to serve as word of God, giving us insight into the ultimate story we are part of, it becomes critically important that we find the genuine meaning of that experience. This is where agencies such as official religious teachers, or Sacred Scripture, or liturgical celebrations, or books about religion come to our aid. They are meant in differing ways to help us interpret more accurately the word of God in our individual lives and in the happenings of our world. As the Second Vatican Council urged Catholics, we are to look carefully and in depth at our religious traditions (the Bible, teachings of the church, etc.), so that we can discern more correctly "the signs of the times." All religious education, taking that term in its broadest sense, is intended to provide us with an individual and community hermeneutic of human experience. Very simply put, all religious instruction should be aimed at helping us understand what is really going on.

At the heart of understanding what is going on in our lives is a correct grasp of what is involved in what we call "divine providence." In general, when people use that expression they are referring to God's watchful and protecting care; but there are many different understandings of how that care works. Many expect God to intervene and block occurrences that would be harmful, or on the contrary to influence forces that affect our lives so that we are happy and successful. In recent years we have become increasingly aware that God affects human lives not by "interfering" with the natural causes of events, but by being present to people. Because of God's personal presence to them, people see things differently, make decisions they would not otherwise make, and so the pattern of their actions and the development of human history are changed. As we will see later in more detail, this divine presence is at the very center of life's sacramentality and of the Christian rituals that celebrate that sacramentality and thereby give a new meaning to human life.

Closely linked with this understanding of divine providence is the notion of "divine revelation," the belief that God has in some special and direct way communicated to humans a knowledge of what human life is meant to be. For Christians this special "word of God" to humans began in the history of Israel, when through Moses and the prophets God revealed the divine action in history and the intent of that activity. Christians believe that in Jesus the Christ this divine communication reached its fullness, for Jesus *embodies* the divine Word. His very existence and life's story as this human Jesus of Nazareth was the parable God told to explain what it meant for humans to live and act in loving relationship to God. What this implies is that any accurate interpretation of human life must be grounded in the insight and the wisdom that God has revealed.

For Christians there is a special problem. As far back as Saint Paul, it was clear that the Christian interpretation of human life might not seem to make sense, to be truly wise. In one of his earliest letters, Paul tells the Corinthians that the paradoxical wisdom of Christianity is a stumbling-block for the Jews and pure nonsense to the Greeks. Only in faith can it be seen as true wisdom. Things have not changed much since Paul's day. The Christian vision of what makes sense, of what is truly and ultimately wise, is widely rejected today, more openly by non-Christians but often in subtle ways by Christians themselves. It is seen as naive and unrealistic. Only when the Christian meaning of life is accepted because of faith in Jesus as the Christ, only when it is genuinely accepted through conversion and lived out practically does it come to be recognized as the answer to human living. Justification of the Christian hermeneutic of experience comes by applying it and then discovering the "new life" as human persons that results.

Briefly, then, each of us needs to develop a personal hermeneutic of experience, an approach to interpreting the happenings in our life as honestly and accurately as possible. Each of us needs this not only in order to be more in tune with the actual world around us, but also to discover who and what we are, to become aware of the practical limits of our free choices and of our potential for achievement, and to establish the context for associating with those other persons who share with us a more or less common "world of events."

One of the greatest barriers to real human community is the fact that people have different stories about reality. People live by quite different mythologies dependent upon whether they are old or young, rich or poor, powerful or powerless, men or women, temperamentally conservative or progressive. Unless we learn to share with one another our particular interpretations of reality, begin to learn from one another and move toward some common elements of interpretation, we will only reinforce rather than remove the barriers that now dangerously divide us.

On the individual level, any growth toward a more authentic self-identification must draw from a realistic understanding of what is actually happening to us. Different interpretations of our human experiences produce different understandings of the meaning of "the human," and different understandings of this meaning cause the very reality of being human to be different. So, to change our mode of interpreting life, our hermeneutic of experience, is to alter our very existence as humans.

Celebration as Hermeneutic

One human activity that plays a major role in developing our hermeneutic of experience is celebration. So basic to our human experience is celebration that the measure of time that we use, the calendar, is derived from the series of civic and religious festivals that marked the passage of the year. Not that life was just one festivity after another for people in centuries past; precisely because life was quite harsh for most men and women, they lived from one feast day to the next.

If they are genuine, celebrations take place on meaningful occasions. The meaning involved may not be very profound or earthshaking. The occasion may be simply "Thank God, it's Friday," but even this has some implications of achievement, some anticipation of the weekend's rest and recreation, some sense of surviving another week. Often, however, celebrations do deal with something a bit more meaningful: a birth in the family, a success of one kind or another, a wedding or an engagement. Because something has happened to us that means something special, we wish to draw attention to it, to share it with one another. In a way, we hope to preserve the impact, the meaning, of this key experience; we wish it to brighten up (to "enlighten") the rest of our lives.

What we do at a celebration depends on the meaning involved. If it is simply T.G.I.F., we don't fuss; we wish simply to relax for the moment without schedules or responsibilities or pressures. We don't want anything fancy or carefully planned; we just want to slow down and be—that is what Friday evening is all about! The Fourth of July is something different. Not that we desire anything all that formal, but we do expect a bit of planning, some organizing of contests or concerts or fireworks. The day has a particular meaning (the birth of a nation), and if nothing draws attention to this meaning, most people are a little disappointed. Thanksgiving, Christmas, New Year's—all of these are celebrated differently; each is basically important and means something quite distinctive, and we try to express this meaning in the way we celebrate. The particular way we celebrate any given event or holiday is part of the formulation of our hermeneutic of experience, for it helps crystallize some aspect of the significance of our individual and social existence.

Celebrations can, of course, be relatively empty and meaningless if we allow them to become routine or if they are exploited for commercial gain. To the extent that this happens, the celebration is not really a celebration; it does not touch the fabric of our daily lives and experience; and so it says little, if anything, to us as individuals or as a group. Genuine celebrations spring from our basic experiences of being human; they give us a chance to express personally but along with others what it means to be a human being. For this to happen to me, I must be able to participate actively in the celebration, participate as the person I truly am, share in whatever is being done as celebration. Unless I am able to do this, I am not part of what the celebration is saying. Neither I nor the others at the celebration can hear the "word" that I am; my meaning as this particular person is not included in what is being celebrated.

Without genuine celebrations to highlight one or other aspect of the meaning of our particular human situation, a vital element in the process of interpreting experience is lacking. Celebrations should be occasions when we have the opportunity to step back for a moment and reflectively express our reaction to life. Not only do we discover more clearly the meaning of what is going on; if we are celebrating that meaning, we are accepting it as good and we are willing to confront the reality involved and respond to its demands by our decisions and our actions.

Take, for instance, a wedding celebration. In every culture we know, weddings are occasions of special celebration. People will make great sacrifices of time, energy, and money to provide the celebration or to participate in it because the occasion has very special meaning for them. The love of the couple, the beginning of a new home, the joy and support and personal growth that the two persons will hopefully provide for one another—these and many other aspects of the new shared life are seen as good things, things to rejoice in, things to celebrate. For the married couples who come for the wedding, the day cannot but make them reflect on the meaning of their own life together and how that meaning has developed over the years of their married life. For the new couple, the celebrations are a pledge of understanding and support from the friends who are gathered. The giving of gifts, the food and drink and dance and song, the special ethnic customs inherited from past generations, the advice from older and presumably wiser uncles and aunts and cousins and friends—all of this is meant to give some expression to what the day means for those who share it.

Role of Ritual in Celebration

Celebrations are, then, important contributors to our hermeneutic of experience. They make us more aware of the significance of the key experiences of our lives, and this significance throws light on the meaning of the rest of our lives. Celebrations give us the opportunity to learn from others: from the men and women who share the celebration with us and whose understandings of life are expressed by the rituals of the festivities, and from the men and women of the past whose insights are imbedded in the traditional elements of the celebrating. In the process of cultural transmission by which the wisdom and insights of earlier generations are passed on to us, few, if any, situations function more importantly than do celebrations. This wisdom of the past finds clarification and enrichment as it absorbs the new understandings of "the human" that we bring to our celebrations of life.

If we truly share with one another in celebrations, if we are able to do things that are commonly meaningful for us, if many of our recurrent celebrations (like Christmas) make it possible to share the inherited cultural wisdom about the meaning of life, this is possible because our celebrating involves ritual. There are certain actions or sayings that take on a stable form, which are then repeated each occasion we gather to celebrate. The meaning of these actions is agreed upon and, if necessary, explained to new participants in the celebration, and they can be shared with some common understanding of what is being said because of this agreed-upon meaning. When children begin the school day with the pledge of allegiance, a basic attitude of loyalty to their country can begin to grow in them because of sharing actively in the significance of this simple ritual. When high school students enthusiastically join in the cheers at a football game, there is a ritual that allows them to express in common their attachment to their school, their desire to win, etc. Simple though it may be, all celebration involves some ritual; without it, people could not celebrate together, could not communicate their feeling and viewpoints.

As is true of celebration as a whole, ritual must be kept alive by retaining its involvement in the actual life experience of the people who are celebrating. There is a common tendency to allow ritual to become the possession of a certain portion of the community. A select group becomes professional ritualizers; most of the others then slip into passive attendance at the ritual, and as they become inactive they lose appreciation for the meaning intrinsic to the ritual. All too often, the ritual, particularly if it touches the religious sphere, can then be viewed as magic. Or it can be seen as some vague civic or religious responsibility that people fulfill by simply attending the ritual.

Recent studies of ritual, particularly those by anthropologists and sociologists, have alerted us to the immense importance of ritual in human societies. While symbols in general play a key role in any culture—one could call them the "motors" of a culture—rituals, to the extent that they are meaningful and alive, have an indispensable role. It is in their rituals that any group expresses its identity, and in expressing it comes to discover that identity more deeply and clearly. Through rituals people express the way they name themselves, the goals they are striving to achieve, their view of the world and of their place in it. However, the very statement in ritual of the group's reality forms their self-understandings, their worldview, their traditions, and the objectives of their communal life and activity. Again, a living ritual functions in unique fashion as a situation and means of communication within the group; in both implicit and explicit ways, people can say things to one another in enactment of rituals that they would find difficult to voice in ordinary situations or for which ordinary language is inadequate. Finally, because they help establish roles and lines of power in a community, rituals can often be very effective instruments of control within a group. We will see each of these functions of ritual being experienced in the various sacramental areas we will study.

If ritual remains alive, it is because the symbolisms involved in it are truly effective. This leads us in our next chapter to the topic of symbolism, one that is vast and complicated, but which we cannot avoid if we are to reach some clearer understanding of the nature and function of Christian sacraments, for these are "sacred symbols."

Summary

Using the term "hermeneutic of experience" as a phrase to focus our discussion, we saw that all our experience includes an element of interpretation. What we understand as happening is our experience of what is happening. So it is important that our interpretation of what is taking place be as accurate as possible, and that the principles of interpreting life's happenings that we learn from our culture, our education, or our own past experiences help us to understand life quite objectively.

These principles with which we face each new situation form our hermeneutic of experience; they provide the basic outlook and attitude with which we give each occurrence a particular meaning. Religion, specifically Christianity, provides us with an ultimate hermeneutic by which we can understand how our life experience is the "word of God." This is expressed in more formal and explicit fashion in religious rituals, which serve the purpose of clarifying our basic human hermeneutic.

Questions for Reflection and Discussion

1. In what way is the interpretation of experience a social process? What role does ritual play in this process?

2. What is meant by "models of thought"? What is meant by "myth"?

3. Can you describe your personal "story"? Your family "story"?

4. Explain the term "hermeneutic of experience." What is your hermeneutic of experience? Where did you get it?

5. How does religious faith affect our hermeneutic of experience?

4

SYMBOL, COMMUNICATION, PRESENCE

There are many definitions of the human being; one of the most recent and probably one of the most accurate is that a human is a symbol-making being. From their earliest moments of human consciousness, humans are engaged in interpreting their experience through symbols, and no waking moment will be without the use of symbols. Actually, the linkage of "human" with symbols goes even deeper; the merging of spirit and matter in our human reality, the fact that we are embodied spirits, means that we exist symbolically.

Not surprisingly, then, the past half-century or so has witnessed an intensive and large-scale study of symbolism. One can without exaggeration say that the principal focus of modern thought has been on the nature and function of symbols. Symbols are intriguing because they are the very stuff of that wondrous and mysterious process we call "human communication."

In communication we are able to share with one another what is inmost to our being, our consciousness. We cannot contact one another, consciousness to consciousness; I cannot enter directly into another's awareness. Yet without in any way losing my own state of consciousness (for example, my awareness of a beautiful sunset)

I can "give" it to another. By the spoken word, by a gesture, by some sign, by a gift, I am able to make another person know how I am now aware. As far back as we can trace human history, people have been mystified by the way words can bridge the spatial gap between humans, can carry to another's thought what I wish him or her to think, and can bring about a shared experience and therefore personal communion.

Signs and Symbols

Basically, all symbols (whether words or other symbols) can be classified as signs. Signs are that kind of reality which, in being themselves known, lead us to know about something beyond themselves. Smoke functions naturally as a sign, because "where there's smoke, there's fire." So, too, water often functions naturally as a sign of death; if a friend of mine dives into a lake and after some time has not surfaced, the meaning is unavoidable.

Besides such natural signs where the link between signs and signified is built into reality, generally because of a causal link between the two (fire causes smoke), there are innumerable signs that humans have devised to carry meanings and intentions from one consciousness to another. For the most part, spoken languages fall into this category, as do letters of the alphabet gathered together to spell words, or a "stop" sign, or a national flag. Generally such signs are referred to as conventional, because their ability to "point" to some meaning is grounded in human agreement or convention.

This description of signs seems simple and straightforward enough; the complication appears when we discuss that distinctive kind of sign called "symbol." However one wishes to name it— and we are here using "symbol" to name it—there is an area of human awareness and communication where what we think and what we say can never be perfectly clear. Not that we are confused, or that we don't know what we are talking about. This is not the area where words like "cat" point unmistakably and clearly to a definite object, where we are dealing with the denotation of words. Rather, we are dealing with the area where a word like "fear" has ambiguities and resonances and fuzzy edges, where a handshake or a hug can say many things, where we use certain words because of their connotation. In this area of symbol, one can describe but never define; we use metaphors and shrugs and various artistic forms as we attempt to share with one another what cannot be put into words.

Symbols differ from simple signs because of the richness of consciousness they effect. They not only give us information and understanding; they touch our imaginations, emotions, desires, and loves and they trigger our decisions and our activity. Any given symbol has this power to resonate with these deeper levels of our consciousness. For example, on some earlier occasion this symbol (a storm) was linked to a particular inner response (fear). Perhaps I was close to the spot where lightning struck and destroyed a large tree; so, the appearance of dark storm clouds conveys to me not just the simple information that it might rain but also a sense of impending danger.

Persons, things, or happenings can be or become symbols. A few decades ago, Adolph Hitler, with his relentless military aggression and particularly with his inhuman hatred of the Jews, became for many a symbol of human evil. In reverse, Mother Teresa has become in recent years a symbol of human concern and compassion. When the nation watched on television the funeral cortege of John Kennedy, the riderless horse with the empty boots in the stirrup served as a graphic symbol of the nation's loss in the assassination of a young president. The sinking of the Titanic still serves as a symbol of human folly in carelessly challenging the forces of nature. For each of us there are certain things, places, persons, or events that have become specially meaning-full and that continue to say something special to us whenever we remember them or encounter them again.

In this process of symbols emerging in our consciousness as retainers and transmitters of meaning, a central role is played by our memory. It is because we can recall past happenings, relive them (sometimes with great vividness) in our imagination, re-experience the joy or anguish or achievements of the past that these can still affect our awareness and our emotions. Along with this, we have the ability, through creative imagination, of sharing vicariously in the meaningful experiences of others. We do this when we see a movie or read a novel or listen to a friend relate a harrowing experience he or she has just passed through.

Because symbols have this power to touch the entire range of our consciousness—rational thought, imagination, emotions, dreams—they are privileged means of expressing our most personal and important and disturbing experiences. The warm handshake of a dear friend, the singing of Christmas carols, the recently-released photos of Hiroshima the day after the bombing,

Picasso's painting *Guernica,* Shakespeare's plays, young lovers walking hand in hand—one could go on with a long list of symbols that speak to us on several levels of insight and feeling. Such symbols speak commonly to all of us and yet speak somewhat distinctively to each of us. When we reflect on it, we realize that such symbols do more than express how we think and feel; they are a powerful force in shaping the way we think and feel.

Perhaps the most basic and important instance of symbols shaping our consciousness is the manner in which our native language affects us. From the earliest moments of our human awareness, the words spoken to us and then, a bit later, the words we ourselves began to speak have been the mold in which our understanding of all reality has been cast. We learned to name happenings and people and ourselves in a particular way, in the way that the people around us had already learned to name them. And so we acquired a particular way of experiencing human life; we developed a particular hermeneutic of experience. Other symbols (like the ones we described above) came in to add to, go beyond, and even challenge the understandings that were attached to our native language, but that language remains the most pervasive and powerful medium for interpreting and sharing our human experiences.

As carriers of meaning from one person's awareness to that of another, symbols are the precious instruments by which we break through the isolation that spatial separation causes between humans. While inanimate objects and even plant life are incapable of reaching outside the particular place they occupy, and animals only partially break through this barrier by sensation and signal, we humans are saved from this solipsism by symbols. We are distinctive because we are symbol-making and symbol-using beings. Because of this, we are able to relate personally to one another, we are able to form community, we are able to be present to one another in love, care, and friendship.

Personal Presence

Before going further in our investigation of symbol and then going on to talk about those very special symbols we call "sacraments," we must briefly ask ourselves what we mean by "presence." On the surface, presence would seem to coincide with spatial proximity, being nearby in a certain place. So, if a roll call is taken at some meeting, a person answers "present." Spatial proximity, however, is not the same as presence for us humans; because we live in a context of space and time, presence is conditioned by some kind of spatial link. If we use the word "presence" strictly, a sharing of consciousness is involved: I am aware of you being aware of me because we are sharing awareness; we are with one another as persons.

Presence is a reality grounded in some form of communication from one person to another. Generally, this is verbal communication, but this is not always the case; some gesture or other sign can convey my consciousness to a friend. Whatever form of communication is involved, one must be careful not to see the word or gesture as simply joining one consciousness to another, as being a bridge the meaning and self-sharing pass over. The communicating is itself constitutive of the presence, for the communicating includes the awareness of the two people. We know immediately that no real communicating is taking place if the speaker is lying, if the words spoken do not mirror what he or she is thinking. And we know that no real communicating is taking place if the hearer is unable or unwilling to understand the words being spoken. The speaker must be willing to give her consciousness to the hearer; the hearer must allow his consciousness to be taken over for the moment by the meaning of the words being spoken.

When I am present to you, the actuality of that presence takes place in your awareness. But it occurs while that awareness is being shaped by my words which carry the "shaping power" of the understanding that I am attempting to communicate to you. Presence is not a static reality; presence is an event, a basic component in that continuing event which is the reality of being human. Our human experience is most importantly and basically the experience of people; every experience of another person is some form of communication. Words and other signs can have a static form, when, for example, they are printed in a book. But one does not print a book simply to have it exist as a book on a shelf; it is meant to be read, that is, to be part of a communication and a sharing of understanding. The words of the book only become words in the full sense when they function in a communication event. And when a book is being read, the author becomes present to the readers.

All this has a most important application to Christian use of the Bible. What we Christians cherish as Sacred Scripture, what we use as guide for our beliefs and our lives is not the printed page of the Bible. What functions for us as word of God is the reading or hearing of the biblical words, the use of this book within the experience and understanding of the believing community. When the Scriptures are used this way by a believing Christian community, there is a situation of special divine presence. It is not the book as such that reveals our God. Rather, the ultimate reality of that god, communicated to us as we use the Bible—and in proportion as we open ourselves to its message—is present now to our consciousness. Strictly speaking, God is not present in the Scriptures, even when they are so being used; but in the use of the Scriptures, God is made present to people.

Presence Conditioned by Symbol

Realizing the role of communication in all presence of humans to one another has brought us again to the need for appropriate symbols. Starting with language, our most common symbol system, all our communication is achieved through some symbols. Since we are embodied consciousnesses, we cannot establish contact immediately from one consciousness to another. If I wish to make another aware of what I am thinking, it is not sufficient to will such a sharing; I must use some symbols as a link to the other person's awareness.

Actually, the need for symbols is even more basic. I myself cannot have any recognizable state of awareness unless I use previously learned symbols from my memory and imagination to give shape to my awareness. I cannot think without images and words. When I wish to express my thoughts, I must do so through symbols. In and through these symbols, which I use to translate my consciousness, a similar state of consciousness will be caused in another person. As a result, each of us will be aware, at least ideally, of what is going on in the other's consciousness.

We say "ideally" because communication does not always happen. More often than we wish, communication breaks down, even between persons who know one another very well. What one thought he or she was saying is not understood, and a misunderstanding results; the symbols used were ineffective in bringing about genuine communication and personal presence. One indication that we today recognize the complexity and difficulty of selecting appropriate symbols is the development of "communications arts" as a special area of research and training.

For authentic communication, for the hearer to become conscious of what the speaker really wishes to say, there must be a commonly understood symbolism. This seems obvious. For a symbol to be understood, it must be a symbol that *can* be understood. Yet, many of the tensions in today's society are rooted in the fact that men and women are not using a commonly understood set of symbols. On the surface, the words we use sound the same, the gestures look alike, the flags and songs and pictures seem identical; but the words do not mean the same to different groups (the joke being told, for example, can have quite a different "ring" for one ethnic or racial group than it has for another), flying the flag can say very different things about one's political convictions, laughter can be "laughing with" or "laughing at." And when we come to those lengthier symbols, the myths or stories we tell to explain the meaning of our particular human experience, there can be very different interpretations of what appears to be the same story. One need only think of the many meanings given the Adam and Eve story as an explanation of evil in human life.

There is no need for everyone to use exactly the same symbols, to tell exactly the same story. But if we are to have any real communication, whether trying to tell the same story or to share different stories, there must be some basic meaning that we all attach to certain symbols above all, to the symbol system that is our language.

At one level, at least, we are quite aware of this need to find and use symbols that say basically the same thing to different people. For example, we use dictionaries, so that we have a common understanding of what words mean, with the result that we then use them in more or less the same way. If we have some dispute about the precise meaning of a word, we look it up in the dictionary so that in the future we will have an agreed-upon interpretation of that word. In the education of our young we are at pains from their earliest years to tell them the meaning, as accurately as possible, not only of words but also of the gestures, social customs, and "signals" we use in our culture. Such education is a key contribution to their hermeneutic of experience, to their ability to interpret the meaning of the various happenings that will make up their human experience and therefore their reality as human beings.

If symbols are to have the kind of impact we have just described, they must have more than an abstract, agreed-upon significance, they must be truly living symbols. They must genuinely relate to the realities of our human experience; they must spring from and remain in contact with that experience. Language—and other symbols even more so—can gradually become empty of meaning. Words can sometimes be used so often and so empty-headedly that they lose the impact they once had. How many people, for example, when they greet someone with the words "How are you?" really wish to learn how the other person is? Words can become faddish and popular and routine, so that people use them without really conveying any meaning. As a matter of fact, some words can become a fashionable way of avoiding any real communication. This is what we refer to as "small talk," a very appropriate term to indicate that there is really very little communicating going on in such a shallow exchange of words.

At times, a particular word or other symbol comes into existence because of some experience that people share, for example, the experience of a war. The symbol, let us say a particular wartime song, said something quite significant to people; it helped to create a common awareness and deeper human community. But a few decades later, when memories of that original situation have dimmed, the same song is incapable of communicating what it originally did; it can no longer function as a medium of communication, except perhaps to indicate to older people who use it nostalgically that they have little in common with a younger generation.

Because human experience is constantly altered with the passage of time and the changing of circumstances, symbols tend to become dulled, get out of date, and have their meaning evaporate. There are ways of maintaining the vitality of some symbols; there are even ways of revitalizing symbols that had grown empty and routine. We will look at those later. For now, though, it is important to realize that symbols must remain alive if they are to help create human community. Only if our symbols grow out of our actual human experiences, give expression to them, and actually help constitute them can they interpret or communicate those experiences.

Honest and Accurate Use of Symbols

In our becoming and remaining truly human, one of the most important things is the ability to handle symbols. A person is able to communicate with others to enter into personal relationships, to be truly present to others, only in proportion as he or she understands and uses the symbol system of their particular culture. When we move into a strange cultural situation, live abroad with unfamiliar language, customs, and usages, we become very aware of this. Until we gradually learn these new symbols, we feel isolated and cannot enter into the lives of the women and men who surround us; we cannot share our own awareness with them except through some gestures that are often ambiguous and misunderstood. Mastering the local symbols is the price of existing in truly human fashion. But when we have paid this price and know another people's language and social customs, we are immensely enriched, because this brings some insights into the meaning of human life that our own native symbol system did not contain. To broaden one's capacity to live with various symbolisms is to deepen one's capacity to exist humanly. This is what happens in all genuine learning.

It is not enough to understand accurately a given set of symbols; we must also wish to use these symbols honestly. There are times when we humans converse but do not wish to communicate. Sometimes this non-communication is quite conscious and deliberate; at other times we do it with very little reflection. Actually, we often do not wish nor do we try to speak all we know about a certain matter. When others have a right to know what we are really thinking and our words do not truly reflect what is in our minds, we are involved in an obvious lie. When others do not have such a right, when, for example, someone is prying into something that is none of their business, we speak evasively or speak so as to mislead the person.

Genuine human communication, all human community, rests on a certain presumption that people will speak honestly. At the same time, we know how difficult it is for people to be completely honest, even with themselves. So we take account of this in our dealings with one another, we hope in not too cynical a fashion. If language is vitiated by too much dishonesty, the entire social fabric of our human existence is threatened. We can, for example, grow completely distrustful of the utterances of our public officials. We cannot then really believe in their good judgment, for we do not even know what their judgment really is; we cannot follow their directives, because we are not certain how sincerely any directive is given; we can neither agree nor disagree with them in any intelligent fashion, because we are not really certain what they are thinking on any given matter. At that point the total breakdown of leadership is imminent; no effective authority functions among the people, though raw power may still be exercised and sooner or later some kind of revolution will replace this intolerable situation with one that promises to provide honest communication and social unity.

No moral precept is more basic than honesty. The very existence of human society depends on it, as does the possibility of persons growing in knowledge and relating to one another in love and concern. The gospels describe Jesus as insisting on only two moral precepts, one of which is honesty. This might seem a minimalistic approach to morality until we realize the all-embracing nature of the command to be honest.

Sexual Honesty

Probably no area of human life illustrates better than human sexuality the extent to which an intelligent and effective approach to morality rests on the honesty of human behavior. This touches not just the moral aspect of sexual intercourse, but all the human interactions in which our sexual identity plays a role. Because our sexuality is intrinsically linked to the fact that we humans exist symbolically—that is, our bodiliness is meaningful and communicative in the most basic sense—sexual honesty is profoundly important. Our sexuality can reveal our relatedness to others, our acceptance or rejection of them as equal human persons, our concern for and our interest in them. Because it is so deeply symbolic, it is critically important that we use our sexuality honestly, perceptively, and sensitively.

We can use our sexuality to "speak ourselves" in a unique way. We can also use that sexuality to deceive, to exploit, to hurt and damage, to oppress. Sexuality can be a unique link between people; it can also be an immense barrier. It can communicate love or hatred; it can provide great security for persons, or it can be a key symbol of one's self-depreciation. It can be used to establish and enrich intimacy among persons, or it can be used as a refuge from and substitute for real personal intimacy.

Inevitably, one's sexuality and one's relationships as a sexual being will be significant. The question is: What will it signify? It should speak positively about one's identity and destiny as a human person; if faced honestly, it will. So, honesty in recognizing the reality of one's own sexuality, honest acceptance of its fundamental goodness and its potential for contributing to personal maturity, honest expression of one's sexuality in dealing with others and in allowing them equal honesty—this is the key to any real sexual morality.

All this is true of our human sexuality precisely because it is an aspect of our human experience that is specially symbolic; one way or another it has a meaning. But it points to something even more basic. We humans are symbols in our very way of being, that is, as embodied spirits. We are symbol-making and symbolically-existing beings. This is so fundamental that we scarcely ever advert to it. Our body is not a box containing our personal consciousness and self-awareness. In our very consciousness we are our bodies, for it is in being bodily that we feel and see and touch and imagine. When we meet a friend, it never occurs to us to question whether the bodily features we observe are today still "translating" the inner personhood of this friend. I take for granted that what I see and hear and touch is my friend. The bodiliness of my friend is a symbol of his or her spirit-being in the most intimate fashion; for body exists as body, not as corpse or machine, by the very life-force of personal spirit. There are not two life-forces, one bodily and one spiritual; there is the one living reality of my friend.

What is present in my "externals," my bodily "contactibility," is my inner being as a conscious person. Yet, even here there are degrees in the extent to which this contactibility functions as a communicating symbol. In my self-awareness, my self-acceptance, my willingness to relate to others, I can be more or less open and honest. I can, for one reason or another, withhold the deeper levels of my selfhood from my being-in-the-world. So I do not allow my bodily contact with others to be a medium of presence and communion; instead, it is an opaque barrier that protects me from being known by others, a mask that hides my genuine self. Mature self-possession and openness to personal intimacy are required for authentic personal relationships. True human community demands individuals who "have it all together," who do not live behind masks.

Summary and Transition

Having taken a quick look at the reality of human sacramentality, our next step is to study the distinctiveness of Christian sacramentality. Before doing that, it might be good to pause and see where we have come.

In effect, our purpose up to this point has been to assemble many of the building blocks we will use in talking about Christian sacraments. If sacraments are transformations of the human, we have to understand better those elements of being human that are in question. And so, we took a look at the role that the meaning of our experiences plays, and saw that this was the very stuff that the concrete reality of our being human is made of. Our experience of ourselves in our world is the reality of our being human. And in this awareness of life we are conscious of happenings as we interpret them to have one or other meaning.

We say that some key experiences have a special role in providing meaning in our lives, that these experiences help build our capacity to interpret what it is that is going on; this is our hermeneutic of experience. And we say that symbols function within these experiences, symbols that we use to interpret what is occurring and to communicate to others our particular life experience.

By the use of such symbols (words, gestures, artistic creations, etc.) we make ourselves present to one another, we share ourselves and our histories and our inmost feelings; we form human community. This means that in our lives and in our persons we are significant; we have meaning for ourselves and for one another. We exist sacramentally. But we saw also that there are many degrees of such sacramentality; we can be for one another very superficially if we communicate very little of what is truly meaningful in our lives, or we can live in open and creative intimacy and express to others (and to ourselves) who and what we truly are.

This leads us to the question: Why do we have Christian sacraments if life, simply because it is human, is already so richly sacramental? What, if anything, can Christian sacraments add to the significance that human experience has for those who are alert and open to its potentiality?

Questions for Reflection and Discussion
1. How are "symbol," "presence," and "communication" linked with one another?

2. How are symbols different from simple signs?

3. Why are symbols a powerful force in our lives and in our culture?

4. Why is honest use of symbols so important?

5. "We exist sacramentally." Explain.

PART TWO

BASIC SACRAMENTS:
CHRIST, CHURCH, FRIENDSHIP

5   INSTITUTED
BY CHRIST

We ended our last section with a question: Why Christian sacraments? Answering that question adequately will take centuries, literally the remainder of the church's historical existence. But we can take an important step toward an answer by trying to understand what we mean by "Christian sacrament," by trying to see what is distinctive about what Christians do in sacrament. Whatever understanding we do arrive at will somehow be related to, be implicit in, the classic statement that Christian sacraments were instituted by Christ.

Historical Reassessment

Like many other doctrinal statements of Christian faith, we have repeated for centuries that "sacraments are sacred signs, instituted by Christ, to give grace" and we have done so without particularly challenging the meaning of what we were saying. Or, if we did explain it catechetically, we often gave it a superficial explanation, even at times a misleading explanation. For centuries, we understood it to mean that Jesus himself, during the years of his public ministry and prior to his ascension into heaven, had directed his disciples to perform various sacramental rituals (baptizing, celebrating eucharist, etc.). There was a centuries-long dispute among theologians as to whether Jesus had himself prescribed in detail the essential liturgical actions (for example, using water in baptism with a trinitarian formula) or whether he had given his disciples only the general forms of sacramental actions and left the details to them. But whether theologians opted for a "specific" institution of sacraments or for a more "generic" institution, there was agreement that the sacramental liturgies were somehow themselves foreseen and mandated by Jesus.

For quite some time this explanation has run into difficulties. In the New Testament accounts of the activity of Jesus there is little trace, if any, of such institution by Jesus, except perhaps for baptism and eucharist. Modern biblical and historical studies, clarifying considerably the picture of what emergent Christianity really was like, have made the "traditional" understanding even more difficult to accept. As a matter of fact, in the light of what we now know about the infant church, it is almost impossible to hold the opinion that the sacramental rituals were foreseen, much less commanded, by Jesus. But what, then, are we to do with what seems to be the deeper and enduring element of Christian belief, that somehow what Christians do in sacraments finds its origin in Jesus' own redeeming activity?

Part of the problem probably lies in the fact that we were looking for the wrong thing when we went back to the New Testament and other early Christian documents. We were searching with too narrow a perspective, looking for liturgical actions that were structured, at least in skeleton form, like our own "seven sacraments." What is helping us now is that we are taking a broader view of our hypothetical understanding of "sacrament": that which effects something by its significance. Sacrament, in other words, is that which gives a new meaning to things. So, our inquiry now becomes: What did Jesus do that has changed the meaning of our human reality? What was there about the significance of his actions that altered the significance of our human experience and therefore the reality of our human existing?

Institution Is Living, Dying, Rising

Let us start with a very general response to this inquiry, and then go on to make it more detailed. Jesus instituted (and continues to institute) the Christian sacramental system by his entire life and especially by his death and resurrection. By living, dying, and passing into a new mode of human living, he has transformed the reality and the significance of what it means to be human. He has poured a new meaning into "human." For this reason he is a new revelation from God as to what humanity is all about. As some theologians are saying today, Jesus is "God's parable," the actual living narrative that explains what both humans and God are all about.

Through his life, death, and resurrection, Jesus has given to the entire course of human experience a "Christ" meaning; he has given to human life an intrinsically filial significance by realizing in his own human development what it means to become increasingly human by responding to the God he experiences as Abba. He has shown how one can become more human by accepting the reality of being God's "beloved one." Of course, his death and resurrection, his passover into new and full human existence, is what throws light on his whole life and reinterprets with new depth the significance of all he had experienced. This was what radically changed the basic sacramentalities of human life, his and ours.

Another way of describing the role of Jesus in instituting Christian sacraments is to say that he is himself the fundamental sacrament of God's saving presence in human history. Speaking about Jesus in precisely these terms is relatively new, but the understanding expressed by those words is contained in the New Testament itself. The categories used by the primitive church, and therefore by the New Testament writings, to understand this sacramental role of Jesus were: 1) Word of God and 2) the New Temple.

Jesus, God's Word

Behind the New Testament theology of Jesus as God's own Word, there lies a long Old Testament tradition of careful religious reflection about God's word. About the time the great prophetic movement emerged in Israel (roughly the eighth and seventh centuries B.C.E.), the idea grew that it was God's word that brought the power of life to human history. Words had mystified and worried people for a long time before that. Why was the word of a law, whether written or spoken, able to cause death or imprisonment or reward? How could those strange signs dug into clay tablets or inscribed on papyrus bring a message hundreds of miles? How could the power of a king be carried through a command? So Israel, made a people by a God who *spoke* to them, particularly in law, became increasingly fascinated by the power of God's word.

The word of God came of necessity through human agents. Most evidently, Yahweh addressed the people through the prophets, whose very function was to speak for God; but more basically God's word directed the life of the people Israel through the law, as this was proclaimed and explained by priests and scribes. This word gave direction and solace; it was a teaching word, but it was above all a word of command that was accompanied by promise or threat.

The word of God carried unique power, especially the power of life. When God calls the prophet Jeremiah to his prophetic ministry, he is told that God's word will be on his lips to build and destroy, to plant and to uproot. No wonder, then, that Jeremiah rather reluctantly proclaims the dire predictions of Jerusalem's destruction. Once gone out of the prophet's mouth, this word of prediction is like a physical force that causes what it speaks. This powerful word is strikingly described in one of the most graphic passages of Scripture (Isaiah 55:9–11):

> For as the heavens are higher than Earth, so are my ways higher than your ways and my thoughts than your thoughts; and as the rain and the snow come down from heaven and do not return until they have watered Earth, making it blossom and bear fruit, and give seed for sowing and bread to eat, so shall the word which comes from my mouth prevail; it shall not return to me fruitless without accomplishing my purpose or succeeding in the task I gave it.

Not only the prophets developed this understanding of God's effective word. In the priestly tradition, as we find it in the opening chapter of Genesis, God's word is the very power of creation. Unlike other ancient myths about the origin of the world, this priestly version sees Yahweh as simply commanding the emergence of the universe. God said, "Let there be light." This word was creative of the world; it was creative of Israel as a people. From a purely sociological point of view, Yahweh's word as believed by Israel, more than any other influence, shaped Israel as a people.

When we come to the pages of the New Testament we see Jesus related to this theology of God's word on several levels. He is a prophet, the great expected prophet who proclaims the definitive advent of the "Day of the Lord." But he is more than that. He realizes the ideal of prophetic vocation as described in the Servant Songs (Isaiah 52-53); he actually recapitulates in his own ministry the history of Israelitic prophetism. But Christian reflection about Jesus pushed even further. Not only is God's word on the lips of Jesus in most exceptional fashion; he is, in his very being as this man from Nazareth, God's saving, creating, and revealing Word.

However, it is good to keep in mind the Christian belief that this mystery of Jesus as the embodiment of God's self-revealing Word continues in history. With his death and resurrection Jesus does not cease to function as this Word, as if his work were complete. Instead, with his resurrection he enters into the full exercise of this function. To be God's Word is to communicate God's self-gift, so that humans can accept this gift and in so doing be saved and enlivened by God's Spirit; and Jesus is forever and irrevocably that Word. So, in studying the incarnating of the Word in Jesus, we are speaking not just of what has happened, but of what is still happening today.

Jesus, the New Temple

Just as Jesus fulfills pre-eminently all Israelitic insights into the word of God, so also he realizes in his person and work the deeper meaning and function of the Jerusalem temple and its priesthood. During the centuries it stood in Jerusalem, the temple built by Solomon played a profoundly symbolic role in Israel's life. Its existence was a sign of Yahweh's confirmation and support of the davidic dynasty, and, through this dynasty, of the people of Judah. As it became gradually the central shrine for all of Israel, and as its priesthood gained an ascendancy over the religious life of the people, the temple became increasingly a unifying center. It was in the temple that the ark of the covenant was kept as a remembrance of the covenant made at Sinai. It was in the temple that the sacrifices to Yahweh prescribed by the law were performed. It was at the great temple festivals that Israelites, gathered together from outlying areas as well as from Jerusalem itself, heard proclaimed and explained the law by which their God guided their life.

This temple was in some sense the special location of the presence of Israel's God. Not that Yahweh was confined to the Holy of Holies, that most sacred portion of the temple; but it was here that God's presence was somehow focused, where one could be assured of the opportunity to contact God, where the smoke rising from the sacrifices assured the people that God was accepting their prayer and responding to their needs. The temple served as a symbol of Israel's continuing fidelity to God; it served no less as a symbol of God's continuing fidelity in protecting and guiding the people.

Given this central and powerful symbolic role of Solomon's Temple, we can scarcely imagine the sense of catastrophe that descended upon the people when the Babylonian armies destroyed it in 586 B.C.E. We can only begin to appreciate the almost obsessive desire of some of the Jews in Babylonian exile to return to Jerusalem and rebuild it.

By Jesus' day, the rebuilt temple had acquired even broader symbolic impact. Although Jews were scattered throughout the Mediterranean basin in the diaspora that resulted from the invasions of Palestine, they found a source of identity and unity in the Jerusalem temple. When possible, they came to this temple to celebrate the great feasts. Even when the journey to Jerusalem was not possible, the very knowledge of the temple's existence was a unifying force among the Jewish people.

As described in the gospels, the conflict between Jesus and the Jewish leadership boiled down finally to the relation between himself and the temple establishment. Not only does Jesus attack the abuses of temple worship, but his ministry also marks the beginning of the end for the temple and all that occurs in it, the end of the special mediatorial role of the temple priesthood. What he accomplished in his life and particularly in his death and resurrection is both replacement and fulfillment of all that the temple was meant to be in the life of the covenant people. Jesus is himself the new "dwelling place" of God's saving presence; he is the new and final "holy of holies." No longer is God's presence to be attached to a sacred place; God's dwelling is to find its focus in the new covenant people, the community that is (in Paul's language) "the body of Christ."

Jesus, the Presence of Abba

When we stop to reflect on these New Testament themes of Jesus as Word and Temple, we can see that Christian faith views Jesus as the basic sacrament of God's saving power in history. Not only is he the visible sign that God is at work in our world; he is God's work in our world. This begins with God's unique presence to the consciousness of Jesus of Nazareth; the Abba experience of Jesus, that unparalleled exposure of his human psyche to the reality of the transcendent, is something we can only dimly imagine. We can refer to it as an immediate vision of God, we can say that he has a face-to-face awareness of God, we can say that awareness of God permeates all his consciousness, but all of these statements are inadequate, even misleading expressions of the mysterious intimacy between this historical personage and the transcendent God he addresses as Abba, the familial and familiar word for father. No Jew of Jesus' day would have used such an intimate word in addressing the God of Israel.

We can draw a faint analogy from some of our human situations of personal intimacy. For example, when I am in conversation with someone I deeply love and I look into that person's eyes, there is an honest immediacy of personal contact and I do not hide myself from that person, and we therefore become very present to each other. In reverse, if I do not really wish to speak that honestly with someone, I avoid direct eye contact. So, we can project that Jesus, with what we could call "the eyes of the soul," lived in intimate conscious exposure and presence to God, and that he did so with the awareness of being, beyond what others could claim, God's own child.

Because this awareness of the transcendent God as his Abba was inseparable from his own self-identification, Jesus lived always in the conscious presence of God; God dwelt in special presence in Jesus. God uttered self as person to this human son; Jesus is that utterance received and "translated" in a human life. Jesus is God's enfleshed word. Quite literally, Jesus could not think about himself apart from awareness of Abba, in relation to whom he formed his own self-identity.

We must not think, however, that Jesus' role relative to this presence of God was an entirely passive one. Presence requires that one be freely open to the person who wishes to communicate; it demands listening in the deepest sense of that term. New Testament thought refers to this aspect of Jesus' relation to his Father in terms of "obedience." He lived in unbroken and unqualified receptiveness; everything in his life was loving response to the love he experienced coming from his Father. The tradition in John's Gospel describes Jesus as "doing always the things that please [his Father]." Concretely, on the level of personal living, Jesus' return of love to his Father was what it meant for him to exist humanly and consciously as son.

Jesus was human and, like the rest of us, the relation involved in being someone's son or daughter was a developing thing. Unfortunately, many a woman or man comes into adult life only biologically and legally someone's child, because they have long repudiated and rejected their parents on the personal level; this relationship is not important to them; it does not lie at the root of their own identity. For all of us, becoming son or daughter is a rather long process, in many instances a difficult process. For Jesus, the process of becoming son to Abba continued throughout his earthly life and through death into resurrection.

This "becoming son" was inevitably conditioned by the circumstances of time, place, and happening that made up the day-after-day experience of Jesus; his relatedness to and acceptance of his Father was lived out quite particularly in the course of his responding to these circumstances. Thus, the individuality of his historical life became, and still is, an intrinsic part of his reality as the incarnated Word of God. It is this human, Jesus of Nazareth, in his particularity, who is the Christ and the Lord.

Because the human development of Jesus unfolds in continuing response to the special presence of his father, we can say that God's personal self-utterance, the Word, is increasingly creative of the man Jesus. It is not only creative ontologically as it is with everything in the universe that it keeps in existence. Nor is it creative only in the way that the intense religious experience of God shapes the consciousness of prophet or mystic. In Jesus it goes beyond this in unique fashion, because it is the very source of his personal self-identification. His human identity is to be the son of Abba.

Jesus, the Sacrament of God's Saving Presence

Another way of expressing the unique being and role of Jesus is to say that he is the sacrament of God's saving presence, which obviously brings us closer to our study of what we mean by Christ instituting sacraments. At the heart of Jesus' sacramentality, and of all Christian sacramentality, lies that special presence of God to Jesus that he knew in his Abba experience, a presence that demanded from Jesus a total openness to his Father's self-giving. As it developed throughout his earthly life, this experience was the fundamental symbol through which Jesus became increasingly conscious of God and of himself.

However, for this transforming and creative presence of Jesus' Abba to become sacramentalized to others, for it to be manifested in a way that would change the meaning of human life, it had to be "translated" on two levels: 1) It had to be part of Jesus' awareness in a way that touched the meaning of everything else he experienced. 2) It had then to be expressed in those words and deeds Jesus shared with those around him to express what life meant for him. His awareness of and openness to his Father must have occurred as an integral element of his continuing experience of being this man Jesus. He experienced his Father as the source, final meaning, and ultimate purpose of all the events that made up his human career. His Father was revealed to him in the midst of and through those events; at the same time, those events were radically different as human experiences than they would have been had they not included this presence of his Father.

Jesus lived a particular historical sequence of human experiences (being a Galilean during the period of social unrest that finally led up to the Roman destruction of Jerusalem, teaching and forming a small group of followers, being opposed by the high priesthood, etc.) in constant exposure to his Father's presence. The reality of being human was, for him, constantly being "divinized." Since his Father was the most basic reality he was constantly aware of, the reality of his Father provided the final meaning of everything else he was experiencing. The self-identity that gradually grew out of this experience was shaped by the relationship to his Father who was known in the midst of the happenings of his life.

In this way the fundamental course of human experience was transformed in its significance, that is, in its sacramentality, by what took place in Jesus' awareness. By this radical psychological exposure to the transcendent, all the basic elements of becoming human—being born and growing, suffering and joy, success and failure, decision and risk and uncertainty, death, fear, hope, and love—took on a depth of meaning they never before possessed. Here in Jesus it was revealed what humanness could be if lived in intimacy with the divine; here in Jesus was revealed the destiny of humanity.

What took place in Jesus' own consciousness was, however, only the first level of "translation." In order that the unique divine Abba presence be sacramental for others, this transformed meaning of human life had to be communicated by Jesus through his words and actions. This is what the gospel narrative of Jesus' ministry and death-resurrection is all about. Through Jesus' teachings and healing actions, but above all through his life-giving encounter with death, he sacramentalized that transforming presence of Abba by which he himself lived.

When we look carefully at the earliest decades of Christianity and at the process of reflection and oral tradition that led up to the composition of the New Testament writings, we can see that the early Christians were quite aware of this "second level translation" of Jesus' sacramentality, though, obviously, they did not examine it in the way we are now doing. Their approach is expressed in the notion that God had done these great deeds: the life, death, and resurrection of Jesus; that this is the culmination of all the great deeds of God that made up the history of Old Testament Israel. What Jesus did was, of course, truly Jesus' doing, but it was also God's work in Jesus: God had sent Jesus as savior, and had vindicated Jesus by raising him from the dead. What Jesus was and did and said must be seen, then, as manifesting God's saving presence and saving intent. To put it in biblical terms, Jesus was and is "the glory of God."

Nothing about Jesus was, therefore, insignificant. In ways that needed (and still need) clarification, Jesus' actions and his very being conveyed meanings that reveal to us the meaning of our own life experiences. The significance of what he said and did challenges the meanings we read into our own experience. His life and, more especially, his death and resurrection are a somewhat enigmatic parable that God gives us as a source of unfolding insight into the human condition. Those who claim to be Jesus' disciples are such by accepting this "Jesus meaning" as their own and making it the "new law" that directs their lives. The insights that come from listening to "God's parable" are for those disciples the most important and controlling elements in their hermeneutic of experience.

Summary

Jesus did not "institute the sacraments" by initiating certain religious rituals himself. Instead, he gave to the entirety of human experience a new significance, because he lived and died and rose into new life under the constant impact of God's intimate presence. God, Jesus' Abba, dwelt with him in unparalleled immediacy, so early Christianity saw Jesus as "the new temple." Jesus was a living embodiment of this saving divine presence, for he was God's own Word, the sacrament of God's saving power in human history.

Though the whole of Jesus' life was sacramental, special meaning attached to his death and resurrection. In experiencing death as the free acceptance of ultimate risk, as complete fidelity to truth and love, as supreme witness to his Abba, and as passage into new life, Jesus gave human existence its full and final significance. This is the Christ-meaning expressed by the Christian sacraments as they trans-signify human life. Jesus instituted these sacraments by being—in life, death, and resurrection—the primordial sacrament of his Father's saving presence.

Questions for Reflection and Discussion

1. How was Jesus' human life experience the source of Christian sacraments?

2. What does it mean to say that Jesus is the sacrament of God's presence?

3. How is Jesus' sacramentality linked to his being God's own Word?

4. How did Jesus' awareness of God as Abba alter his human experience?

5. In what way did Jesus institute Christian sacraments?

6 CHRISTIAN COMMUNITY: SACRAMENT OF CHRIST

Discipleship in earliest Christianity became something quite distinctive in the history of religions. It involved more than the cherished memory of a beloved master they were still devoted to. It was not just the careful retention of the master's teaching and continuing dedication to the task of spreading the message that he brought. It was all this, but more basically it was a personal attachment to one who was still present to them in that new way of human existing they called "resurrection." Jesus' earthly career was seen by these first Christians as uniquely significant; indeed, they realized as never before the profound meaning of that career. But they viewed his risen existence as yet more significant, for its meaning gave ultimate meaning to everything that was human. Christian discipleship, from its inception, is more than devotion to a memory or to a message; it is devotion to a living person.

The meaning that these early disciples of Jesus discovered in his life and new life could, of course, be seen only through faith. Others who had known Jesus but had not accepted him as the Christ of God did not see his life as so significant. It was only a small group of believers who held this faith in common, who shared it with one another, and who became the early Christian communities out of which historic Christianity developed.

Emergence of these Christian communities made it possible for God to continue acting through Jesus, the Christ, in sacramental fashion. Because sacraments operate as signs, they must be humanly observable. Clearly, the risen Jesus, even as truly experienced by his believing disciples, was not normally visible or tangible, and so could not immediately sacramentalize the saving presence of his Father. What has continued in human history as an observable reality is the Christian community, the church, which, at least in the context of Christian faith, can signify the saving presence of God and of the Christ.

Thus, the institution of the church, its emergence out of the life, death, and resurrection of Jesus, made it possible for the new meaning of "human," which came with Jesus, to continue in history. Christian communities could be seen and heard. For those who came to believe in Jesus as the Christ, the experience of being a member of such a community included the experience of the presence of the risen Lord. The experience of Christian discipleship was sacramental of Christ's presence. As a Christian, one could, along with the other members of the community, "sense" the presence of the risen Lord whenever the community assembled (for example, for the "breaking of the bread"), and this awareness could then extend to the whole of life.

Whoever came into contact with one of these believing communities was truly in contact with the presence of the risen Lord. And if this person could then accept in faith the reality of this presence, the community was effectively acting as a sacrament of the risen Christ. While certain actions of the community—its eucharistic gatherings—could be considered sacramental in a special way, it was the entire existence and activity of the community that was sacramental. So, the institution of the church and the institution of the sacraments are one and the same process. Jesus could not have instituted sacraments without bringing into existence a sacramental community.

Institution of the Church

How exactly did Jesus institute the church? For a long time now, our response to this question had stressed Jesus' role in initiating the official structures of the church, the way authority was first given to the twelve and then passed on to their successors, the way "the power of the keys" was promised to Peter and through him to those successors we call the "popes." The impression given by such an explanation was that Jesus foresaw a structured religious group that would carry on his work after his death, and that Jesus himself actually began the process of bringing those precise structures into being; he himself, for example, appointed the twelve as the beginning of the episcopacy.

In recent years, careful historical study of infant Christianity has indicated that things happened somewhat differently. One can find a rooting for ecclesiastical structures in Jesus' own actions. But that action of Jesus from which those structures developed, along with everything else in the church, was precisely his passage through death into resurrection. Christianity began not as women, men, and children who belonged to an organized religious group or who thought of themselves as starting any new religious movement, but as people who shared an experience of the risen one, shared a vision of what human life was all about, and shared Christ's own Spirit.

The earliest Christian communities were relatively small groups, held together by a shared faith experience. What they had in common, what held them together, what they shared with those who joined their ranks, was the conviction that God's definitive act of salvation had occurred in Jesus' death and resurrection. They were communities of resurrection faith, communities animated by the Spirit, given them in a continuing Pentecost by the risen Christ. Because they embodied this presence of the risen Lord and of his Spirit, they were sacramental of this presence, and their actions as communities were sacramental. What Jesus did to bring about this situation, that is, to "institute the church," was not to establish formally any particular community structures, but to become the risen one and to share with them as risen Lord his own Spirit of new life.

These early Christian communities (and for that matter any genuine Christian communities in later times) existed evangelically; their very being proclaimed the gospel of God's saving presence in human history. God's creative Word, now uniquely expressed in the risen Jesus, was specially present in their midst. In conjunction with their own free and believing receptivity, this Word was continuously creating them as the church. And because they were an evolving creation and expression of God's Word, they were a prophetic people; they lived as a community by the Spirit of prophecy.

What we have just been saying points to the fact that the unity that bound together the early Christian communities was not so much a unity of structure and organization as it was a unity of life; they shared a common life. Obviously, when we use the term "life" here, we are referring to the kind of life that social groups have, or beyond that to the kind of conscious life (thought, feeling, and love) that persons can share with one another. That does not mean that we are using "life" in some secondary sense. The life of consciousness shared by persons is the most real kind of life; this is life in its most important and basic sense, the kind of life that finds its full expression in the God who by thought and love creates all that exists.

Jesus instituted (and continues to institute) the church by shar-ing life with it, sharing his life-giving vision and his life-giving Spirit. This is the mystery of God's presence through the risen Christ that the Gospel of John describes in the imagery of a vine and its branches. In the Johannine description of Jesus' last supper with his disciples, Jesus tells the disciples that he is the true vine and that they are the branches. To remain alive and fruitful, they must remain united to him. Leaving aside the very rich symbolic references to Israel's past and the rich theology of Jesus' fulfilling the past that this passage contains, we can simply focus on the most obvious level of meaning in the text. Just as life exists in the branches of a vine only when they are joined to the main stalk, so disciples of Jesus must "abide" in him if they are to share his life. If they remain faithful to him, there will be one life force that will flow through all of them, and a life unity that will bind them into one living reality. In this living reality, the fruitfulness of the branches will make apparent, will sacramentalize, the life force present in the main stalk.

Christian Community: Body of Christ

In the Pauline letters, one finds the same notion of a living unity between the risen Christ and the members of the community, but the Pauline literature uses the figure of a *body*. The Christian com-munity is the body of the risen one; Christ is the head of that body, the church. Because describing the nature and role of the church according to this notion of "body" is another way of stating that the church is the sacrament of the risen Christ, it might be worth-while to take a more detailed look at what it can mean to say that the Christians who make up the church are in some real way the body of Christ.

One of the things we must all do in approaching this question is to free ourselves of the notion that "body" refers primarily, even necessarily, to the quantified solidness that we associate with our own bodies. "Body" as used in the Pauline metaphor refers much more to the functional aspects of our bodiliness. What do our bodies do for us as personal beings? Without claiming that the list is complete, we can point to three indispensable functions that our present bodiliness provides for us.

1. Our bodily being locates us in space and time so that we can relate to and deal with the other created realities around us.

2. For each of us, our bodily dimension acts to translate our spiritual dimension. For example, our thoughts and feelings are translated through the gestures we use and the words we speak; even more basically, we take it for granted that the external appearance of a friend means that that person is really present to us.

3. Our bodily powers of action are the "instruments" through which our inner ideas and choices find concrete realization in the world.

Our bodies locate us, they identify us, they are indispensable elements in our becoming part of our world and our human society. Without this bodiliness, no one of us could be part of history or have any impact on it.

When we use "body" in this functional way, we can see the implications of calling the Christian community "the body of Christ"; we can see the appropriateness of Paul using this comparison as a way of explaining Christ's continuing presence to human history. First, having once passed into the new Spirit-life of resurrection, Jesus' existence no longer fits the limitations of our space-time continuum. This immediately raises the question: How, then, does he contact and relate to those who are in that continuum? In three ways:

1. The people who, at any given point of history, are the Christian community act as "body" to locate the risen Christ in space and time. This makes it possible for people throughout history to come into contact with him.

2. This community of disciples, accepting as it does his values and goals, implements in the concrete circumstances of human life the vision and purposes of the risen Christ. The church is, as it were, the instrument through which Christ continues to carry out his saving activity. Christ's ministry did not end with his death; in reality, it increased in intensity and breadth of coverage and effectiveness with his death and resurrection. But it could do so only

because the communities of women and men who formed the church were the means of his saving power reaching the lives of people.

3. The Christian people are meant to act as "the face of Christ," as the perceptible manifestation of what and who Jesus is as risen Lord. As our bodies symbolize our personal identity, so the Christian communities manifest the presence of the risen Christ in their midst. Or to say all this in another way, Christians exist in community as the sacrament of the risen Christ.

The church is, then, of its very essence a sacramental reality. Indeed, it is the focal sacrament that makes the saving presence of God manifest in human life. This means that all the activity of Christian communities is sacramental, even though certain actions, the sacramental liturgies, may be more formally and explicitly singled out as "sacraments." In many ways, this parallels what is true of the rest of our human life. Though everything we do is human activity, there are some actions, such as friendly conversation, that are more fully and distinctively human. And just as the frequency and depth of these distinctively human activities raises all our existence to the level of the genuinely human, so the church's celebrations of sacramental liturgies should intensify the sacramentality of the church's whole life. To the extent that the Christian community's existence in history is authentically sacramental, genuinely signifying the presence of the risen Christ and of his Spirit, God's saving action in history achieves its purpose.

Church as Sacrament: New Idea?

Once we think about it, understanding the church as the basic and continuing sacrament of Christ's presence to history seems quite logical. It fits into all our traditional insights about Christ and Christianity, but in a way that challenges us and forces us to go deeper into our understanding and appreciation of the church. And when we think about Christianity in this way, we tend to forget just how recent and almost revolutionary a designation of the church "sacrament of Christ" really is.

Less than a half-century ago, the universal Catholic approach to describing Christian sacraments was to think of them as "channels of grace," liturgical situations the faithful came to in order to be sanctified, which for practical purposes meant to people that these were the occasions when they were freed from their sinfulness and received whatever fortification ("graces") they needed to avoid sin in the future. The sacraments existed to be causes of this forgiveness of sin and granting of grace. These actions were performed by the church (and in that context "church" meant the ordained clergy) in order to bring needed grace to the faithful. The role of the church was to be an instrument of God who caused this grace through them and their activity as celebrants of sacramental liturgies.

What happened in sacramental actions, then, was viewed in very individualistic terms. The individual Christian who participated in a sacramental ceremony as "the recipient"—the infant being baptized—was changed "spiritually" by a vertical flow of grace from God through the ordained celebrant and the sacramental act he performed. The purpose (and effect) of performing sacramental liturgies was to provide the means of salvation for those Christians who came to the sacraments as "fonts of grace." This corresponded neatly with the instruction given people regarding the purpose of their lives and of their Christianity: "God made me to praise, reverence, and serve him and thus save my soul."

Such emphasis on the individual was not, however, limited to religion or to sacramental practice. It was a characteristic of modern thought generally. Much of this emphasis was good, for it made us more aware of the worth and importance of each human; but all too often it led in the direction of rugged individualism, the view that a person owed responsibility only to oneself and could not be asked to forego any personal advantage for the sake of the common good. For reasons that are complex and not completely clear, perhaps to some extent because we saw some of the dangers latent in an uncontrolled individualism, a shift set in toward greater appreciation of the communal aspect of our human life. We became more aware of the social forces that shaped us even as individuals; we became aware that being individually personal and sharing with one another in society were inseparably intertwined.

This move toward greater insight into the community aspect of our human lives touched our religious thinking. Though the word carried for a long time a rather vague denotation, we began to refer to the "ecclesial" aspect of the church's life and its sacramental acts. In sacramental theology this was not entirely new. The great medieval theologians had already spoken about the church's contribution as a community to the effectiveness of sacraments and had indicated that participation in sacraments did somehow touch one's adherence to and role in the church. But this ecclesial element in Christian sacraments was never developed in theological study, and with the modern emphasis on the individual it was largely overlooked until quite recently. Since World War II, however, there has been increasing attention paid to clarification of this aspect of sacraments and their effectiveness.

Along with this renewed awareness that sacraments always involved the entire church and had an effect on the whole church there came the awareness that such realities as "grace" and "salvation" had to be thought of in much more social fashion. True, it was individual Christians who made up the church, and it was actual men and women and children who were related to Christ and were transformed and supported by grace. But we began to see that individual Christians started their lives of faith in communities of Christians, that they depended continuously upon those communities for the survival and development of that faith, and that faith itself was a life of sharing Christian discipleship with the others who formed a Christian community.

This new appreciation for the communal dimension of Christian faith and life interacted, of course, with the increased understanding of "community" that was taking place throughout the contemporary world. Social scientific analysis was beginning to filter into popular knowledge of what human community is and how it works, psychological reflection was making quite clear the interdependence of individual and community, and the rapidly shifting patterns of human habitation were making identification with and membership in community a very practical problem for millions of people. So, people were talking about "community," bemoaning its absence in so many situations of human life, trying to find means of creating or nurturing community—and all this rubbed off on Christianity.

At the same time, a development was occurring that would eventually intersect with this emphasis on community. Both historians and theologians in the area of liturgy were regaining the early Christian insight that the principal agent of any sacramental action was the risen Christ. While it was obvious that the Christians who celebrated sacrament were performing the liturgy, the deeper reality was that the risen Christ acted through them as his body. What helped us once more view liturgical actions this way was the fact that just at this time we also recovered the understanding that "the resurrection of Jesus" meant that he is still alive and in our midst and that he had not left Earth to "go up to heaven." So, if he is still alive in our midst, even though not visible, we could much more easily understand that it is he who does sacraments through us.

But did the risen Christ act in sacraments through the celebrant alone or through the entire group of assembled Christians? While we still tend to think of the celebrant alone as performing the sacramental liturgy (for example, at eucharist), we are more and more realizing that the community as a whole, though with different members playing distinctive roles, does the sacramental liturgy. And the community has this active role precisely because it is the body through which the risen Christ acts.

All this is still quite new to us. We have scarcely begun to think in this way about ourselves as Christian communities "doing" sacraments rather than simply "receiving" sacraments. Nor have we done more than begin to translate this understanding into our celebration of the sacramental liturgies. But as we do come to understand and implement our role as the body of Christ, joining the risen Lord in his redeeming praise of his Father, we will come to realize what it means for us, the church, to exist as the sacrament of the risen Christ.

Summary

The classic phrase "instituted by Christ" as applied to the Christian sacraments can now be seen to refer essentially to what Jesus did in his entire life and especially in his death and resurrection. The significance of that passover mystery, Jesus' passage through death into new Spirit-life, is the new meaning that human life now bears. However, it is through the believing community, the church, that this significance is preserved and expressed in history. It is this community's faith that makes the risen Christ, himself the primordial sacrament of God's saving action, present in history. The church does this by living faith-fully and significantly, by expressing in its being and its activity the presence of Christ. The church is the sacrament of Christ, who himself is the sacrament of his Father.

But how does the Christian community actually go about living out this sacramentality? This is the practical question that will occupy us for the remainder of this book as we turn to those areas of key significance that are associated with what traditionally we have called "the Christian sacraments."

Questions for Reflection and Discussion

1. Explain: The institution of the church is the institution of the sacraments.

2. How did Christianity actually begin?

3. How did Jesus institute the church?

4. What kind of life is referred to by the "life symbol" of the church as body of Christ?

5. The purpose of the church is to make God's saving power present in human history. Explain.

7 HUMAN FRIENDSHIP: BASIC SACRAMENT

In the traditional short definition of Christian sacrament, the third element is a brief statement about the effectiveness of sacraments: "Sacraments are sacred signs, instituted by Christ, *to give grace.*" Sacraments are meant to do something. What they do is essentially God's doing; in sacraments God gives grace. We will devote the remainder of this book to studying how the various Christian sacraments give us grace, beginning with the sacrament of marriage. Before looking at the sacramentality of human friendship and of marriage in particular, it might help to talk briefly about the kind of transformation that should occur through sacraments.

In trying to explain what sacraments do, we have used various expressions: celebrants of sacraments "administer the sacraments" to people; people "receive sacraments" and "receive grace" through sacraments; sacraments are "channels of grace." The official statement of the Council of Trent, which has governed Catholic understandings for the past four centuries, is that "sacraments contain and confer grace."

The traditional understanding of grace and sacraments would include at least the following. The grace given was won for us by the death and resurrection of Jesus. Without depending upon misleading images such as a "reservoir" or a "bank account," it seems that there must be some way that the graces flowing from Jesus' saving action are "stored up" so that they can be distributed to people who participate in sacraments. The grace given in sacramental liturgy is, at least for baptized Christians, a needed resource if people are to behave in a way that will lead them to their ultimate destiny in the life to come.

Beneath all such formulations—which we are all familiar with in one form or another—lurks a basic question: What is this "grace" we are speaking about? It is all well and good to say that we receive the grace we need when we come to sacramental liturgy, and that we receive it in proportion to our good will. But what do we have in mind when we use this word "grace"? We have already begun to see that "sacrament" should be understood in a much broader sense, one that extends far beyond the liturgical ceremony that is the focus of a particular sacramental area. Now, with grace also, a deeper examination leads us to the conclusion that grace touches everything in our lives; it pervades everything we are and do.

This book's final chapter will deal in detail with the reality of grace, but some brief discussion of grace at this point may help us to understand better the effectiveness of the various individual sacraments as we study them. In trying to get a more accurate notion of grace, it might help to remember a distinction that was sometimes made in technical theological discussions, a distinction that unfortunately received little attention and so was scarcely ever mentioned in catechetical instructions about grace. This is the distinction between "uncreated grace" and "created grace."

"Uncreated grace" refers to God's graciousness toward human beings; "created grace" refers to that special ("supernatural") assistance God gives to humans to heal and strengthen them and to raise them to a level of being compatible with their eternal destiny. For the most part, our previous theological and catechetical explanations stressed created grace as a special help that enabled persons to live morally good lives, an assistance to guide and support them when they faced temptations. There was also a frequent reference to "the state of grace," the condition of being in good relationship to God and therefore in position to move from this present life to heaven, rather than to hell. But there was practically no mention of uncreated grace.

During the past few decades, there has been a renewed interest

in and study of grace. We have learned to pay much more attention to uncreated grace, that is, to the reality of God who in the act
of self-giving and precisely by this self-giving transforms and heals
and nurtures our human existence. Along with this new emphasis
on God's loving self-gift as *the* great grace, there has been more use
of the notion of "transformation" to aid our understanding of
created grace. Under the impact of God's self-giving, we humans
are radically changed; this fundamental and enduring transformation of what we are as persons is created, sanctifying grace.

In various ways, sacraments—in their broader reality as well as
in their liturgical elements—are key agencies for achieving this
transformation. Although the effectiveness of the different sacraments is quite distinctive, each area of sacramentality touches and
changes some of the significances attached to human life. As these
significances are transformed, the meaning of what it is to be human is transformed; our human experience is therefore changed,
and with it the very reality of our human existing.

This process of transformation is what we now turn our attention to, hoping to discover what sacraments are meant to accomplish in the lives of Christians.

Sacrament of Human Friendship

Explanation of the individual sacraments traditionally starts with
baptism. Apparently it is the first sacrament Christians are exposed to, and the one all the others rest upon; it is the one that in-
troduces the person to Christianity, etc. However, as we attempt to
place the sacraments in a more human context, there is at least the
possibility that we should begin with another starting-point.
Perhaps the most basic sacrament of God's saving presence to human life is the sacrament of human love and friendship. After all,
even the young infant who is baptized after only a few days of life
has already been subjected to the influence of parental love (or its
lack), which in the case of Christian parents is really the influence
of the sacrament of Christian marriage.

Sacraments are meant to be a special avenue of insight into the
reality of God; they are meant to be words of revelation. And the
sacramentality of human love and friendship touches the most basic level of this revelation. There is a real problem in our effort to
know God. Very simply put, it seems all but impossible for humans to have any correct understanding of the divine as it really is.
God is everything we are not. We are finite, God infinite; we are in

time, God is eternal; we are created, God is creator. True, we apply to God the ideas we have drawn from our human experience; we even think of God as "person." But is this justified? Is this the way God is?

Some fascinating and important discussion of this problem is going on today among Christian philosophers, but let us confine our approach to those insights from the biblical traditions. As early as the writings of the first chapter of Genesis (which is part of the priestly tradition in Israel that found final form around 500 B.C.E.), we are given a rich lead. Speaking of the creation of humans by God, Genesis 1:27 says that humans were made "in the image and likeness of God." That is to say, somehow the reality of human persons gives us some genuine insight into the way God exists. But the passage continues—and it is an intrinsic part of the remark about "image and likeness"—"male and female God made them." This means that the imaging of God occurs precisely in the relationship between humans, above all in the interaction of men and women. To put it in contemporary terms, some knowledge of the divine can be gained in experiencing the personal relationship of men and women (and one can legitimately broaden that to include all human personal relationships).

The text provides still more understanding, for it points out that from this relationship life is to spread over Earth; humans in their relation to one another (primarily in sexual reproduction, but not limited to that) are to nurture life. And humans are to govern Earth for God; they are to image and implement the divine sovereignty by this nurture of life that is rooted in their relationship to one another. As an instrument of divine providence, human history is meant by the creator to be effected through human community, through humans being persons for one another.

Though the first and immediate aspect of the relationship between Adam and Eve as life-giving is their sexual partnership, the text does not confine it to this. Rather, Genesis goes on to describe the way Adam's own human self-identity is linked with Eve's. As Adam is given the chance to view the other beings in God's creation, he is able to name them, but he is unable to name himself until he sees Eve. The very possibility of existing as a self is dependent upon communion with another.

Implicit in this deceptively simple biblical text is a profound statement about the way human life is to be conducted. If life is to extend to further life, either by creating new humans or by creating new levels of personal life in already existing humans, it will happen on the basis of people's self-giving to one another. And, if women and men are truly to "rule" the world for God, they will do this by their love and friendship, and not by domination. To the extent that this occurs, the relationship of humans to one another will reveal the fact that God's creative activity, which gives life and guides its development (in creation and in history), is essentially one of divine self-gift. Humans have been created and are meant to exist as a word, a revelation, of God's self-giving rule; but they will function in this revealing way in proportion to their free living in open and loving communion with one another.

Whatever small hint we have regarding the way God exists comes from our own experience of being humanly personal. Our tendency, of course, is to think of the divine in human terms, even carrying to God many of the characteristics of our humanity that obviously could not apply directly to God; for example, changing our minds as to what we intend to do. Excessive anthropomorphism has always been a problem in human religious thinking and imagination; we have always been tempted by idolatry. Even today, when our religious thinking has been purified by critical and scientific thought, we still fall into the trap of thinking that God exists in the way we think God does. This does not mean, however, that we must despair of ever knowing God. On the basis of biblical insights (like those in Genesis 1:27 and even more in New Testament texts grounded in Jesus' own religious experience) we can come to some true understanding of God by reflecting on our own experience of being personal.

For us to be personal—aware of ourselves and the world around us, aware that we are so aware, relating to one another as communicating subjects, loving one another, and sharing human experience—is always a limited reality. We are personal within definite constraints of time and place and happenings. Even if our experience as persons is a rich one, through friends and education and cultural opportunities, it is always incomplete. For every bit of knowledge there are immense areas of reality I know nothing about; I can go on learning indefinitely. Though I may have a wide circle of friends, there are millions of people I can never know; I can go on indefinitely establishing human relationships. There are unlimited interesting human experiences I will never share. In a sense I am an infinity, but an infinity of possibilities, infinite in my incompleteness. Yet, this very experience of limitation involves some awareness of the unlimited; our experience of finite personhood points toward infinite personhood and gives us some hint of what that might be.

God Revealed as Personal

What lets us know that the divine is indeed personal in this mysterious, unlimited fashion is the fact (which as Christians we believe) that this God has "spoken" to humans; God has revealed not just some truths about ourselves and our world, but about God's own way of being personal in relation to us. God in the mystery of revelation to humans is revealed as someone. What this means can be grasped by us humans only through our own experience of being human together. In our love and concern for one another, in our friendships and in the human community that results, we can gain some insight into what "God being for us" really means. These human relationships are truly insights into God, but not just in the sense that they are an analogue by which we can gain some metaphorical understanding of the divine. Rather, humans and their relationships are a "word" that is being constantly created by God. In this word God is made present to us, revealing divine selfhood through the sacramentality of our human experience of one another.

One of the most important results of this divine revelation and genuinely open relationships to one another is the ability to trust reality. This might seem a strange thing to say, for reality is a given. Yet, the history of our times has been one of growing uncertainty and strong distrust of the importance and goodness and even the objective reality of the world that surrounds us, especially the world of people. Great world wars, among other things, have made many humans cynical about human existence and have made many others unwilling to admit that things are as they are. There is abundant evidence that our civilization is increasingly fleeing toward fantasy, taking refuge in a world of dreams, so that it does not have to face the real world. It is critically important, perhaps necessary for our sanity, that we find some basis for trusting life and facing reality optimistically and with mature realism.

Most radically, a culture's ability to deal creatively with reality depends on its view of "the ultimate," of God. We must be able to trust this ultimate not only as infinitely powerful but also as infinitely caring, as compassionate and concerned. The only ground, ultimately, for our being able to accept such an incredible thing—

and when we stop to reflect, it is incredible—is our experience of loving concern and compassion in our human relationships. If we experience the love and care that others have for us, beginning with an infant's experience of parental love, and experience our own loving concern for others, this can give us some analogue for thinking how the ultimate might personally relate to us. Jesus himself drew from this comparison. "If you who are parents give bread and not a stone to your children when they ask for food, how much more your Father in heaven. . . ."

Experiencing love in our human relationships makes it possible for us to accept the reality of our lives with a positive, even grateful attitude. And this in turn makes it possible for us to see our lives as a gift from a lovingly providential God. If we have friends, life has some basic meaning; we are important to them and they to us. What happens to us and them makes a difference; someone cares. If love exists among people, there is genuine, deep-seated joy, because joy shared by people is the final dimension of love. If this is our experience of being human, then our existence can be seen as a good thing and accepted maturely and responsibly.

All of this means that our experience of being truly personal with and for one another is sacramental; it is a revelation of our humanity at the same time that it is a revelation of God. This experience of human love can make the mystery of divine love for humans credible. On the contrary, if a person does not experience love in his or her life, only with great difficulty can the revelation of divine love be accepted as possible. Learning to trust human love and to trust ourselves to it is the ground for human faith and trust in God.

To say that human love is sacramental, especially if one uses that term strictly (as we are doing), implies that it is a mystery of personal presence. Obviously, in genuine love there is a presence of the beloved in one's consciousness; the deeper and more intimate the love, the more abiding and prominent is the thought of the beloved. To see this as truly sacramental of divine presence means that human love does more than make it possible for us to trust that God loves us. The human friendships we enjoy embody God's love for us; in and through these friendships God is revealing to us the divine self-giving in love. God is working salvifically in all situations of genuine love, for it is our consciousness of being loved both humanly and divinely that most leads us to that full personhood that is our destiny. Such salvation occurs in our lives to the extent that we consciously participate in it, in proportion to our awareness of what is really happening and our free willingness to be part of it.

It is instructive to note that when Jesus, immediately after being baptized by John, was given a special insight into his relationship to God as his Abba, the word used in the gospel to describe his experience of his Father's attitude toward him is the Greek *agapetos*, "my beloved one." This was the awareness of God that Jesus had, an awareness of being unconditionally loved, an awareness that became the key to human salvation. And John's Gospel describes Jesus at the last supper as extending this to his disciples. "I will not now call you servants, but friends."

Marriage, Paradigm of Friendship

Among the various kinds of human friendship and personal love, the one that has always been recognized as a paradigm of human relationship and love, and at the same time a ground of human community, is the relation between husband and wife. There is considerable evidence that humans have never been able to explain or live this relationship satisfactorily, basic and universal though it is. In our own day, there is constant and agitated discussion of the way men and women are meant to deal with one another, and there is widespread talk of a radical shift taking place in the institution of marriage. As never before, the assumptions about respective roles in marriage are being challenged. Marriage is seen much more as a free community of persons rather than as an institution of human society regulated for the general benefit of society; equality of persons rather than respect for patriarchal authority is being stressed. And with considerable anguish in many instances, people are seeking the genuine meaning of the relation between women and men, and more broadly the relationship of persons to one another in any form of friendship.

Questioning the woman-man, and especially the husband-wife, relationship is not, of course, a new phenomenon. As far back as we can trace, literature witnesses to the attempt to shed light on this question. What complicates the issue is the merging of two human realities, sexuality and personal relatedness, in marriage, a merging so profound that people often are unable to distinguish them. We know, however, that in many ancient cultures there was little of what we today consider love between spouses; marriage was a social arrangement for the purpose of continuing the family

through procreation. In not a few instances, there was so pronounced a cleavage between love and sexuality that the wife was
considered the property of her husband and she was abandoned if
she proved unable to bear him children. If men sought human
companionship, they sought it outside the home. Apparently the
marriages in which something like a true friendship existed between wife and husband were relatively rare.

Sacramentality of Marriage in Israel

In ancient Israel an interesting development began at least eight
centuries before Christianity. Surrounded as they were by cultures
and religions that worshipped the power of human sexuality, the
Israelites assiduously avoided attributing anything like sexuality
to their God, Yahweh. At the same time, these neighboring erotic
religions were a constant temptation to the Israelites; the great
prophets of Israel lashed out repeatedly against participation by
Israel's women and men in the ritual prostitution of the Canaanite
shrines. In this context it is startling to find the prophet Hosea using the example of a husband's love for his wife as an image of
Yahweh's love for his people Israel.

Apparently, Hosea was one of those sensitive humans for whom
marriage was more than a family arrangement; he seems to have
had a deep affection for his wife, Gomer. The love was not re-
ciprocated; his wife abandoned him for a life of promiscuity with a
number of lovers; perhaps she became actively involved in some
situation of shrine prostitution. At this point, Hosea was obliged
by law to divorce her, which he seems to have done. But then "the
word of the Lord came to Hosea," bidding him to seek out and
take back his errant wife. And all this as a prophetic gesture that
would reveal Yahweh's forgiveness of an adulterous Israel that
had gone lusting after false gods.

Once introduced by Hosea, the imagery of husband-wife becomes the basic way in which the prophets depict the relationship
between Yahweh and the people Israel. Tragically, the image often
has to be used in a negative way. Israel is the unfaithful spouse
who abandons Yahweh to run off with "false lovers," the divinities
of the surrounding fertility religions. Yet, despite this infidelity on
Israel's part, Yahweh is a merciful God who remains faithful to his
chosen partner. "Faithful" becomes a key attribute of this God of
Israel. Yahweh is a faithful divinity who keeps promises to Israel.
And the husband-wife relation becomes in the prophetic writings

an alternative to the king-subject relation that the rulers of Israel and Judah (for their own purposes) preferred as a way of describing the covenant between Yahweh and Israel.

Our particular interest, however, is not the manner in which the use of the husband-wife imagery altered Israel's understanding of the covenant between people and God. Rather, it is the manner in which, conversely, the use of this imagery began to alter the understanding of the relation between a married couple. If the comparison husband-wife/Yahweh-Israel is made, the significance of the first couplet passes into understanding the significance of the second couplet, but the significance of the second passes also into understanding the first.

The understanding the people had of their god, Yahweh, and of Yahweh's relationship to them, the depth and fidelity of his love, the saving power of this relationship, slowly became part of their understanding of what the marriage relationship should be. Thus, a "Yahweh-significance" became part of the meaning of married relatedness. The sacramentality of the love between husband and wife—and indirectly the sacramentality of all human friendship—was being altered. It was, if we can coin a term, being "yahweh-ized." The meaning of God's relationship to humans became part of the meaning of marriage, and marriage became capable of explicitly signifying and revealing this God. This meant that human marriage carried much richer significance than before; it meant that the personal aspect of this relationship was to be regarded as paramount; it meant that the woman was neither to be possessed as property nor treated as a thing; it meant that marital fidelity was expected of both man and woman. Thus the "institution of the sacrament of marriage" begins already in the Old Testament.

Marriage as a Christian Sacrament

With Christianity another dimension of meaning is infused into this relation between wife and husband, the Christ-meaning that comes with Jesus' death and resurrection. Several New Testament passages could be used to indicate this new, deeper meaning, but the key passage probably is the one in Ephesians (5:21-31) that traditionally forms part of the marriage liturgy.

Be subject to one another out of reverence for Christ. Wives, be subject to your husbands as to the Lord. For the husband is the head of the wife, just as Christ is the head of the church, the body of which he is the Savior. Just as the church is subject to Christ, so also wives ought to be, in everything, to their husbands. Husbands, love your wives, as Christ also loved the church and gave himself up for her. . . . In the same way husbands should love their wives as they do their own bodies. He who loves his wife loves himself. For no one ever hates his own body, but nourishes and tenderly cares for it, just as Christ does for the church, because we are members of his body. "For this reason [in the words of Scripture] a man will leave his father and mother and be joined to his wife, and the two will become one flesh."

In dealing with this text it is important to bear in mind what the author of the epistle is doing. As so often in the Pauline letters, the purpose is neither to challenge nor to vindicate the prevailing structures of human society as they then existed. Just as in other cases the Pauline letters do not argue for or against an institution like slavery. The passage in Ephesians takes for granted the commonly accepted patriarchal arrangements of family authority without defending or attacking them; in a patriarchal culture all authority is vested in the husband-father. However, Ephesians insists that in a Christian family this authority structure must be understood and lived in an entirely new way. The relation between the risen Christ and the Christian community must be the exemplar for a loving relationship between the Christian couple.

This text contains a rich treasure of sacramental and christological insight that has scarcely been touched by theological reflection. Mutual giving of self to one another in love, not only in marital intercourse but also in the many other sharings that make up an enduring and maturing love relationship, is used in this passage as a way of understanding what Jesus has done in his death and resurrection. He has given himself to those he loves. His death was accepted in love as the means of passing into a new life that could be shared with those who accept him in faith. Jesus' death and consequent resurrection was the continuation of what was done at the supper when Jesus took the bread and said, "This is my body [myself] given for you." Ephesians 5 tells us that we are to understand this self-giving of Jesus in terms of the bodily self-giving in love of a husband and wife, and vice versa, that we are to understand what this marital self-gift is meant to be in terms of Jesus' loving gift of self in death and resurrection.

One of the important things to bear in mind in studying this text is that Jesus' self-giving continues into the new life of resurrection. Actually, his self-giving is intrinsic to this new stage of his human existence. The very purpose and intrinsic finality of his risen life is to share this life with others. The risen Lord shares this resurrection life by sharing what is the source of this life, his own life-giving Spirit. For Jesus to exist as risen is to exist with full openness to and full possession of this Spirit. So, for him to share new life with his friends means giving them his own Spirit. What emerges from this Spirit-sharing is a new human life of togetherness, a life of un-expected fulfillment, but a life that could not have been reached ex-cept through Jesus freely accepting his death. So also, a Christian married couple is meant to move into a new and somewhat un-expected common existing, which cannot come to be unless each is willing to die to the more individualistic, less unrelated-to-another, way of life that they had before.

Christ's self-giving to the church is more than the model ac-cording to which a man and woman should understand and live out their love for each other. The love, concern, and self-giving that each has for the other is a "word" that expresses Christ's love for each of them. The fidelity of each to their love is a sign that makes concretely credible their Christian hope in Christ's fidelity. In lov-ing and being loved, each person learns that honest self-appreciation that is the psychological grounding for believing the incredible gospel of God's love for humankind. In their re-lationship to each other, and in proportion as that relationship in a given set of circumstances truly translates Christ's own self-giving, the couple are a sacrament to each other and a sacrament to those who know them.

In this sacramental relationship, a Christian man and woman are truly "grace" to each other; they express and make present that uncreated grace that is God's creative self-giving. Although there certainly is mystery in this loving divine presence, it is revealed in the new meanings discovered in the lived relationship between Christian wife and husband. The trust required by their un-qualified intimacy with each other and the hope of genuine ac-ceptance by the other, which accompanies this intimacy, help bring about a new level of personal maturity. But this trust and hope are grounded in the Christian faith insight that open-ended love can lead to new and richer life. Perhaps even more basically, a Christian couple can commit themselves to this relationship, believing that it will not ultimately be negated by death. Instead, Christian hope in risen life supports the almost instinctive feeling of lovers that "love is stronger than death."

Psychological studies have detailed the ways a truly mature married relationship, one that integrates personal and sexual love, fosters the human growth of the two people, and it is not our intent to repeat such reflections here. But these same studies point also to the indispensable role that continuing and deepening communication with each other plays in the evolution of such a relationship. In a Christian marriage the communication is meant to embrace the sharing of faith and hope in that salvation that comes through Jesus. The Christian family is meant to be the most basic instance of Christian community, people bonded together by their shared relationship to the risen Jesus.

All of us can think of marriages where this ideal has been to quite an extent realized, where husband and wife have over the years supported and enriched one another's belief and trust in the reality and importance of Christianity. Various challenges can come to Christian faith, if it is real faith and not just a superficial acceptance of a religious pattern. These challenges can change shape over the years, they can come with suffering or disappointments or disillusionment or boredom, they can come to focus with the need to face the inevitability of death. At such times of crisis, when faith can either deepen or weaken, the witness of a loved one's faith and hope is a powerful and sometimes indispensable preaching of the gospel.

Perhaps the most difficult thing to believe over the course of a lifetime is that one is important enough to be loved by God. Nothing makes this more credible than the discovery of being important to and loved by another human. The fidelity of one's lover—not just in the critically important area of sexual fidelity but also in the broader context of not betraying love by selfishness, exploitation, pettiness, dishonesty, disinterestedness, insensitivity—makes more credible the Christian trust in God's unfailing concern.

One could go on indefinitely describing how a Christian couple "give grace" to each other, because the contribution to each other's life of grace (their being human in relation to God) involves the whole of their life together. The sacrament of Christian marriage is much more than the marriage ceremony in the church; that ceremony is only one important element in the sacrament. Christian marriage is the woman and the man in their unfolding relationship to each other as Christians; they are sacrament for each other, sacrament to their children, and sacrament to all those who come to know them. The meaning of what they are for each other should become for them and others a key part of what it means to be a human being.

Before ending this reflection on the sacramentality of Christian marriage, it is good to return to what was said earlier: All genuine friendship, and in a particular way the friendship between people who share faith in the God Jesus revealed, is sacramental. While marriage, because of its society-recognized pledge of lifelong fidelity and its creation of new human life, does play a paradigm role for friendships, deep friendships also play a paradigm role in reflecting the personal relationship that marriage should be. It is important for those who, for one reason or another, are not married to realize that the essence of marriage's sacramental power, the transforming power of human love, is open to them also in proportion to their mature care, concern, and affection for others. Married and single are meant together to form one community of friends.

Summary

If we restrict "sacrament" to certain liturgical rituals, it is logical to think of baptism as the initial sacrament. If, however, we realize the fundamental sacramentality of all human experience and the way Jesus transformed this sacramentality, there is good reason for seeing human friendship as the most basic sacrament of God's saving presence among us. Human friendship reflects and makes credible the reality of God's love for humans; it gives us some insight into the Christian revelation that God is a "self."

Within human friendship there is a paradigm role played by the love between a Christian wife and husband. Building on the transformation of marriage's meaning that began with the Israelitic prophets, Christianity sees the love relationship of a Christian couple as sacramentalizing the relationship between Christ and the church, between God and humankind. God's saving action consists essentially in the divine self-giving. This is expressed by and present in the couple's self-gift to each other; they are sacrament to each other, to their children, and to their fellow Christians. This sacramentality, though specially instanced in Christian marriage, extends to all genuine human friendship.

Questions for Reflection and Discussion

1. What is meant by "uncreated grace"?

2. Why can we say that human love is the most basic sacrament?

3. What is the revelation expressed in Genesis 1:27?

4. How do we know that God is personal? What does "personal" mean when applied to God?

5. When and how was the sacrament of Christian marriage instituted?

6. The Christian couple are the sacrament of marriage. Explain.

PART THREE

EUCHARISTIC *COMMUNIO*

8

EUCHARIST AS COMMUNION

B efore beginning to study various aspects of eucharist (which we will do later in this chapter and in the following several chapters), it would be good to discuss a topic that most Catholics have come to see as central to eucharist: the presence of Christ brought about by the change of bread and wine. Today we are trying to give a somewhat simpler, more direct, and perhaps more understandable explanation of that change and the presence it causes, an explanation that does not mystify people by the use of terms like "transubstantiation" that they do not understand or perhaps even misunderstand.

A major step in the shift in official teaching about Jesus' eucharistic presence came with the letter of Pope Paul VI, issued during the Second Vatican Council. In this letter the pope, while in no way denying a special presence of Christ attached to the transformed bread and wine, drew attention once more to the presence of Christ to the assembled congregation. This gave us an important signpost for the direction we are now pursuing.

Christ's Presence Received in Faith

First of all, let us briefly review what we saw earlier about the reality of presence. While connected with spatial location, presence is something other than that, for presence occurs in the awareness that persons have of one another. When I am present to a friend, my presence occurs in the consciousness of that friend who pays attention to me and allows me to be the object of his or her awareness. I cannot be present to a thing, for there is no consciousness there; presence can happen only between persons.

Such a presence to another's awareness happens because of communication. I speak or gesture or use some other symbol to share with that person my ideas, enthusiasms, intentions, etc. In a context of genuine friendship, my communication shares not only my consciousness but my very self-presence to a friend; it always involves my self-gift. Clearly, this can occur only if that friend is willing to truly listen, truly willing to accept my self-gift, and to do so by giving himself or herself as a friend.

To apply this to the risen Christ's presence to believers: Because the risen existence that Christ now enjoys does not place him in our limiting context of space and time, he obviously is not immediately observable to us. He is not "somewhere," so he can be neither close nor distant in our ordinary understanding of those terms. However, Christians believe that his more spiritual mode of being human not only allows but facilitates his personal presence to those who believe in him. Christian belief has from the very beginning attached this presence in a special way to eucharistic gatherings. "Where two or three are gathered in my name, there I am in their midst."

The communication that causes presence can occur for the risen Christ because the believing community, functioning as his body, provides the symbol through which Christ's own Spirit is communicated to his followers in history. The community by its very being, by its faith, and in various ways through its activity, is a "word" that speaks the enduring presence of the risen Christ to his disciples.

Christ's Presence to the Eucharistic Community

When a group of Christians gather for celebration of eucharist, the risen Christ is already present to them before the ritual action begins. Since they are believers, they already have the open minds and hearts which are the "receptacle" for Christ's self-gift to them; and Christ already offers to them his friendship, shares with them his own Spirit. If not, they would not be a portion of the church which is the body of Christ.

What this means is that the presence of Christ connected with eucharist is basically his presence to the people who are there. As we will see later, this presence is reinforced, deepened, and nurtured by the various elements of ritual as it unfolds. The entire eucharistic liturgy, somewhat like a dramatic presentation, carries a developing message, the message of human life redeemed and transformed by the power of God working through the death and resurrection of Jesus the Christ. The whole of the Mass is "liturgy of the word"; and it does what words do: provide that communication from which presence flows.

But if the liturgy as a whole is a symbol that makes Christ present *to the people*, what is the function of the consecrating of bread and wine? What sort of presence does Christ have in relation to the consecrated species? Do these truly become body and blood of Christ? Is there really a basic change that the bread and wine undergo with the eucharistic words of consecration, "This is my body," "This is my blood," a change for which the term "transubstantiation" has been used? A quick response is: Yes, there is a basic change; yes, the bread and wine do become body and blood for the risen Christ and enable his presence; yes, this happens through transubstantiation.

Now to expand that answer. It helps to maintain a functional point of view in dealing with these questions, especially since the Semitic mentality that Jesus shared with his culture emphasized what things and persons (including God) did, rather than what kind of being they were. So, as we mentioned, Jesus in saying "This is my body given for you" was in effect saying "Here I am for you." As a result, the bread began to function for him somewhat the way our bodiliness functions as we give ourselves to one another in friendship—by smiles, handshakes, hugs, and marital intercourse. While the bread was still bread—something that was necessary if it was to symbolize what Jesus meant to say: that he wished to nourish their life—it was now more than that because it had begun to function as a "word" by which Jesus communicated his in-depth presence to his friends. The bread was truly changed; it had not previously been a presence-causing symbol as is our human bodiliness.

So also with the wine become blood for Christ. In a cultural perspective that believed that blood was life and that the cup shared at a Passover dinner was memorial of the covenant enacted in blood at Sinai, Jesus was saying to his friends, "This is my life, the life of the *new* covenant that I am sharing with you." In eucharist as Christians share the cup, the risen Christ shares with them the Spirit-life he now possesses in fullness and in so doing becomes more intensely present to them. We humans share our spirit life with one another as we communicate through words and other symbols; Christ does this in eucharist as the wine functions to speak his continuing gift of new Spirit life.

What are we to understand, then, by the term "transubstantiation"? First of all, it is important to remember that we do not have to use this word, though it is appropriate if one understands it accurately. The term "substantiation" came into use only around the twelfth and thirteenth centuries and is a particular, philosophical way of trying to explain the reality of Jesus' presence in eucharist. In that philosophical point of view, which came from Aristotle, "substance" is the "depth dimension" of a thing that lies beneath all the physical properties such as weight and size and shape. So, while in that view "substance" is the ultimate ground of a thing's reality, it is almost exactly the opposite of what people today understand by the word "substantial": something solid and tangible. What is involved, then, in transubstantiation is not a physical change but a metaphysical change—which means what?

What it means is that the ultimate meaning and purpose of something is changed; it now exists differently because of that changed purpose and meaning. An example: Suppose it is the day before Valentine's Day and it suddenly occurs to me that I have bought nothing to give my "significant other." So, I rush to the nearest candy store and there on the shelves is a large assortment of tempting chocolates. For the moment all they signify is the prospect of delicious pleasure, also the possibility of gaining weight, etc. However, as I make my presentation the next day, the box of chocolates now exists in a different way than it had; now its purpose in existing is to be a symbol of my love. Everything else that was true about it before is still true, which means that it can be an appropriate symbol, except that its very be-ing is different: It is now a gift, a symbol of my self-gift in friendship. So also the bread and wine in eucharistic action exist differently after the words of consecration; from this point on they exist to speak Christ's self-gift as source of new life.

God's Eucharistic Presence

Despite our interest in Christ's presence to us in eucharistic action, it is good to remember that beyond it lies the mystery of God's presence through Christ and in the gift of their common Spirit. This connects us with the widespread discussion nowadays of "creation spirituality" and "incarnational theology." These developments are important because they draw to our attention the manifestation of the divine glory in creation, remind us of our responsibilities as stewards of Earth to preserve and develop rather than despoil it, and challenge us to regard creation and especially humans as good. At times, however, some of the enthusiasm for the beauty of the world and a desire to overcome some earlier tendencies to make God an abstract and distant transcendent divinity have led in the direction of pantheism. There is a consoling reality to the immanence of God, but this must be seen in terms of divine presence to creation rather than creation itself being God.

Hopkins wrote ". . . nature is never spent./There lives the dearest freshness, deep down things" and there is no doubt but that the beauty of nature at times leads us to imagine the beauty that must characterize nature's creator. However, the Bible uses the term "God's glory" to point beyond the divine power that brings the universe into existence and sustains it in being; it points to a God personally interested in saving humans from evil. The specific meaning of "the glory of God" in the Old Testament texts is "God's manifested saving intent." So the burning bush that signaled to Moses that Yahweh was about to save his people is called "the glory of God"; so also the bright cloud that stood before the opening of the tabernacle or that at a later period filled the temple at its dedication. In the New Testament it is Jesus who is described as "God's glory," for he is the temple's replacement. Besides, a careful study of the healing actions of Jesus, actions intended to sacramentalize and therefore reveal the God whose Spirit works in Jesus, has led us to realize that "creation," "revelation," and "salvation" are the one same divine action.

What underlies and unifies these three processes is the divine saving intent. Because of modern reflection, philosophical and psychological, on the reality of "intentionality," we are being helped to understand God's creative and saving activity as divine self-giving. Throughout the entire process of creation there runs God's gift of self, but it is only with the emergence of personal creatures that this divine self-giving can find a commensurate personal response. This gift of God to human persons, while obviously touching the individual psychic life of individuals, is directed to the formation of human community, which itself flows from people's self-communication in word and love. This community in turn is meant to be the sacrament of the community between God and humans. In speaking this way we are clearly talking about the mystery of God's presence, a presence that is grounded in God's sharing of truth in the Word and of love in the Spirit.

This divine self-giving works creatively. Old Testament thought, particularly in the prophetic and priestly traditions, had already worked out a sophisticated theology of God's word, which brought into existence that of which it spoke. John's Gospel pushes this further when it identifies Jesus with that Word. This divine Word works throughout history but through creatures, especially through humans, sustaining the existence of things and of the active and passive powers by which they interact with one another. In humans this creative action occurs as people's consciousness grows through the sharing of truth and their affective life develops as their mutual desirability draws them into enriching relationships. Without bypassing the power and activity intrinsic to created reality, the divine creative intent takes shape in the forms of nature and the emerging patterns of human life.

However, a level of divine involvement and self-gift that is deeper than the sustenance of things in their existence comes with divine presence. While not isolated instances, the prophetic experience of Israel's great charismatic prophets is a paradigm of this divine "intrusion" into the conscious life of humans. Jeremiah, for instance, found himself unavoidably and unexpectedly aware of the God of his people in unmediated exposure to the divine reality, so "swamped" in his consciousness by God's being-for-him and present to him that it wiped out awareness of the sensible world around him. Though it triggered in his memory those images, ideas, and words that he had previously applied to the God revealed in Moses, the reality of God as he was immediately confronted with it challenged and shattered all those previous patterns of religious insight, because it was incompatible with their inevitably limiting (idolatrous) character. Yet, although this God he now knew in an entirely new way did not "fit" into Jeremiah's worldview, the prophet now understood as never before his Israelite tradition and history and God's present guidance of the people. As the prophet's oracles were gradually accepted by the people some generations later and began to shape their religious understandings, this communication of God-self gave their history a new direction, one that was more in line with the divine intention.

Christians believe that this creative presence of God to human life took unique expression in Jesus of Nazareth. The New Testament texts make it clear that the people looked upon Jesus as a prophet and that he thought of himself as the eschatological prophet, the prophet who would announce and help introduce God's decisive intervention in human affairs. By the time of John's Gospel, understanding of Jesus as the Christ had progressed to the point where Christians realized that this Jesus they had known was and remained the very embodiment of God's Word. This incarnating of God's revealing word of self-gift found its central manifestation in Jesus' human awareness in which, as he grew into mature years and like any human gradually clarified and established his personal identity, the divine Word found every developing embodiment. What this meant was that in Jesus' awareness there was an unparalleled presence of God to a human; Jesus was truly the basic sacrament from which all Christian sacramentality flows; in him the divine intentionality for creation found its focus and source of realization.

Jesus did not cease functioning as God's Word, God's self-expression, as he passed beyond history in his resurrection. Indeed, that function continues even more broadly in the risen Christ's presence to those who receive him in faith, who therefore make up his body which is the church. In being present to Christians, especially when they assemble for eucharist, Christ still proclaims the kind of God his Abba is, still functions as God's Word communicated to humans so that God can be salvifically present to them. This is the ultimate level of presence that is celebrated when Christians gather for eucharist: The Christ who is present in the assembly of those who are present to one another in faith makes present to them his Abba and theirs—which is why in eucharist we pray "Our Father in heaven. . . ."

Self-Giving

In his symbolic use of bread at the last supper, Jesus crystallized the link between Christian marriage and Christian eucharist, a link so close that neither can be understood adequately without the other. What Jesus did was to combine into one action the two most central human symbols of love and concern. He took the giving of food, which is the most basic action of parents (beginning with a mother nursing her baby), and he united its symbolism with that of the gift of the body in marital intercourse. Taking the bread, he said, "This is my body given for you."

Just as the community of the human family springs from this twofold symbolic giving, so the Christian community is meant to develop out of Jesus' continuing giving of himself in the symbol of bread-become-body. This notion of the church emerging continuously from the celebration of eucharist tends to challenge the somewhat static view of the church that we have developed in Western Christianity. In the West, the church has been seen more as a religious organization, as a structured institution, in contrast to the ecclesiology of Eastern Christianity where there is more emphasis on the idea that the church is constantly coming into existence through the celebration of eucharist.

Actually, both points of view represent genuine understandings, and both are rooted in the New Testament word *koinonia* that is used (for example, in Acts) to describe the early Christian communities and their worship gatherings. What we need to regain is a greater sense of the dynamic implication of "communion" and "community," an awareness that what is involved is a process of sharing and that eucharist and the community that celebrates eucharist are authentic and effective insofar as a genuine sharing is taking place. But what kind of sharing are we talking about?

Christian history and the eucharistic liturgies that have come down through that history indicate quite clearly that what Christian communities share most when they gather for eucharist is the risen Christ himself. Though it would be an error to confine the word "communion" to the single action of the faithful receiving the consecrated bread and wine, the fact that the word has come to be associated especially with that one element of eucharistic action suggests that people have in faith recognized that Christ himself is what they share with one another in eucharist.

Eucharistic Origins

It was the experience in faith of the risen Lord that first brought the early Christians together in the days after Jesus' death. Almost instinctively they met to share with one another the presence and the Spirit of their crucified and now risen master. We do not know the exact shape of those earliest Christian gatherings. We do know, though, that out of these gatherings there very quickly developed those memories and traditions that coalesced into the gospels and those worship forms that soon are recognizable as eucharist. So it is clear that these men and women came together with a common sense of being Jesus' disciples, with a common desire to share memories of his life and works, and with a common need to share their belief that he was risen and present among them. There was the recounting of recollections and explanation of what it all meant. There were songs and prayers of praise for what God had done in this Jesus, and there was the sharing of bread and of the cup in memory of him as a sign of their living unity as his body.

These early Christian gatherings, which were more or less "eucharistic," were informal professions of discipleship. Each of the persons present knew that each of the others was there precisely because of her or his acceptance of Jesus as God's son and minister of salvation. There was a shared identification as "Jesus people," an identity that set them apart from the rest of the world, and that, at least on occasion, made them the object of suspicion and persecution. It was the assembled group of believers that was the key sign of Jesus' presence; it was the group's expression of faith and hope through their song and prayer that was the sign of the Spirit being poured out on them. Rather quickly, stylized ritual actions would take on special and enduring symbolic power, particularly in the use of the bread and the wine; but from the beginning it was the assembled believers who were the central and most important symbol. This leads us to a fundamental principle of sacramental liturgies, particularly eucharistic liturgies: The most important sacramental symbol, the most significant reality, in any liturgy is the people who perform the action.

Eucharist is a human action. True, it is also the action of God who is manifested through word and Spirit; it is the action of the risen Christ who still gives himself as source of life to those who believe; but this deeper level of the action can take place only in and through, and in proportion to, the action of the assembled Christians. Moreover, any given eucharist is not the action of humans in general; it is the action of a particular group of people who have come together to profess their discipleship and to share the Lord. As that particular group, they have very specific meanings for one another as individuals and very specific meanings as a group. In their lives they might perhaps be very indifferent and unconcerned about one another, so in their eucharistic gathering they can scarcely function as signs to one another of loving Christian care and service. We would hope the opposite would be the case, that their real care for one another could truly sacramentalize Christ's own concern for each of them, and that their concern as a group for the world around them could be a sign of Christ's redeeming presence.

What particular people in a particular eucharist communicate to one another as persons may be very different from what is said in another eucharistic gathering. In one case people can signify hostility and division, class and economic animosities, distrust, and even fear of one another. In a second case, people can be seen as open and concerned for one another, as warm and trustworthy, as genuinely sisters and brothers in Christ. Clearly, these two groups will perform eucharist quite differently. In the one, there can be genuine sharing in what it means to be Christian; in the other case, any such communion is all but impossible.

Elements of Eucharistic Communing

So, the notion of sharing or communing is basic to genuine eucharistic celebration. If one scans, even quickly, the sequence of actions that make up a eucharist, one can see that "communing" is intrinsic to all of them.

1. The coming together of men, women, and children for eucharist, let us say on a Sunday morning, is something they do in common; they come to the same place, at the same time, to do more or less the same thing. While we seldom pay attention to it when people gather on a Sunday morning, they are there as an assembly called together by the word of God; they are a "called people" and their "call" stands in a direct line with the vocation of Israel out of Egypt to become the people of God. The very fact that they are there together to celebrate eucharist is already a symbol of the faith, heritage, and identity they share with one another.

Of course, the symbolism of this gathering runs deeper. As we already saw, a community of Christians, because it is body of Christ, signifies the presence of the risen Christ, and of his Spirit. Probably the gospel saying, "Where two or three are gathered together in my name, I am there in their midst," is to be understood in terms of eucharistic gathering. And the sacramentally effective action of eucharist begins as soon as people start coming together to share this action—and not only when the ordained appears on the scene. In simpler times, there probably was much more sharing of life's experiences among people as they met and conversed before going into the church building; and the meaning they had for one another passed unnoticed but importantly into what they then did during the liturgy. If, for example, someone learned before

Mass that a friend's young daughter was dangerously ill, that was certain to be part of that person's Prayer of the Faithful. Perhaps we should try to regain some of this interchange among the assembled group, even capitalize on it to make the entire eucharistic celebration more personally meaningful.

2. Listening to the proclaimed word of the Scripture readings is another important element in the communing that goes on in eucharist. While only the lector is publicly active, the attentive hearing of the readings is its own important kind of activity. In human relationships, listening is one of the most important things that people can do; it is half of communication. And we all know that it is often difficult to listen; relatively few people are good listeners. Even when it is a question of hearing the word of God, as this happens in the early portion of the liturgy, people can hear the words without really accepting them as something they wish to understand and make their own.

If, however, a group of Christians gathered together for eucharist really do listen to the Scripture readings for that liturgy, this means that at least for that short time they are sharing a common awareness. They have a more or less common mentality because the same passage of the Scriptures is for that moment shaping their consciousness. They are at that moment professing a common faith by the very fact of listening together. They are sharing the vision of human life revealed by that particular portion of Old or New Testament. One can see how early Christianity placed great weight on this unifying role of the proclaimed Scriptures. Being a lector was recognized as a distinct ministry, which received public recognition in an ordination ceremony.

3. One of the key elements in achieving communion among a group of Christians assembled for eucharist is the homily, or sermon. Any real sharing of a common action demands that the group of people understand what they are doing. In eucharist this is the function of the homily. While a good homily does include an explanation of the Scripture readings that is appropriate to the particular group gathered for eucharist, it is meant to go beyond that and help the people understand the meaning of the entire eucharistic liturgy on that occasion. What is the significance on this day of their coming together as Christians? What does it mean in the concrete circumstances of their lives, at this time and in this place, for them to be disciples of the crucified and risen Christ? How is that view of human life that comes with Christian faith to be translated

into the demands and possibilities of their lives? What is "the word of God" that is addressed to them and to which eucharist is meant to be response?

By responding to such questions, by clarifying the particular meaning of a given eucharist, the homily plays an indispensable role in shaping the shared awareness of the people. More important than any theoretical clarification of a preacher is that person's own faith witness; the preacher is meant to help initiate that sharing of faith that will make the assembled people a true community of believers. And the homily should lead into the Prayer of the Faithful, so that this can be a time of sharing needs and hopes, praying together for common goals, becoming more aware of one another's sorrows, joys, and hopes. One of the things all Christians—for that matter, all humans—have in common is a need for salvation, a need for divine assistance if they are to reach their destiny despite the barriers we encounter. This shared need for God's help finds expression in the eucharistic Prayer of the Faithful.

4. Though we have long become accustomed to thinking of the Eucharistic Prayer, the Canon of the Mass, as the portion that is proper to the celebrant, such is not really the case. Even when it was recited in Latin and said silently, its introduction stated that is was to be prayed in common by celebrant and people. Now, with the use of the vernacular, all can understand and respond to the invitation, "Lift up your hearts to the Lord." "Let us give thanks to the Lord our God."

Even though the celebrant speaks the Eucharistic Prayer, he does so as the voice of the assembled people; it is the prayer of the entire people, not just the celebrant's. This is why the entire community agrees by its solemn "amen" at the end of the prayer.

Obviously, there cannot be a real communing in this Eucharistic Prayer unless the Christians assembled for the celebration actually join their consciousness to the celebrant's as they silently pray with him. But if there is such a united awareness, the Eucharistic Prayer becomes a corporate ritual in which all join, rather than a performance by a celebrant that others watch. All the assembled Christians are meant to commune in the act of acknowledging (that is, worshipping) the God revealed in Jesus as the Christ.

Unless the Eucharistic Prayer becomes this kind of shared praise of God, a true faith community will not emerge from the eucharistic action. This particular prayer is the most ancient and most basic profession of faith. For people to join in praying it means that together they are professing their faith; there is a real communing in faith; there is taking place that process of sharing which is the dynamic meaning of "Christian community." And because the solemn consecration of bread and wine takes place in the course of the Eucharistic Prayer, the assembled Christians are professing their faith not just in the saving events of the past, but also in the saving event happening in their very midst.

5. Finally, there is the sharing of the consecrated bread and wine, the portion of the eucharistic liturgy to which we ordinarily give the name "communion." Limiting the use of the term "communion" to this particular act was quite understandable, because sharing the bread consecrated as the body of Christ could clearly be seen as "receiving the Lord," as the moment in the liturgy when Christians could most clearly experience the mystery of Christ giving himself to them. This is the moment of the risen Lord's most intimate presence to those who believe in him, the moment of most intense communing between Christ and Christian.

Because the sense of the sacredness of this reception of the Lord grew strong and especially meaningful to each Christian who received communion, there was a tendency to stress this individual aspect of the action, with the consequent loss of any social significance. The social meaning—that this is primarily an action of sharing with others—was largely forgotten. Still today, it is not very widely understood that the reception of the eucharistic bread and wine is something that Christians at eucharist are meant to share with one another. They are a community because they come into union with the same Lord; he relates to them as individuals but he also relates to them as a group. It is as a group, a community, that they are body of Christ.

One indication of the extent to which the social character of "receiving communion" was forgotten is the fact that for centuries there was a rather complete loss of the notion that eucharist is a sacred meal. Instead, especially in Catholic circles, emphasis was placed on the teaching that eucharist was a sacrifice; it was commonly called "the sacrifice of the Mass." Ironically, it was also forgotten that the very thing that makes eucharist a sacrificial action is its reality as a sacred covenant meal. Overlooking this meal character of the action led theologians to many strange theories to explain what was meant by calling eucharist "a sacrifice," theories that have now been largely discredited and abandoned. This does not mean that the sacrificial nature of eucharist is unimportant, or that concentration on it was a mistake. Indeed, it is important from several points of view, and so it is worth our giving more detailed attention to it, trying to profit from the recent shifts in theological understanding of what the word "sacrifice" means when applied to Christianity.

Summary

Though many Catholics associate the word "communion" only with reception of the consecrated bread, the notion of "communing" applies to the entire eucharistic action. From this communing the Christian community's faith should grow in clarity and intensity.

Various elements of the eucharistic action provide distinctive ways of communing: Gathering for eucharist reflects people's share in God's election and their shared response; listening to the proclaimed Scripture enables the group to share a common understanding of the gospel, and the homily is meant to insure such an understanding and to relate it to people's lives; the Eucharistic Prayer itself is the shared prayer of the entire community, even though the ordained celebrant prays it aloud in their name; and sharing of the consecrated food and drink is a specially symbolic communing.

Questions for Reflection and Discussion

1. How did the celebration of eucharist originate?

2. Why are people the most important symbolic element in any eucharist?

3. How do people commune with one another in eucharist?

4. How does eucharist celebrate Christians' identity as body of Christ?

5. Explain: Eucharist is the action of the entire assembled group.

9   EUCHARIST: COVENANT SACRIFICE

If one examines the metaphor of the husband-wife relationship that the Israelitic prophets used to describe the way their god, Yahweh, dealt with this people, one discovers that the underlying reality the metaphor is meant to clarify is a relationship, which that Israelitic tradition calls the "covenant." This means that the use of the husband-wife/Yahweh-Israel imagery stands at the very center of Old Testament thought, because no category of religious understanding is more central to Israel than "covenant."

The event that established Israel as a people, the Exodus from Egypt, focused on the covenant that the people under Moses made with their god at Mount Sinai. What held the twelve tribes loosely together during the disorganized period of the Judges was some sense of a shared covenant with this one divinity. The new situation of the kingship under David and his successors was legitimated in terms of a special covenant made between Yahweh and the Davidic dynasty, a covenant that was inserted within the older Mosaic covenant as a further step in Yahweh's special election of this people.

And it was appropriate that the prophets, beginning with Hosea, should turn to marriage as an image for understanding this covenant between Yahweh and Israel, since marriage itself was seen by the peoples of that time as an important instance of covenant. It was an alliance (or contract) between the two people involved, but it was also an alliance between two families, or if the man and woman had a special role in society (for example, king and a princess from another nation), an alliance between tribes or nations. Once introduced into Israelitic thinking about the covenant with their god, the husband-wife imagery was a constant connotation in any reference to that covenant.

Covenant and Sacrifice

This means that the husband-wife significance passed into Israelitic understandings of what they did in their sacrifices in the temple. We place the term "sacrifice" on the rituals performed in the temple; the Israelites themselves did not use this generic term. Instead, they listed a number of worship acts, and among these none were more basic than the peace offerings. The essential structure of these peace offerings is that of a covenant meal between Yahweh and the people, a ceremonial meal like the one (described in Exodus 24) at Mount Sinai that first formalized the Mosaic covenant.

One of the worship situations classified by the Bible as a peace offering was the Passover dinner that was shared each spring by Jews throughout the ancient world. Jesus is described as sharing this meal, whose purpose was to keep fresh in Jewish memory the Exodus and the covenant with Yahweh, with his closest disciples on the night before he died. The centrality of covenant on that occasion is clear from the words Jesus used over the cup: "This is my blood, the new covenant . . ." And since Christian eucharist is meant to link Christians in memory to what Jesus did at that last supper, the "covenant" meaning, with all its marital overtones, is basic to the understanding of the eucharistic liturgy.

Covenant Meal as Sacrifice

Thinking about the eucharistic action as a covenant meal is not yet all that common among Catholics, although some of the Reformation churches have kept a bit more of the notion. For centuries, until very recently, the emphasis in Catholic understandings of eucharist was on "sacrifice." We commonly referred to "the sacrifice of the Mass," and in so doing we were following the lead of the Council of Trent (1545-1563), which had used "sacrifice" as its basic way of describing the eucharistic action. At the same time, we had considerable difficulty finding a satisfactory theological justification for employing this term.

"Sacrifice" seemed to imply dying, being destroyed, immolation, shedding of blood. Even when we used the word in an applied sense, it connoted giving up something. Since the eucharistic action has always been seen as the recollection of Jesus' redemptive death, it seemed correct to categorize both the death on Calvary and its eucharistic commemoration as "sacrifices." However, recent biblical and historical study has forced us to reconsider our understanding of "sacrifice" as it applies to Old Testament Israel, to the action of Jesus that begins at the supper and continues into his death and resurrection, and to Christian enactment of eucharist.

Old Testament Sacrifice

In examining the ritual of Israel, specifically that carried on in the Jerusalem temple, we have had our previous explanations of Old Testament sacrifices challenged.

1. In temple rituals involving the offering of an animal, the killing of the animal was not an intrinsic part of the liturgical action and so, when circumstances demanded it, anyone could kill the animals. What did pertain to the ritual was the use of the animal's blood. Since the blood was the life, it belonged to God; and so there was the ceremonial pouring of the blood (either at the base of the altar or on its four corners) as a public recognition of God's sovereignty over life.

2. There was no generic category of "sacrifice" applied to the various liturgical rituals. Among the diverse celebrations mentioned, none was more basic than the peace offering, which in its essentials was a covenant meal shared by Yahweh and the people. This covenant meal intensified and reiterated the covenant relationship or, if it had been violated by Israel, served to restore the covenant. Thus, a central act of what we would call "the sacrificial system" of the Israelites was a meal; and what the people (or their representatives, the priests) did to participate in the sacrifice was to share in the meal.

3. Classified among the peace offerings was the annual celebration of the Passover, which was carried out not in the temple but in Jewish homes. Quite clearly, what people were doing in this situation was sharing a meal together. But just as clearly this meal was

a recollection and restatement of the Mosaic covenant. All the ritualized use of foods was accompanied by an explanation of their Exodus and covenant significance. The prayers celebrated Yahweh's covenant love for the Israelites, and the assembled members of the family remembered and identified with their Israelitic traditions.

Jesus' Sacrifice

Jesus' last supper with his disciples before his death is described in the gospels as just such a familial gathering for the Passover. By eating together, Jesus and his friends were performing the Paschal peace offering; and it was this action that Jesus "transignified" by the new meaning he gave to the sharing of the bread and the cup, that is, the sharing of himself.

Can we, then, legitimately speak of "Jesus' sacrifice"? What would we mean when we speak this way? Traditionally, Christianity has looked upon Jesus' death on Calvary as sacrificial. And somehow, both the action of Jesus at the supper and Christian celebration of eucharist share in what happened on Calvary. Yet, in trying to fit Christ's and the church's actions into the category of "sacrifice," we ran into serious questions, and we resorted to notions such as "unbloody sacrifice" and "spiritual immolation," which only raised more questions. Wrestling with these questions has helped us, with the aid of theological reflection, to see things in a somewhat new light.

We first begin with a principle that has many applications to Christian theology. We must allow what Jesus did to remain distinctive and not force it into some already formulated category (such as "sacrifice"). While such categories may help us understand Jesus' actions somewhat, they cannot deal adequately with the radically new thing that happens in Jesus. Applying this to our present discussion: What did Jesus actually do in the action of his Passover, beginning with the supper and extending through his death into his resurrection? Basically, he gave himself to his friends. This is what he says in breaking the bread with them, "This is my body [that is, myself] given for you." This is how his passage through death into risen life is described in Ephesians 5, a gift of self to his disciples that can be compared to a Christian married couple's self-gift to each other.

One can apply to this profound self-giving of Jesus the term "sacrifice," though the application changes drastically the understanding one has of this term. "Sacrifice" refers to an action in which something, often referred to as a "victim," is put aside, usually permanently, for a sacred purpose. Such "removal" of the victim from the realm of the ordinary or secular is intended to recognize and honor some divinity. In the case of Jesus' Passover, what happens is that by going freely to death in order to be the instrument of humankind's salvation, Jesus is placed irrevocably beyond the ordinary world of space and time we live in. He lives with a new and fulfilled form of human existence, so that he can share this fuller life with all persons of faith. This giving of new life to others is the sacred purpose that acknowledges his Father, who is glorified in his "adopted sons and daughters."

"Sacrifice," then, refers to the combined act of death-resurrection. If we apply the term to what Jesus does today, it means that the risen Christ is giving himself in new life to his friends. This self-giving by the risen Lord is his continuing action of "offering sacrifice." And the corollary of this is that Christians' action of "offering sacrifice" consists in their loving self-gift to their fellow humans which, because it is a recognition of their relationship as brothers and sisters, witnesses to their common relationship to that God who is the Father of our Lord, Jesus Christ. This relationship, among humans and between them and God, a relationship that finds its center in the risen Christ, is the new covenant.

When Christians gather for that covenant meal they call "eucharist," they are pledging their "being for" one another by sharing in this meal, by accepting the covenant relationship to one another, by identifying themselves to one another as members of the same family of God. As individuals and as a community, they join themselves to the risen Christ, present in their midst, as set aside for the sacred purpose of bringing new life to their fellow humans. This is what it means for them to "offer the sacrifice" of eucharist.

Summary

Christian eucharist is, then, a continuing celebration of the new covenant, which is lived out by the community of the risen Christ and his disciples, joined together as one body, bringing new and unending life to all who do not refuse it. But what eucharist celebrates is that the entire life of these Christians, if lived out in loving concern for and genuine self-gift to their fellow humans, is a living sacrifice. Because this loving self-gift must take ever-changing form as the circumstances of life change, the covenant must be constantly renewed and "translated" in a somewhat different fashion. This process of eucharist renewing and adapting the covenant to history as it unfolds will occupy us in a later chapter when we study eucharist as initiation into Christian decision.

Questions for Reflection and Discussion

1. How does the image of husband and wife relate to "covenant" in biblical thinking?

2. What is meant by "Jesus' sacrifice"?

3. Is Jesus' resurrection a "sacrifice"? In what sense?

4. How do Christians "offer the sacrifice of the Mass"?

5. How do you understand "sacrifice" as applied to eucharist?

PART FOUR

CHRISTIAN INITIATION

10   INITIATION INTO CHRISTIAN COMMUNITY

As soon as Christianity began and communities came into being through faith in the resurrection of Jesus, the need arose to introduce new members into these communities. When it describes the first Pentecost, the second chapter of the Acts of the Apostles says that five thousand were baptized. While we do not know exactly how converts to the new faith were initiated in those earliest decades, it is clear that there was some form (or forms) of indicating that the community received them and that they were joining the community. The New Testament writings make it clear that baptizing developed very early as the one common way (that is, ritual) for this initiation.

Before long, however, the understanding that Christians had of the baptizing ceremony shifted away from emphasis on "entry into the Christian community." Some of that significance inevitably remained, since it was rather obvious that a baptized person was becoming a new member of a particular Christian group. But Christians began to think about baptism much more in terms of "removing sin," "setting one on the path to heaven," or "washing away a stain."

Very importantly, the development by the fifth century of a theology of "original sin" had a decisive and not entirely beneficial effect on the understanding of Christian baptism. As the story in Genesis about the sin of Adam and Eve came to be interpreted as description of an actual individual historical happening—which was not intended by the scriptural authors—a number of theological puzzles arose. The sinful happening in Eden was seen to pass down somehow through all human history, though no one could explain satisfactorily how. Each human, by the very fact of being conceived, was marked by this sin. Without any personal guilt, each human entered life in the state of grave sin because of this universal inheritance from our "first parents."

Given such a picture of the human condition, the inevitable question was, How can a person be freed from this inherited evil? This is where baptism came as a "solution." It was the merciful means provided by Jesus through his death, so that in baptism the stain of original sin could be removed from a person and the possibility of reaching one's eternal destiny could be restored. Baptism was, then, an indispensable means of reaching salvation. It proved almost impossible for Christian theologians to explain how God, who willed the salvation of all humans who did not deliberately reject it, could grant salvation to the millions of humans who had no access to this Christian sacrament.

Without rejecting the deeper insights of tradition contained in this centuries-long explanation about baptism and its effect, careful study of this tradition (especially in its biblical formulations) has allowed us to see "original sin" and baptism in a broader context. There is a certain universality about human sinfulness that carries the history of such sinful folly back to the very origins of humanity. Besides, each human must pass from identification with this "kingdom of sin" (what Paul refers to as the time of the "first Adam") to identification with that "kingdom of God" which is established definitively by the death and resurrection of the "second Adam," Jesus Christ. To put it into the symbolic language used in the baptismal liturgy, one must "renounce Satan and all his works and pomps."

Salvation from sin comes, then, through adhering to the kingdom of God, a reality that extends beyond the church. Baptism, on the other hand, initiates a person into the church, into a community dedicated to bringing the kingdom of God to fulfillment, a community that is part of but does not encompass the whole of this kingdom. More aware now of this distinction between the church and the kingdom of God, we have been brought back to a renewed awareness of baptism's function as initiation into the community of Christian faith and life.

One clear benefit of recovering early Christianity's understanding of baptism is our movement away from the individualism that characterized a baptism theology that focused almost exclusively on "removal of original sin." There has been an accompanying movement away from the excessive concentration on human sinfulness that marked many centuries of Christian conscience. Sin is a reality of human experience. Human malice and moral weakness are all too evident in our history, but Christianity is meant to bring into existence a human situation that is a positive alternative to sin and suffering, that is, God's kingdom of love, justice, and peace. Baptism is meant to initiate a person into a Christian community, which exists to help create this positive alternative.

Initiation: Basic to Life

Christianity is not unique in having initiation rites. Depending on the nature of the human group involved, every community of people needs some way of incorporating new members. Even in the family, where the basic introduction into the group comes through birth, there are various ways cultures celebrate the acceptance of a new member. Obviously, this initial act of celebrating birth does not completely introduce the person into a family. Such introduction will take many years; in some ways it is a life-long process that takes somewhat different forms as one goes through the various "passages" from one stage of life to another. This process of initiation will include many happenings, the making of many decisions, the development of many human relationships; it will be inseparable from a person's life experience and growth into maturity.

Reflecting on what entry into a family really means, a years-long and relatively difficult process of becoming part of a genuine community of people, helps us understand more clearly what is involved in initiation. There are, of course, relatively superficial instances of initiation, for example, the ceremony that still takes place on ships crossing the international dateline when those doing so for the first time are initiated by the "old timers." But when something more serious is involved, there is always a personal element in the initiating. Because persons do not become "something new" instantaneously, genuine initiation into a group always takes some time; it is always a process. Usually it is helpful to have an initiation ceremony, but this ceremony only promises what will take place as the individual is gradually integrated into the social group.

Though religious initiation is a very distinctive type of social process, it might be helpful to look at some of the elements that are common to all situations of initiation. Since any social grouping exists for some reason, a new member coming into a group will wish to and be expected to share this purpose. This means, then, that the initiate must be informed about the group's goals, must be convinced of their motives in seeking these goals. Since such goals are generally somewhat unspecified—for example, to do something about arranging some good recreational facilities for youth in a neighborhood—and need to be spelled out in detail over a period of time and in response to concrete circumstances, the new member only gradually comes to understand what the group really seeks to accomplish. In addition, the new member discovers over a period of time how serious the group really is about its stated purpose and whether, therefore, one should really commit one's time and energy to the group's activities.

Another thing a new member is meant to share is the group's identity. This is usually the first question a person asks when invited to join some group: What kind of a group is it? And the underlying hesitation in the person's mind: Would I wish to be identified that way? If, for instance, a group sees itself as militant terrorists, one might not wish to become such and to be so known, and so would have no inclination to join the group. On the other hand, if a group identifies itself as a political party committed to working for certain social goals through active participation in normal political processes, a person might be quite happy to share such a social identification.

One of the ways groups clarify for themselves their identity and their goals is by myths, but myths in the positive sense of the story an individual or group tells to explain what is happening or has happened. Any group of humans has its story of what it has been and now is. It generally refers to this story as the group's "history," but the fact that those not in the group might explain those same happenings in a different way lets us know that there is always a certain interpretation, a certain creativity that enters into such accounts. It is interesting to watch the national political conventions that precede presidential elections as the parties struggle to find some common identity and purpose they can agree on (their party platform) and to notice the way speaker after speaker appeals to the story that the party has used to describe itself: It is the party that has always supported labor and fought for social reform, or it is the party that has always tried to balance the budget and establish conservative economic policy.

Naturally, any group tries to tell its story as convincingly as possible to prospective members. Unless the person entering the group really accepts the group's myth, there will be no genuine identification with it. Unless there is such genuine and growing identification, and unless that person's individual story is integrated with the group's story, the initiate will become only a nominal member and will never share the group's existence and activities.

One of the most effective ways some groups introduce prospective or newly initiated members to the group's identity and purposes is to immerse them as quickly as possible in some of the group's activities, and in the midst of it explain the group's self-understanding and purpose. There is a way of knowing what a group is all about that comes only in the experience of doing what the group does. This is an understanding that no theoretical explanation can give. If a group can arrange such experience prior to the individual's entry, it gives the group an opportunity to appraise the desirability of admitting that person, and it gives the person a chance to decide if entry into that community of people is good.

Many groups do not have any formal initiation rituals. Yet there seems to be an almost instinctive tendency to devise some regular formula to say that the group is accepting the new member and that the new member is seeking and accepting membership in the group. Primitive peoples have initiation rites for young men and women as they come to puberty; college fraternities have their hazings; service clubs have their special luncheon meeting to welcome new members. New citizens are recognized as such and accept their new civic responsibilities in a public ceremony. And throughout history religious groups have developed special rituals of initiation.

Even though its approach to liturgy was strikingly informal in the early decades, Christianity has followed this pattern. There is clear evidence that from its earliest days Christianity has used some form of baptizing to introduce neophytes into the community.

Religious initiations usually are the most solemn and significant, at least if the religion is alive and its ritual has not become empty and formalistic. In Christianity, initiation is associated especially with two liturgical acts, baptism and confirmation. Actually, initiation should be seen as a life-long process that involves but is not limited to these two sacramental rites. Christian initiation is the process of becoming Christian. This, obviously, requires a growth in faith and commitment that takes place over a lifetime and can in no way be achieved by one or two liturgical rituals. Unless this more basic "entry into the Christ mystery" does occur, the rituals of baptism and confirmation by themselves are largely meaningless and therefore ineffective. Really, the process of initiation is identical with what is sometimes called "religious formation" or with what should be the formation of conscience.

Revised Rite of Initiation

Because it is so fundamental, the process of initiation is being studied and revitalized in the Christian churches today. In Roman Catholicism, for example, the recent revision of the rite for the Christian initiation of adults (R.C.I.A.) has already proved to be one of the more significant and enriching developments in the contemporary church. This new rite regards adult baptizing as the paradigm instance of initiation, because the adult initiate is personally expressing the decisions intrinsic to Christian faith. Inevitably, then, the rite draws attention to the psychological aspects of initiation: the understandings, attitudes, intentions, and hopes of the person being baptized, as well as of the community receiving him or her into its midst.

If the baptism liturgy itself is to function in this way as an authentic statement of the person's decision to be Christian, it is clear that it must be preceded by a period of careful preparation, in which the person is informed about the nature and demands of Christian life and can discover and accept Christian faith. So, the revised rite has restored the adult catechumenate, the preparatory lead-up to baptism, which was such a notable element in the life of early Christianity. Already there are signs that this catechumenate, both in its more limited form as an actual preparation of adults for entry into the church, and in the more extended form of adult education aimed at authenticating the faith of already baptized women and men, will have beneficial and far-reaching effects on the church.

In terms of our broadening the notion of "initiation" to include the entire process of people becoming Christian, it is important to remember that the catechumenate is itself already part of this process. Before the formal ritual of baptizing, the new Christian is starting to share the Christian community's life and purposes and self-understanding. Even during the centuries when "forgiveness of original sin" dominated the church's thinking about baptism, the church retained some notion that a person in the period of preparation was already "partly in the church." If, for example, a person who was a catechumen died suddenly without any opportunity to receive sacramental baptism, that person was considered to have "baptism of desire" (a somewhat misleading term) and so to have obtained salvation.

Infant Baptism

However, the bulk of Christians being introduced into the church are infants who cannot yet enter personally into the conscious profession of faith. Baptizing such infants, which the church has done from the earliest centuries, has always raised questions about the nature and effectiveness of baptism. These questions were so basic that, beginning with the time of the Protestant Reformation in the sixteenth century, some Christian churches rejected the baptizing of children until they were able to make their own decision to become Christian. Basically, the difficulty boils down to this: Christian baptism is an act of conversion, a person's free decision to profess Christian faith. Therefore it requires enough human maturity to understand what beliefs are being professed and to make the free choice of becoming a Christian. None of this is applicable to an infant.

This problem needs some honest confrontation and some relatively satisfactory answer, since most of the persons being introduced into most of the Christian churches are infants. Fortunately, there is a good deal of thought being given to this, especially among religious educators.

In the case of infants, there is an informal but extremely important initiation into the Christian community that begins with their birth and is meant to be continued in various ways (including liturgical rituals) right into adult life. Although the new rite for the baptism of adults does not develop this theology of infant initiation, it provides some precious guidelines, particularly in the way it indicates that an understanding of the church as personal community must underpin any authentic theology of Christian initiation.

This all seems to say that any discussion of the sacraments of baptism and confirmation must take account of the broader reality of Christian initiation, the process of introduction into the Christian community and into the mystery of Christ. It is this process, then, that we will examine a bit more closely in the next chapter. After doing this, we can go on to see how the respective sacramental liturgies contribute to this "growth in Christ."

Summary
Present explanation of baptism has moved away from earlier concentration on "removal of original sin." Instead, in line with the new rite for adult baptism, there is more attention being given to initiation into the community, to growth in understanding, and to the free decision involved in faith. What this means is that initiation rituals, whether for adults or infants, must be seen as part of a larger reality, the initiation of a person into the mystery of Christ through initiation into the life of the Christian community.

Questions for Reflection and Discussion
1. How do human groups initiate new members? How does this happen in the church?

2. What is a Christian initiated into?

3. Explain what is meant by saying that Christian initiation is a process.

4. How is this process of initiation related to "formation of Christian conscience"?

5. Is there any justification for infant baptism? Explain.

11   SIGNIFICANCE
OF *COMMUNIO*

T he most obvious significance of the rite of Christian initiation has always been that of entry into the community.
Perhaps because it was so immediately obvious, and because people had been gradually led to think of sacramental liturgies as ceremonies that worked very mysteriously and through
God's hidden activity, this significance of the rite tended to be obscured by meanings such as "removal of original sin."

Yet, if one looks at baptism theologically, one can see that "entry
into the Christian community" has an intrinsic primacy among the
significances of the ritual. After all, it is by being introduced into
the believing community that one comes to Christian faith. One
carries out his or her responsibilities for fulfilling the mission of
Christianity by sharing this mission with others in some Christian
community. As a matter of fact, it is difficult to find any genuinely
Christian activity that is unrelated to a believing Christian group;
even the prayer of a hermit in his or her geographical isolation is
meant to be as a member of the church and in union with all the
praying of the church.

A basic significance of Christian initiation, then, is that of entering a community. Before we go any further with this idea, we should make more precise our use of the term "community." In an earlier chapter we mentioned briefly that the term has more than one meaning, especially as it is applied to Christianity. As early as the second chapter of the Acts of the Apostles we can notice an ambiguity. In that passage, which describes how the earliest Christians gathered into groups to share their faith and life, the Greek word *koinonia is* used. This word can refer to the group of people who are gathered and to whom we usually apply the word "community." But the word can also (and in this case probably does) have an active meaning: "the communing," the sharing that goes on within a group.

In Christianity there clearly is (and must be) a visible community of people, and there are observable structures of their existence as a community. But sharing their faith and their prayer and their Christian activity with one another is more basic. This is their active communing. The group grows out of this sharing and finds appropriate structures to implement this sharing. The more active meaning of *koinonia*, then, is paramount.

Because it is so easy to lose sight of this more action-oriented understanding of the term, it might be helpful if (somewhat artificially) we use two terms in our discussion: "community" to refer to the group of people, and the Latin word *communio* to refer to whatever aspects of communing we are describing. Christian *communio* is a very distinctive kind of sharing, setting Christianity apart from other human groups. Each of these other groups, to the extent that it is a genuine community, has its own distinctive *communio*.

Christianity is an organized, institutionalized, religious group; more basically, it is a movement in which people share faith and life. Because the activity in which Christianity is engaged is complex, there are a number of different aspects to the sharing (the *communio*) that takes place among Christians. As in any community, there is a sharing of the group's vision or "myth," a sharing of its mission and purpose, a sharing of the values espoused by the group, a sharing of its identity, and a sharing of the spirit animating the group. This chapter will look at specific ways in which these five sharings are meant to occur in the church.

Sharing the Christian Vision

Christianity began with a new vision of what human life was all about. With the experience of Jesus' resurrection, the earliest disciples saw everything differently. Even the story of what God had been doing in the centuries of Old Testament Israel was now understood in the light of what Jesus had done. It took time for these earliest Christians to sort out what had happened but they knew that it was something utterly unprecedented. Somehow a new humanity had come into being, a new creation was in progress, a new and definitive phase of the kingdom of God had been inaugurated. Above all, they began to see that a radically new understanding of what it meant to be human had been revealed in Jesus, especially in his death and resurrection.

So, they began to tell a new story about the ultimate realities of our human existence and destiny; in other words, they began to tell the distinctively Christian myth. Naturally, the first place this story was told and retold was in the Christian communities themselves. As the early disciples of Jesus recalled the things that Jesus had said and done, and as they tried to fit all this together with their Jewish beliefs about God's care of Israel and fit it also to their present experience of the risen Lord and his Spirit, the story developed into what we call the New Testament Scriptures.

Though we have very few details about the earliest years of the church, something like an incipient catechumenate must have come into being very early. Many persons were attracted to this new faith, this new way of life, and before these people would have become Christian they would certainly have received some instruction. They would have been told, at least briefly, what God had done and continued to do in Jesus as the Christ. The communities shared with these prospective members the Jesus-as-Christ story about humanity and its salvation.

Actually, even this preparatory explanation, the beginnings of Christian catechesis, must have been preceded by some initial preaching of the Christian message. That there was such a first proclamation of the good news of Jesus' resurrection is clearly attested to by the Acts of the Apostles. This book is not a history in the ordinary sense, but it is rooted in the actual happenings of those early years. Time and time again it describes Christians announcing the gospel to both the Jew and Gentile who had not yet heard it. As a matter of fact, from Acts we can learn what the kernel of this early preaching ("kerygma") was: Jesus of Nazareth, who had been put to death, was now risen and present to and through the community as Christ and Lord.

The principal task of the early Christian communities—and it remains the principal task of the church throughout its history—was that of sharing its myth, its gospel, the good news about what God had done in Jesus. No aspect of this sharing is more critical than the introduction given those who were immediately preparing for entry into the community. Very early there developed a catechumenate program, a regular pattern of instruction, blessings, and prayers that led up to the initiation liturgy.

Today, the same need that the early Christians faced must be met by our Christian communities. If people are to become disciples of Christ intelligently and freely, if they are to participate productively in the life of the church, if their faith is to be an integral part of their outlook on life, they must accurately and thoroughly understand what Christianity really is. This is the need the renewed catechumenate is directed to fill. If this results in a greater sharing of the Christian vision, it will help produce Christian groups that are truly communities of faith.

What elements of Christian vision must people be introduced to, what elements of understanding must they increasingly grow in, that is, be continuously initiated, if they are to become truly Christian? 1) Most importantly, they must come to know who and what Jesus of Nazareth was and is, to understand what it is that he has done to bring salvation to humans. 2) They must come to know what God is really like, come to know how God was revealed to us in the life, death, and resurrection of Jesus, what God does in the lives of people to guide them toward their destiny. 3) They must come to know through a combination of instruction and their own experience of life what they as Christians should do for themselves and for others, what responsibilities they share because of the gift of faith.

One could continue to spell out more of the understandings that must be shared in community if the church is to grow and fulfill its mission, but let us mention just one more because of its central importance. It is essential that Christians be led to understand what is going on when they assemble for the eucharistic celebration. What is happening? What is the particular role of the celebrant? What is their own share in this key liturgical act? What exactly is meant by the special presence of Christ that is connected with this action? How is this action meant to function as the key to their faith and life as Christians?

When one looks at the elements of understanding that one needs in order to share the Christian vision, it is clear that initiation into the Christian community must be a lifelong process of deepening one's grasp and appreciation of the gospel. As we will see later, the liturgies of baptism and confirmation play an indispensable role in this initiation, but they are only key moments in a much longer and more inclusive process. The more each individual and each Christian community enters into the Christian vision of human life, the more they will become part of that *communio*, that sharing of human consciousness, which is the essence of the living church.

Sharing the Christian Mission

One of the basic elements in understanding what it means to be Christian is the realization that the church (and each of its members) shares the saving mission of Jesus. To be a Christian is to be a disciple, to join with the risen Christ in his continuing work of bringing into being the kingdom of God, which is the ultimate well-being of humans. Obviously, one must know about this mission in order to share it. But sharing in the mission is more than just knowing about it; it is an awareness of being sent to do something and the consequent sense of responsibility for accomplishing that goal. Sharing the mission is the lived-out choice to participate in the community's activities in order to achieve the mission.

The Christian mission is a distinctive one proper to this community, the church. It is the historical continuation and implementation of Jesus' own mission. The New Testament describes Jesus as sent into the world to announce and to bring into being the final stage of the kingdom of God. He is sent to teach and to heal, to correct the misunderstandings people have about the God he knew as Abba, and to reconcile people with one another and with God. But the New Testament also indicates quite clearly that the earthly career of Jesus is but the beginning of the final stage of the kingdom. What is begun in Jesus is meant to be carried on in history by subsequent generations of disciples until the final destiny of human history is accomplished.

Such a description of the church's mission seems simple enough, but it is still very general and abstract. It needs to be spelled out for each group and for each individual within that group in terms of the actual set of historical circumstances they live in. A Christian community is not meant to heal people in general; it is meant to heal the people it comes into contact with, the people it bears responsibility for. It is not meant to work for social justice and peace in some vague fashion, but by undertaking precise measures that are calculated to come to grips with the actual situation it finds itself in. As a result, the practical understanding of the mission of a particular Christian community can be discovered only in the course of trying to carry out that mission.

How, then, is a person to be initiated into the mission of Christian community? Certainly in stages; but at each stage there should be a combination of instructions and experience. There must be the developing experience of what it means to translate Christian faith and vision into actual life; but as this experience unfolds there must be a continuing clarification of the way God's own saving action is occurring in and through the community's actions. Ideally, the very first stage of this double initiation will come with a person's decision to participate in the catechumenate. A more definitive stage of participation in the community's mission should come with the baptism ceremony. Then a gradually deepening commitment to this mission will find expression in the ritual of confirmation. And each celebration of eucharist (as we will see in a later chapter) should be a step in further identification with and involvement in the community's Christian mission.

If a person genuinely accepts her or his mission as a member of a Christian community, it means that that person's personal life goals become integrated into this mission. The person really makes the goals of the kingdom of God the primary goals of his or her own life. This demands a firm but flexible decision to "live for Christ," that is, the decision to be authentically a disciple of Christ. This in turn demands that one's own personal myth, the story one tells about one's own identity and destiny, be seen as an integral part of the larger Christian myth. If one is to commit oneself to seeking the kingdom of God as life's primary objective, one must truly understand that only the Christ-myth can make sense of one's own personal story.

Initiating new members into a community's mission presupposes that that community itself is actively involved in pursuing its mission. If the new member cannot become part of fulfilling that mission because the community in question is not really committed to that goal, that person will be unable to acquire any sense of sharing the mission of Christ. One can have a feeling of joining a religious organization, a congregation, a friendly group of people, but one cannot experience *communio*, cannot have the sense of being part of a dynamic movement, of sharing a mission.

Sharing a Values System

One of the more striking moments in the liturgy of baptism is the renunciation of Satan. But what really is being renounced? Certainly much more than an open allegiance to Satan. What is involved is a choice against the temptation to follow a false set of values, a choice to follow instead the gospel's values.

In the long process of initiation into Christianity, nothing is more practically important than discovering those values that underpin the Christian way of life, and then gradually accepting the values as one's own. People do what they do, make the decisions they do, live in a certain style because of the values they have. Some people value power more than anything else; others give personal friendship a higher priority; others prefer a simple and unencumbered life; others value service to those in need more than their own enjoyment. And so persons with different value priorities live quite different lives and become quite different persons.

Any group of people who forms a genuine community in which there is real *communio* shares a basic values system. Where there is authentic Christian *communio*, the shared values system is that exemplified in the life, death, and resurrection of Jesus, and in the lives of his disciples. Such a community marches to a different drummer. The New Testament description of all this was to say that Jesus followed a different wisdom, which was neither that of the Jewish teachers of his day nor the wisdom of the sages of Greece. Jesus' wisdom was ultimately a very paradoxical wisdom, for what sense does it make to say that one has to die in order to live?

One of the gospel passages where the distinctiveness of Jesus' values system is emphasized is that of Jesus' temptation in the desert immediately after his baptism by John. The tempter (Satan) does not even suggest any of the crasser attractions that ordinarily divert humans from becoming what they should; he takes for granted that Jesus is determined to do good and to bring salvation to his fellow humans. What he suggests to Jesus are "better" ways of accomplishing this task. He suggests that Jesus win a following by performing startling magical deeds (changing stones to bread), that he try sensational but foolish things to gain attention (such as jumping from the top of the temple and expecting God to preserve him miraculously from harm), and—the real "clincher"—that he be sensible enough to seek his goal through wealth and power.

Jesus rejects all of these as paths to human fulfillment, as means of salvation. Instead, he taught that poverty, simplicity, honesty, freedom of spirit, concern for others, and ordinariness are to be valued. Above all else, persons—all persons—are to be valued.

How such enigmatic values are to be expressed in any given set of historical circumstances depends on the judgment made by Christians who understand the Christ-myth and are committed to the mission of Christianity. In any set of circumstances those judgments and the values that underlie them will be regarded as "naive," "impractical," "unrealistic." As Paul told the first community at Corinth long ago, the wisdom of Christ is "a stumbling block to the Jews and foolishness to the Greeks."

If people are to follow this Christian values system, they need the support of one another, precisely because so many others will reject these values. People can embrace Christian values only if they are introduced into and increasingly become part of a real Christian community where one of the elements of *communio* is a sharing of these values. If this happens, people will learn by experience that the way of life grounded in such values truly brings peace and joy.

Sharing Christian Identity

Some years ago a prominent sociologist of religion conducted a survey across the U.S. to determine how important religious faith and affiliation were in people's thinking. The question he asked was simple: "How do you think of yourself: as an American, a worker, a man or woman, a member of this or that religion?" He found that the particular religious faith of people came quite far down the list, which seemed to indicate that being Christian (or a particular form of Christian, such as Catholic) did not play as prominent a part as we had imagined in the way that people identified themselves. People thought of themselves as *being* American, or as *being* physicians or lawyers or as mothers and fathers of a family, or as *being* rich or poor. They did not particularly think of themselves as *being* Christian; rather, religion was something they *had*, such as membership in a service organization, or an education.

Of course, such surveys are always difficult to appraise; one must be careful not to draw too many conclusions from them. However, it does seem that religious communities such as the Catholic church have not been too successful in creating in their members a sense of Christian identity. This has become increasingly a problem in the U.S. as immigrant groups, among whom ethnic and religious identity were intertwined, become more assimilated and ethnic identities become dimmed. The church, then, faces a basic task: How can men and women come to share personally the distinctive identity of the Christian community?

Difficult though the task is, the objective is quite clear and simple. The earliest Christians thought of themselves as disciples; this was the identity that dominated their individual and community life. So, too, must any later generation of Christians come to identify itself. Christian discipleship should be the fundamental context of awareness and activity within which other identities—nationality, gender, social class, professional activity, etc.—are experienced. One long-standing indication that this should be so is the naming of a person at baptism. She or he, on the occasion of entry into the Christian community, is given a Christian name, that is, a new sign of personal identity.

Even though we associate a person's identity with her or his name, the name by itself does not provide a person with conscious identification. Establishing one's identity is a lifelong process (as we saw earlier) that lies at the very center of our life experience. So, too, giving one a Christian name is only a symbol of the hoped-for process of truly Christian identification. Acquiring such an identity requires discovery and choice on the person's part, discovering exactly what discipleship entails and choosing to accept the implications of such discipleship. So, this identity is one into which a person must be gradually and consistently initiated.

But how can a Christian community more effectively lead its members into such a basic self-identification? For one thing, it must share with the individual the Christ-myth, that explanation of the ultimate meaning of human life by which the church over the centuries has understood itself and its purpose. However, presenting this community story to a new member must be inseparable from the community's explanation of its own identity, the way it thinks of itself as a group of people who are disciples of the risen Lord.

If a group of Christians does not really think of itself in this way, it is incapable of initiating new members into Christian self-identity. If, on the contrary, a community of Christian men and women does really share a sense of being disciples of Christ, this will be something that it cherishes and will wish to share with those who enter the community. And to the extent that members, both old and new, share this self-understanding, there will be a genuine Christian *communio.*

One other element of this initiation into Christian identity should be mentioned, the introduction into the community's mission, discussed earlier. An essential part of authentic Christian identity is the awareness that as a disciple of the risen Christ, one is sent, as is the entire community, to help carry out Christ's work of establishing the kingdom of God. Such a sense of being sent can come only through the experience of sharing the community's mission activities. It is in actually being sent that a Christian can come to realize that this is basic to his or her purpose in life. One comes to think of oneself as a Christian by doing Christian things.

Sharing the Community's Spirit

Inseparable from any group's self-identity is that group's spirit. We speak of a class having "school spirit," or about the spirit of a football team, or about the "company spirit" that explains why a certain business is successful. Obviously, it is the individual members of each group who possess the interest, enthusiasm, and commitment referred to as the group's "spirit." Yet there is a corporate aspect to such spirit; a group as a group has something that goes beyond the sum of people's individual attitudes. There is a spirit that is shared, that makes this group distinctive. This spirit animates the group, gives it a group personality, and is the moving force that helps bring the group to its goals.

Everything that spirit does for a group must, of course, be done for any Christian community, if it is not to be a dead group, unenthusiastic, going no place, and dis-spirited. What is special about Christian communities and about the church as a whole is that, beyond all the ordinary human elements of spirit, the deeper animating and moving force is Christ's own Spirit. The church came into existence with Jesus' gift of his own life-giving Spirit. This Spirit, now shared with all those who accept Jesus as risen Lord, is in Christ himself the very source of risen existence. Although we sometimes think of Pentecost as a one-time happening a short time after Easter, it is in reality a continuing event that started with the resurrection and is unending, because it is inseparable from Jesus being risen.

This, then, is the deepest level of *communio* in Christianity. To be a Christian, a disciple of the risen Jesus, is to be a "Spirit-ed" person, to live already to some extent in that new Spirit-way of being human, which is risen life. But there is only the one Spirit given to the Christian people as a group; a person does not possess this Spirit on an individual basis, but precisely by sharing in this Christian community. In initiating a new Christian into its own corporate existence, a Christian community enriches that person's life by sharing with him or her the Spirit of unending life. Thus, the sacramental liturgies of Christian initiation have always been seen as the occasion when the initiates receive the holy Spirit.

Summary

Having seen earlier that the focus has shifted in our theology of Christian initiation from emphasis on removal of sin to emphasis on entry into the Christian community, this present chapter examined some of the elements of such initiation into the community, stressing the person's initiation into the *communio,* the sharing that is meant to occur in any Christian group.

A new Christian is meant to share the community's vision of what human life is and is intended to be, a vision revealed in the life, death, and resurrection of Jesus. This is a sharing of the community's myth, its story of what it is, its "good news" of humanity's salvation in Jesus. The initiate begins to share also the community's mission, to exercise his or her own active discipleship. Along with this, the new Christian is introduced to the values system espoused by Christianity that this person must come to accept personally as a criterion for moral decision. So that the initiate can take on a Christian identity, the community shares with him or her its own identity as a group of people who believe in the resurrection of Jesus and are committed to Christian discipleship. Most importantly, the community shares its own Spirit given by its risen Lord, the Spirit by which it lives and is united in faith, hope, and love.

Questions for Reflection and Discussion

1. What elements are contained in the vision of life that Christians are meant to share?

2. What is meant by "the Christian myth"?

3. Explain: Christian initiation is a lifelong process of appreciating the gospel.

4. What is the mission that Christians share?

5. What does it mean to share Christian identity? To share Christ's Spirit?

12   LITURGIES
OF INITIATION

I f, as we have been saying, initiation into Christianity is essentially a process engaging the entirety of a person's life and experience, where exactly do liturgies of initiation—baptism, confirmation, and first communion—fit into the picture? What do they *do* that is not more basically done by living out daily experience in the light of Christian faith? And if there is some distinctive contribution that such liturgies are meant to make, how is this to be achieved?

Guidelines from the New Rite

Although it is no final word on the subject, the relatively new *Rite of Christian Initiation of Adults* does provide us with valuable principles for understanding and celebrating the liturgy of Christian initiation. Building upon the theology of Vatican II, especially upon the insights in the *Constitution on the Sacred Liturgy*, the rite points toward an understanding and a practice quite different from what has characterized Catholic baptizing and confirming during recent centuries.

1. It is clear from the new rite, particularly because of its restoration of and emphasis on the catechumenate, that initiation into the

Christian community is meant to be understood and personally accepted. This raises the well-known difficulties attached to the baptizing of infants, but the principle is still applicable: Those baptized in infancy are meant to be guided by the community toward a personal understanding and acceptance of the meanings contained in the baptism liturgy, and any community baptizing an infant is pledging itself to provide such guidance.

This principle would seem to be self-evident. People, obviously, ought to know what they are doing. Yet, there is a particular need to state that the emphasis for so long has been placed on some mysterious conferring of grace and removal of original sin that, as a result, there has been little, if any, grasp of the way the ritual action itself was Christianizing the individual. And if there was little understanding of how the ritual as such was accomplishing this "transformation into Christ," it follows that there was even less understanding of how the individual, or the attendant community, if there was such, could be active in this transformation.

Actually, the ritual is not only meant to be understood; it is an act of understanding shaped by the liturgical form itself. And it is in the sphere of this new understanding, that is, faith, that the person's growing introduction into the Christ-mystery is to occur. But if the new state of awareness is shaped by the liturgical ceremony, it is also and even more deeply shaped by the person's own acceptance of the "word" of the ritual. To express it another way, the experience of willingly accepting public reception by a believing Christian community is a key moment in the process of consciously becoming a Christian. It should be one of those key experiences we discussed in an earlier chapter.

2. The new rite makes it clear also that the liturgical initiation is meant to be a public commitment to radical and ongoing conversion. Preparation leading up to the initiation liturgy would, we hope, have already have achieved a substantial re-orientation of the person's outlook and values. Yet, the liturgy itself is intended to provide that critical symbolizing situation in which this conversion is both stated and crystallized. In describing the initiation of an adult, which the church now sees as the prime example, the model, for Christian initiation, the new rite details the manner in which this conversion is to be fostered by a rather lengthy catechumenate. Even the acceptance into the catechumenate is to be a special act: on the part of the community a willingness to admit this person to the group of catechumens, and on the part of the in-

itiate a decision to prepare for full entry into the community. While all this, obviously, cannot be realized in the case of infant baptism, the baptism ritual is still a public commitment to that ongoing conversion that will lead the newly baptized toward adult faith.

3. The baptism ritual is an act of election, a formal election of the individual by the community receiving the person, and more profoundly an election by God, which is sacramentalized in the community's act. What we now clearly see in the ritual is the reiteration of that sequence of happenings that the Bible describes as God's way of working with people. God begins the action by calling (for example, calling the people under Moses out of Egypt), but the people must respond by their conversion from a previous way of life (as the Israelites did in crossing the waters as they left Egypt), and only then as they formally state their acceptance of God are they chosen, elected, as God's own people (as the Israelites were at Mount Sinai).

Guidelines from Vatican II

Since the revisions of sacramental ritual in the Catholic church are a continuation of the work of Vatican Council II, we can gain further understanding of what these rituals are and are meant to accomplish by examining some elements in the outlook of that council. While many of the documents have some bearing on our understanding of sacraments, the two decrees that have most direct relevance are the *Constitution on the Sacred Liturgy* and the *Dogmatic Constitution on the Church*. These spell out for us the kind of liturgy needed for effective initiation of persons into the mystery of Christ, and the kind of believing community needed to celebrate such liturgies.

1. While a Christian community and the church as a whole needs some structure and organization, its more basic reality is to be a community of people who share faith in Jesus as the risen Lord. By its faith it is to proclaim in varying situations of human life the good news of Jesus' resurrection. It is to be prophetic, a sign of God's saving presence in history. Though a Catholic community should cherish its own special traditions of Christian belief and life, it should live in open concern for and sharing with Christians of other denominations. Rather than continue the centuries-long alienation from fellow believers in other Christian churches, a community of Catholics—if it follows the dictates of Vatican II—

should work toward the ecumenical reunion of all Christians. So, a new Christian is received into a particular Catholic community but is also being received into the broader reality of the church of Christ, the *oikumene*, a truly catholic people of God.

2. Vatican II has crystallized a return to thinking about the church in terms of the risen Christ. Though the notion was never totally forgotten, there had been for many centuries relatively little emphasis placed on the idea that the church is body of Christ, the continuing sacrament of the presence of the saving Lord in history. Now the council has reminded us that any Christian community is meant to be such an embodiment of the continuing mystery of Christ's saving act. By entering a particular community of Christians, then, an individual is by that very fact being initiated into this body of Christ, being initiated into the mystery of Christ's death and resurrection. This presupposes, of course, that the initiating community is itself aware of being such an embodiment of Christ and thus able to share this understanding with new members.

3. Another reversal of attitude that came to full expression at Vatican II was the abandonment of the notion that Christians should hold themselves aloof from their world and keep their gaze fixed as exclusively as possible on "the world to come." Instead, the council, particularly in the *Pastoral Constitution on the Church in the Modern World*, indicates a wide scope for Christians' involvement in building a future that befits humans, and it urges all Christians to become part of this ongoing human endeavor. A new Christian who is being received into this "rediscovered" Christian enterprise is embarking upon a task shared with the other members of this community, and is committing himself or herself to participating in the work of reshaping human history according to the principles of the gospel. Again, for such an understanding of initiation to function in any given case, the community into which the person is being introduced must itself have an awareness of this history-creating mission it is meant to pursue. No community can share a sense of Christian mission unless it possesses it.

4. In its ground-breaking *Constitution on the Sacred Liturgy* the council gives several critically important guidelines for the revitalization of Christian sacraments. None of these is more fundamental than the insistence that liturgical ceremonies are meant to function as "words," that is, they are meant to convey certain understandings about God and God's saving activity, so that people

participating in the liturgy can hear this "word" and respond to it by their faith and conversion. Sacraments are, after all, actions that have their effect precisely through the significance they contain, through the meanings they convey to people's awareness. Sacraments are word-situations.

What this says about the liturgies of Christian initiation is clear enough, though the implementation may be quite difficult. These liturgies must convey to people the interpretation of human life that is intrinsic to Christian faith. While initiation into Christianity does have a deeper and mysterious level as entry into Christ's death and resurrection, it is meant to be a deliberate and therefore understood acceptance of the meanings attached to Jesus' life, death, and resurrection. Being an acceptance of Jesus as God's saving gift to us, this liturgical action is a response to God who offers that gift. The liturgical ceremony must, therefore, function as a communicating word that informs the initiate of this offering.

Specific Liturgical Acts of Baptism

Having glanced at some of the principles underlying the recent revision of initiation ritual, we can now go on to examine in more detail the significances that are meant to be attached to different moments of the initiation liturgies. There is no doubt that the revision of rites sees the baptism of adults, rather than that of infants, as the model for initiation. However, because the vast majority of baptisms are still those of infants, it may be practically more valuable to use the ritual of infant baptism as our principal basis for reflection, although we hope we can weave in some of the most important elements contained in the adult ritual.

Reception by the Community. Ideally, the ceremony will take place in the presence of a fairly representative group of the local community, since it is a reception of the new Christian by the community. The rite, therefore, recommends that it take place on Sunday when the church is celebrating the paschal mystery. While in adult initiation the new Christian is presented to the community by a sponsor who attests to the neophyte's readiness, in infant baptism a nucleus community, the parents and godparents, has already accepted the child into its Christian community existence, and now presents the child for admission into the larger community.

If possible, the celebrant of the liturgy will meet the child at the door, so that the entry into the church building can help convey the significance of entry into the community. Here, in greeting the child's parents and godparents, a very brief compression of the "election" occurs.

In the initiation of an adult, there is a long process of preparation leading to the point where a candidate formally chooses intensive catechumenate formation, and the community approves his or her public status as a catechumen. This is symbolized by inscription of the person's name in the list of those desiring baptism; the catechumen is now one of the "elect." In the ceremony for an infant, the celebrant simply asks the name of the child and, after a brief explanation of the responsibilities laid on parents and godparents to provide for the Christian formation of the child, designates the child as one of the "elect" by signing the child with the sign of the cross. Significantly, the parents also sign the child, for it is they, in the years ahead, who will effectively introduce the child into the wider Christian community and into the mystery of Christ.

There are several aspects of this initial action that merit our reflection. 1) It is an action of welcome. It says that the new Christian is from this point onward the object of the community's love and concern and responsibility. Hospitality has been from the earliest generations of Christians a virtue to characterize Christian communities; the baptism neophyte is now experiencing this for the first time as a full member of the community. 2) Though the external circumstances do not always indicate it, receiving the new Christian is the action of the community represented by the celebrant. Logically, then, the local community into which the baptized is received should accept responsibility for continuing the initiation of the person. 3) The cross signed on the infant's head by celebrant and parents is a symbol that this person is now marked as a Christian. However, what will mark him or her socially as a Christian will be the outlook and lifestyle that person will adopt in the years to come. That the child will be "marked" in this way will depend in great measure on the values and lifestyle these parents hand on to the child. 4) The election of the child by the community is sacramental. The deeper reality is that God, who still saves humans by sending Jesus as risen Lord, is adopting this person who now publicly is identified as a disciple of Jesus.

Scrutiny and Exorcism. In adult baptism, several liturgies of "scrutiny" are prescribed for the period of Lent, in which the candidate is led to greater awareness of personal sin and of the community's support (expressed in its prayers for the candidate) in coming to liberation from sin. These liturgies also contain rites of exorcism intended to free the candidate from sin through the Spirit. Again, this is compressed and modified in infant baptism. The liturgy of the word, which is intended to clarify the significance of the baptism, is directed at the parents and godparents; the community's prayers for the initiate look toward growth in faith rather than the present conscience of the person; and the renunciation of values and lifestyle opposed to Christianity is expressed by the child's sponsors.

Still, the underlying significance of the action remains the same. The baptized is embarking on a course of life that grows out of a vision and a set of values that is not shared by most people. These Christian values stand in direct opposition to "the sin of the world," that inherited backlog of hostility, exploitation, injustice, and dishonesty that vitiates human existence and stands as a barrier to human fulfillment. Each Christian must make, and continue throughout life to remake, a personal choice against this sin of the world. Yet, in living out this difficult "renunciation of Satan and all his works and all his empty promises," a Christian needs the support of a concerned Christian community and the power of God's own Spirit, which is ultimately the only force able to overcome evil.

Christian belief, building upon the faith insights contained in the Old Testament, has always held that the reality of sin is something beyond the frailty or malice of a particular person. Somehow, there is a corporate or social aspect to sin; somehow it has a universality that touches all humans. This universality extends back to the very origins of human history. As long as there have been humans, sinfulness has been part of the human condition. Even when one realizes that the story of Adam and Eve is just that, a story that illustrates a truth rather than a description of one historical occurrence, the meaning intended by that text remains profoundly true. Sin goes back to the very origin of human existence and has a continuity that carries through to our own day. More than that, the mysterious reality of sin has a cumulative history. Although each generation is touched by the "original sin," this strange "wound" in humans' capacity to act authentically, it also makes its particular contribution to the history of evil, to overcoming or increasing the alienations that are the residue of sin.

Happily, this pervading power of sin is more than matched by the power of God's Spirit flowing from the risen Christ—such is Christianity's faith. In Christian initiation, particularly as it comes to a climax in the baptism liturgy, the person joining the Christian community becomes one of those who are basically freed from this force and committed to its overthrow.

Profession of Faith. Whereas in adult initiation a person is led through several stages of discovery and acceptance of the Christian faith the community is sharing with her or him, in the case of an infant the sponsors speak for the child and profess their own faith as well as the incipient faith of the child. Ideally, other members of the community are participating in the liturgy and join in this profession of faith, thereby linking themselves with previous generations of Christians who have used this same creed to state their belief in Jesus as the Christ, in his Father, and in their Spirit who is sent into the Christian community as its animating principle.

In the early centuries of Christianity, the verbal statement of belief and the immersion into the water coincided as one single profession of faith. As the person stood in the baptismal pool, he or she was asked the three questions: "Do you believe in God, the Father of our Lord Jesus Christ . . . ?" "Do you believe in Jesus Christ . . . ?" "Do you believe in the Holy Spirit . . . ?" As the person responded "I do believe" to each, she or he was immersed in the water, a symbolic statement of belief in the saving power of Jesus' death and resurrection.

This might be a good place for us to take a closer look at the questions about infant baptism, particularly the questions regarding the infant's faith, and those that have led some Christian churches to reject infant baptism. How can the infant be said to join a believing community, especially if we stress the active meaning of "community" (as we have been doing), when the child is incapable of sharing faith with others? Unless one wishes to see sacraments' effectiveness as completely hidden and mysterious and automatic, how can one talk about the infant "receiving faith" through this liturgical ceremony?

One could reply by saying that the sponsors, on behalf of the child, give a pledge of future believing, but that seems to postpone the real participation of the child in Christian *communio*. One could say also that the principal agent of the baptizing is God, which is certainly true, and that God lays claim on this person as one of the elect. But then the question is: In what does this "laying claim" consist? How is the child changed by this liturgical act?

While it would be foolish to pretend that one can give complete-ly satisfactory replies to the real difficulties connected with infant initiation, it does seem that we can give enough explanation not only to justify the practice but even to suggest that some initiation of infants is advisable. Two insights regarding Christian faith itself may help us deal with this question.

1. Faith is a life process involving human consciousness. It grows into mature fullness along with consciousness itself, and like full consciousness it emerges from preconscious psychological perception. Thus, there must be elements of "preconscious faith" growing quietly in the child's psyche long before anything like personally chosen faith appears.

2. Christian faith is much more than a rational acceptance of the fact of Christ and a deliberate willingness to accept Christian teaching and live by it. Because Christian faith is a personal ac-ceptance of Jesus of Nazareth and the God revealed in him, be-cause it is essentially a friendship, it involves the whole range of knowledge, feeling, sense perception, imagination, and affectiv-ity—with each of these elements conditioning each of the others.

All this indicates that the beginnings of that life process start with birth itself. And, as we suggested earlier, the psychological impact of the parents upon the child is the initial and continuing sacramental force that is meant to condition the child's emerging consciousness so that it can be open to a more explicit embrace of the word of God. While this family community is first and ir-replaceable, the child's world must be broadened, and that bigger world will impinge on the child in terms of Christian values or their opposite. Thus, the early entry into a Christian community which at least in theory lives out those values, should mean that that group of Christians becomes an evangelizing reality in the child's prerational life. So, in the baptizing liturgy the child really does enter into the Christian *communio* on the level of those crit-ically important psychological resonances that condition all our formal consciousness. The earliest stages of Christian faith can be truly present, depending on the extent of sacramentalizing that oc-curs in the liturgy itself. As a matter of fact, the development of these "seeds of faith" in a child's prerational years would—other things being equal—seem necessary preparation for the later emer-gence of truly personal acceptance of Jesus as the Christ.

What this implies, of course, is that the baptism liturgy must be seen as only one early step in the process of a community guiding this child toward genuine Christian faith. Liturgy is but one moment, though a specially significant moment, in the sacramental process. What that entire process entails becomes clearer if one studies the new rite for initiating adults, and catechists must turn to this guide as they help the baptized child toward full faith.

Even though we now separate a person's verbal acceptance of the Christian creed from the baptism of water (in which the community's ministering representative uses the declarative form "I baptize you in the name of the Father, and of the Son, and of the Holy Spirit"), these two actions still form one continuing profession of faith shared by the neophyte and the initiating community.

Baptizing with Water—Entry into Christ. So, even though the liturgical ceremony of baptizing with water is intrinsically linked with the initiate's verbalization of belief, it has a richness of symbolism we can profitably examine, particularly since it also plays a key role in our annual celebration of the Easter Vigil. Pointing to the death and resurrection of Jesus, water is a natural symbol. In situations such as a storm at sea, water unmistakably speaks of death; in situations such as the growing of crops, water just as clearly signifies life. But during the history of Israel water acquired a rich symbolism that sprang from the people's crossing of the waters when they fled Egypt. Water used liturgically by later Israelites recalled the Exodus and allowed the celebrating group to accept into their own lives the covenant established during this journey from Egypt to the promised land. So, a convert to Judaism (a "proselyte") was baptized to supply for the fact that his ancestors had not passed through Exodus waters. So also, in the baptism of John, which Jesus accepted, the water signified the person's decision to live out the covenant of God and the people, and in Jesus' case that meant accepting his new exodus journey toward death and resurrection.

From its earliest days, Christianity has seen baptism as a particularly appropriate ritual to initiate new members into the community by linking them symbolically with Jesus in the mystery of his dying and rising. For practical reasons, the Catholic church (among others) generally uses the pouring of water instead of immersing the baptized in a pool, as was done in the early days; but the symbolism remains the same: One goes down into the water (as sign of Jesus' death) and then emerges from it (as sign of Jesus' risen life). As Paul told the early Christians, one is baptized into the death and resurrection of Christ. But what does this beautiful phrase mean? How can one enter into another's death and new life? Five things need to be said on this point.

1. The saving force of Jesus' death and resurrection lies in his experience of dying and rising and in his free acceptance of and involvement in it. His willingness to go through death in order to provide new life for his friends is the saving sacrament of his Father's life-giving love. If the new Christian "enters into Christ's death and resurrection," this must mean that this person is somehow sharing this experience of loving even unto death. To share with Christ this willingness to so love others is, of course, the very heart of Christian discipleship.

2. This identification with Christ's own acceptance of death and resurrection is not primarily directed to the past events of Jesus' death on Calvary and the consequent rising from the dead. Resurrection for Jesus is a continuing reality, involving an unceasing sharing of himself and his new life. "Behold, I am with you all days, even to the end of the world." This here-and-now experience of the risen Lord is what the Christian is meant to identify with; one enters into this experience much as one shares the enthusiasms and projects of a close friend.

3. To the extent that one shares "the mind of Christ, " a person is marked in his or her consciousness as Christian. This is the deeper reality symbolized by signing the initiate's forehead with the sign of the cross.

4. But there is the other side of this mystery. The symbol of water baptism points also to Christ's incorporation of this person into his new risen existence. If the Christian can share in Christ's new life, it is only because the risen Jesus initiates the sharing by communicating his risen consciousness to the person. The community's initiating action, in which the externals of the liturgy performed by the community as body of Christ quite literally function as Christ's own word, communicates Jesus' self-giving. The liturgy is truly sacramental of the presence of the life-giving Lord.

5. Christ's sharing of his risen existence is nothing more or nothing less than *the sharing of his Spirit*, the very source of this new life. The Spirit expresses for him his relation to his Abba, his own self-identity, and his love for his human brothers and sisters. All this the risen Lord shares by sharing his Spirit. Christian tradition has always stressed this giving of the Spirit as the very heart of what

happens in baptism. The initiate receives the Spirit as source and pledge of unending life.

There is, then, a deep mystery connected with the baptismal entry into Christ. But the mystery consists not so much in the hiddenness or strangeness of what happens, but rather in the "unbelievability," the wonder that God should so love us as to bring us with Christ into this new way of being as his "beloved." The entry into the death and resurrection of Jesus is essentially, then, an entry into a friendship that is meant to grow into an unending life of personal love between the initiate and Christ.

Baptismal Chrismation. Immediately after baptizing with water, the new Christian is anointed on the head. In the case of adult initiation, the anointing is the second step of initiation, which traditionally in Western Christianity we have called "confirmation." About this we will reflect in just a moment. In the baptism of infants and of children old enough to be catechized and to make their own profession of faith, the formal "confirmational" anointing is reserved for a later occasion. What takes place is an anointing whose symbolic purpose is to indicate that baptismal gift of the Spirit we referred to above. This action is not separate from what immediately precedes it, as if the Spirit is not given until this ritual action. Giving the Spirit is intrinsic to the whole action of initiation, but this anointing draws explicit attention to the "sealing" of the person by Christ's Spirit.

Conferring of White Garment and Lighted Candle. The symbolism of the two actions the ritual closes with is rather obvious. Having "put on the Lord Jesus" and received the new life of grace, the new Christian is a new creation, with an innocence that is not that of Eden but rather the purification that flows from charity and the Spirit. So, the initiate stands in the midst of the community, a reminder to all of that newness of life they all share. And the conferring of the candle, lighted from the Paschal Candle, which signifies Christ as the light of the world, says quite clearly that the light of faith is to be treasured throughout life but also carried into the world to free others from darkness.

Confirmation

Except for the case of adult initiation when confirmational anointing is an integral part of the ceremony which includes baptizing and first full participation in eucharist, the special anointing with chrism by the bishop, confirmation, takes place at another, usually much later, date. Giving a satisfactory theological explanation of confirmation as a sacrament apart from baptism has always baffled religious educators and theologians. Part of the difficulty, at least, comes from the fact that the separation of these two rituals of initiation, which originally formed two steps in one liturgical ceremony, was somewhat accidental.

As Christianity spread from the cities where a bishop resided who could be present at the yearly Easter Vigil to smaller communities in the countryside where the bishop visited only occasionally, Christians were baptized without the bishop being there. Because the act of chrismation had long been seen as the proper role of the bishop, there was no "confirmation" in the Western church for those baptized in the outlying communities. Instead, when the bishop came to visit the community, he "completed" the baptism initiation by solemnly anointing the recently baptized. Out of this evolved the distinct sacramental ritual we have known as the sacrament of confirmation. In Eastern Christianity a different decision was made. Even in the case of infants the chrismation remains intrinsic to the baptism initiation. If the bishop is not present, the presiding presbyter performs the chrismation.

The *Rite of Christian Initiation of Adults* stresses once more for the Western church the intrinsic link of chrismation with baptizing as parts of one process of initiation, so it is probably not profitable to search for some distinctive meaning for confirmation. Basically it is confirmation, a reiteration on the part of both initiate and community of the commitments already made in baptism. The celebrating bishop does add a new dimension of symbolism, since as a member of the worldwide episcopacy he provides a link with the larger community, the whole church, which shares its faith with this Christian mission of the church. The person is, we hope, now committed to the worldwide mission of the church with fuller understanding and more mature personal decision.

Liturgy for the sacrament of confirmation is quite simple and straightforward. After some appropriate readings from Sacred Scripture, the candidates are presented by name to the bishop. He then addresses them briefly, explaining the significance of the scripture readings they have just heard and of the action they are sharing in. As the suggested homily in the *Rite of Christian Initiation of Adults* implies, this instruction by the bishop should draw attention to the gift of the Spirit, which the confirmed are receiving, and to the active involvement in the church's life, which the confirmed are pledging. In response to this instruction, the candidates renew their baptismal profession of faith and their renunciation of "Satan and all his works and all his empty promises." The bishop then extends his hand over the heads of those being confirmed, praying that the power of the Spirit be given them. He then anoints each on the forehead with chrism as a sign of the community's sharing its Spirit with this person.

Both the bishop's hand extended in blessing and the anointing are traditional Christian symbols for the giving of the Spirit. There have been some attempts to explain the "special" effect of confirmation as the gift of the Spirit, but this can be true only if one admits that baptizing itself was already a sharing of the Spirit with the initiate and that what occurs in confirmation is meant to be a further step in the process of initiating the person into the community and into its Spirit. What is important to remember is that this occurs sacramentally, that is, there is a deeper sharing of the Spirit only if there is truly an increased sharing of Christian faith and life by the community that celebrates confirmational liturgy, and if the candidates for confirmation are truly open to living according to the Spirit and to fulfilling the responsibilities of Christian adulthood. The liturgy does not act magically.

For the past few decades there has been a great deal of debate about the proper age for confirmation. There are good liturgical reasons for placing it between baptism and first communion. As a matter of fact, there are good liturgical reasons for once more combining baptism and confirmation into one ceremony. However, there are good pastoral reasons for having confirmation at a later age, when the young person can knowingly and freely choose Christian faith. But in this latter case, some argue for the sacrament occurring early in adolescence and others argue for the ceremony being celebrated toward the end of adolescence.

Perhaps the fact that each of these positions has good arguments suggests that we should reconsider the entire matter in the light of what we discussed earlier, namely, that we are involved with a lifelong process of initiating a person into Christ. There seems to be no reason, liturgically, theologically, or pastorally, why more than one liturgy could not be celebrated as confirmation of the baptismal choice—perhaps one around the age of seven or eight, when children really need to choose among the competing values they are exposed to; perhaps again at the beginning of adolescence, when lifestyle and involvement with one or other peer group can be decisive for the years ahead; perhaps again when the young person stands on the threshold of adult life. Each of these moments of passage occurs after a period of considerable change in experience and at the beginning of a risky new period.

To pick up a notion we discussed earlier, the young person at each of these passage points needs a Christian hermeneutic of experience, that is, a set of understandings, attitudes, motivations, and desires that equips one to face new life situations and to make appropriate Christian decisions. While sacramental liturgies by themselves cannot provide such a hermeneutic of experience, they should be occasions when the process of developing such an outlook on life comes to focus and is publicly celebrated.

To some extent the solution to this liturgical problem about the proper age for the sacrament of confirmation is secondary. What is basically more important is that we learn to guide young Christians in freedom toward authentic faith, and that we create liturgy appropriate for nourishing that process. From beginning to end, Christian life is meant to be a continuing initiation into the mystery of Christ. Sacramental liturgies have to help achieve that goal.

Summary

Placing the liturgies of baptism and confirmation into the broader context of "initiation into Christian life" makes it possible to give a more pastoral explanation of these liturgies, and to deal more intelligently with such questions as infant baptism and the appropriate age for confirmation. This has been greatly facilitated by the guidelines contained in the new rite for Christian initiation, which spell out Vatican II's commitment to the reform of liturgy. The new rite expresses the elements of initiation we have already studied: reception into a believing community, personal acceptance of and commitment to the risen Christ, introduction into a lifelong process of Christian discipleship. All of these are sacramental of God's "adoption" of the individual through the gift of the Spirit, and sacramental of the person's entry into the new life of faith.

Questions for Reflection and Discussion

1. What significance should be conveyed by the liturgy of baptism? By the liturgy of confirmation?

2. What guidelines are provided by the new *Rite of Christian Initiation of Adults?*

3. What does the liturgy of baptism commit a person to?

4. How is the baptismal liturgy a profession of faith?

5. What does it mean to say that one is baptized "into the death and resurrection of Christ"?

13   EUCHARISTIC INITIATION: CREATION OF CHRISTIAN HISTORY

I
n the earlier portions of this book we saw how human experience is at once a discovery and a creation. Through what
happens to us we discover who we are and what our world is
all about; but we always interpret these happenings, and to some
extent this interpretation is the result of our own decisions. Now
we can apply this insight to the Christian celebration of eucharist,
seeing how it is meant to be the central current of a continuing process of discovery-creation on the part of Christian communities
and of the individuals who make up those communities. Eucharist
should be a continuous reshaping of that distinctive hermeneutic
of experience that flows from and shapes Christian faith.

One way of investigating this function of eucharist is to examine
the way people are constantly being introduced into the Christian
myth, that story about what is happening to humans that dis-
tinguishes Christianity from other religious belief systems.
Humans live by one or other ultimate story, and if they form communities this always involves some sharing of an ultimate story.
Because we attribute to this story a considerable amount of ob-
jectivity—we claim that this is really what has happened and is
now happening—we usually refer to this story as "human his-

tory." So also, when we talk about "Christian history," we are referring to that interpretation of human life based on what has happened in the life, death, and resurrection of Jesus of Nazareth.

Clearly, as a person is introduced into the Christian community, that individual is, or at least should be, given an explanation of what has happened in Jesus. But this is only part of the initiation into the Christian explanation of life. This community of believers, the church, has a two-thousand-year experience of trying to understand who Jesus is and of trying to translate Christian discipleship into the changing circumstances of life. Consequently, it has a long tradition, an acquired wisdom, to share with new generations of Christians. While one can theorize about Christianity's explanation of "the human," even refer somewhat loosely to a "Christian philosophy of life," the fundamental and only ultimate Christian explanation is the story about itself and its Lord that has been a lived experience for these past two thousand years.

Throughout their lives as Christians, men, women, and children are learning more about this community story and either making it their own "ultimate myth" or refusing to do so. In proportion as they accept this story as their own and fit into it their individual stories, their interpretation of life is genuinely Christian. And as they share with their fellow Christians this Christian interpretation of their own human lives, they are part of the historically continuing process of creating the Christian myth. Eucharist is the center of this sharing.

Eucharist as Storytelling

From its beginnings, the Christian eucharistic gathering has been a "story-telling" event. The New Testament enables us to reconstruct to some extent those earlier generations when the immediate disciples of Jesus gathered in small groups to recall what Jesus had done and said, to attempt some interpretation of his death and resurrection that would fit into their story of God's dealings with humans, and to make present through eucharistic commemoration the abiding presence of this risen Lord.

It was very largely from such eucharistic gatherings that the gospels emerged. So, within a very short time, the reading of sections of the New Testament became an established part of the eucharistic celebrations. Justin (around 150 C.E.) speaks of readings from "the memoirs of the apostles" at the Sunday liturgy. From that time until our own day, people who gathered for eucharist hear the New Testament story of humanity, but they hear it as explained by two thousand years of Christian reflection on the meaning of those texts.

This means that the story told at eucharist extends well beyond what is mentioned in the New Testament, for that can be considered the story of Jesus and the first couple of generations of his disciples. Eucharist celebrated in the late twentieth century tells its own story, for it is the gathering together and the celebration of the Christian life story of the people who share a particular eucharist today. It does include that ancient story we name "early Christian history," for today's Christians identify themselves with the faith of those of old and absorb the wisdom inherited from them into their own interpretation of life. But the Christian community of today understands and reinterprets that tradition in the light of its own experience of trying to live out Christian faith and discipleship.

Discovering Christian Discipleship

Initiation into the church and into the mystery of Christ's death and resurrection is most fundamentally a growth in understanding. Even in the case of an adult convert, the period of catechumenate only begins the process of discovering what Christianity is all about. Knowing what it means to be a disciple of the risen Jesus involves a considerable amount of information and theoretical understanding; of equal importance is the knowledge that comes from experience: One learns what it means to be a Christian by being a Christian.

The reason why this knowledge through experience is so central to the understanding of Christianity is that one's self-identity is involved. If people are to think of themselves as Christian, the experience of existing and acting as Christian must be an integral part of the experience of being who they are. Otherwise, Christianity is merely something they know about, just as a non-Christian knows about Christianity but does not identify with it.

One only gradually comes to know what it means to be Christian, for the very reason that being Christian is not something apart from and added to our lives. Rather, it is a particular way of being everything else we are; it is being who and what we are in relationship to the risen Christ. So, it is only in the day-after-day sequence of happenings through which we live out this relationship that we discover what it means to be a human who is Christian—to grow and mature as a Christian, to suffer and rejoice as a Christian, to live and be concerned and hope as a Christian, to succeed and fail and risk and decide as a Christian.

In the early stages of one's life as a Christian, one usually has little insight into the nature or demands of Christian discipleship. This is perhaps truer today than it has been for many centuries. Until quite recently it seemed quite easy to answer the question, "What does it mean for you to be a Christian?" but today that is changed. We are more aware that mere performance of regular religious duties, such as attending Sunday liturgy, is not enough. Nor does it suffice to be a fairly active member of a parish, sharing in projects and financial support.

Actually, faithful living out of Christian principles as a disciple of the risen Christ can be difficult, even painful. As we saw, a baptized person commits himself or herself to following a set of values at odds with those espoused by much of the world. This can demand some painful decisions. This was strikingly exemplified in the life and death of Dietrich Bonhoeffer, an influential German Lutheran theologian who, though a committed pacifist, was led by his Christian convictions to share in the attempt to overthrow Hitler. He paid for it with his life. Faced with the stark contrast between what most people around him in Germany were doing and what he felt his Christian conscience required, Bonhoeffer wrote his famous book, *The Cost of Discipleship.*

A case like Bonhoeffer's illustrates not only the price that discipleship can demand, but also the extent to which the reality of discipleship must be learned as we go through life. Certainly, as a young theologian studying and teaching in Germany in the years before the rise of Hitler, Bonhoeffer never dreamed that discipleship for him would involve giving witness by his death under the Nazis. The same was true, though less dramatically, of most of us. Thirty or forty years ago, we had little, if any, anticipation of the changes in the world and the church that have come after World War II. The understanding we then had of what it means to be truly Christian, while probably still applicable in large part, is no longer sufficient for this changing world we live in. All of us have had to learn that genuine Christian discipleship is a bit more costly—but also more precious—than we had thought.

Since our discipleship is something we do within and as part of a Christian community, an important element in the discovery of what it means to be a Christian is the gradual discovery of what the church is as a special human community. Such discovery has been an unsettling experience for many people these past few decades. For many, especially but not only for Catholics, the church had seemed to be a prime example of unchangeableness. Dogmas of faith were immutable; the principal elements of church structure were divinely instituted and therefore perennial; liturgy was meant to be universally homogeneous and unchanging. Then something happened, and this church that had been a symbol of stability became an increasingly changing community.

It is not our purpose here to evaluate this recent change. Instead, we recall this experience only to illustrate the continuing need for Christians to grow into an understanding of the genuine nature of the church. If people were surprised, even upset, by the fact that the church changed with a changing world, this was because they had misunderstood the nature of the church, not because the church "had started to go to the dogs." All Christians today need to learn from careful study of history and from our own experience much more about the church than we know. Again, however, our own experience is basic to this unfolding understanding, for we are the church, and no experience is more basic, more constant, and more important than the experience of eucharist.

Christian Experience Confronted by the Gospel

Our experience of life is the word of God, but its Christian significance and its dictates are not immediately evident. To know what life is telling us about ourselves and about the God who is revealed in our experience, we must turn to the revelation contained in the life, death, and resurrection of Jesus, and to the enduring faith of Christians over the past two millennia. Life and the gospel must be brought into creative encounter with each other; this is what should occur in each eucharistic celebration.

Each eucharist is somewhat distinctive because of the particular group of Christians who gather to share this action. Each of these persons has a significance for the others, and together they have a certain corporate meaning. When these people hear the word of God in the liturgical act, they hear it in the light of their own life experience of being human and Christian, and so this word says something distinctive here and now that it says nowhere else and at no other time. On the other hand, the word of the liturgical act is giving a new meaning to the life experience of the gathered

Christians. Life and liturgy interact as complementary and reciprocally interpretative words to shape in ongoing process the hermeneutic of experience by which these people will understand and create their future. Life and eucharist throw light upon each other; each is meant to be understood through the other.

Two examples of such interaction between life and eucharist illustrate and clarify this point.

1. Humans have always felt some need for salvation. In greater or lesser degree, their life experience has been touched by the presence of evil, and they have needed to be freed from the forces of oppression and enslavement. Eucharist responded to this experienced need for salvation by proclaiming that salvation comes through the death and resurrection of Jesus. But what salvation meant to any particular group of Christians gathered for eucharist depended on the particular form of the evils they struggled against. Perhaps it was physical sufferings and dire poverty, actual slavery, moral and social corruption, but whatever it was, the gospel proclaimed at eucharist spoke to that particular need. It was in terms of that particular salvation that eucharist itself became meaningful.

Today, we understand the problem of evil, of injustice, of oppression, much more in systemic terms. Obviously, it is human beings who do evil, but because of the complication and vast organization of life today, much of the evil that afflicts people happens through the vast and impersonal systems that are so much a part of contemporary life. As a result, when we listen to the gospel today, hoping to find guidance and consolation in our lives, we are more attuned than previous generations to a basic gospel principle that speaks directly to this threat of systemic oppression, the clear superiority of persons over the structures of society. According to those Christian principles we celebrate in eucharist, no man, woman, or child is ever to be subordinated to any institution of society, political, industrial, economic, or religious. The meaning of eucharist speaks to our need for liberation from systemic enslavement, but eucharist has that meaning for us today precisely because our life experience has told us that this is the form of salvation we need.

2. People who come to eucharist today still share in large part the myth that most humans have always believed, that the key to human history lies with those who possess power; those who wield this power are the more important people, and, at least to

some extent, this is the way that God has established things. This explanation of human existence, however, is being radically challenged in many quarters today. There are some indications that this previously taken-for-granted view of power and authority, of a hierarchically structured world governed by patriarchal domination, may give way to a new understanding of human life in which people will no longer accept such power as the controlling force in their lives.

Conditioned by this new understanding of possible liberation from oppressive power, Christians can then hear, perhaps more clearly than ever before, that element of the eucharistic word that challenges this situation. Jesus himself rejected the claims of such dominant power. In Jesus' temptations in the desert, a scene describing the chief decisions Jesus and his disciples would have to face if they wished to work for humanity's salvation, worldly power is explicitly refused as a way Jesus could fulfill his messianic mission. Instead of accepting Satan's offer of "all the kingdoms of this world," Jesus goes on to his death and resurrection. This is what every eucharist proclaims: Salvation will come only through death and resurrection. Eucharist has always proclaimed this, but because it interacts so clearly with our life experience, this element of its "word" is more specially heard today.

This interaction of human experience and eucharistic meaning is the reason we celebrate eucharist day after day and year after year. Eucharist is a recurring sacramental liturgy precisely because life is continuously unfolding, with ever-changing meaning. This continuing course of experience needs to be constantly interpreted by the meaning embodied in the death and resurrection of Jesus. Eucharist is meant to be an all-encompassing convergence of meanings and of the symbol systems that carry these meanings. It is this in proportion to its being authentic eucharist.

Deepened Experience of Christ

Any interpretation of human history in the light of Jesus of Nazareth is controlled by what we think of him. The most basic question posed to Christians always is "Who do you say that I am?"—the question Jesus asked the twelve. So, if there is to be a developing Christian interpretation of human life, a Christian myth that provides a distinctive insight into history, there must be a growing insight into the identity and role of Jesus. The celebration of eucharist is meant to provide such a deepening understanding.

However, we must be careful in talking about the church's deepening experience of Christ over the course of the centuries. While there can be a growth in the church's insight into the Christ mystery, as we will soon see, this does not mean that a Christian of an earlier century did not have just as profound an experience of Christ as someone has today. Because the experience is that of a personal relationship, and because Christ remains the same for all time, each Christian's relation to Christ is unique and ultimately dependent only on that person's depth of faith and personal maturity.

Yet, for any Christian, as well as for the church as a whole, the repeated celebration of eucharist is meant to be a growth into Christ. One comes to know a friend by experiencing that friend, by relating to that friend amid a variety of happenings, learning that friend's fidelity and support and encouragement. So also, over the course of the years as life unfolds, a Christian who relates in friendship to Christ in the experience of eucharist comes to a deepened understanding of and appreciation for this friend. This is intrinsic to eucharist, because it is basically a situation of the risen Christ's self-gift to those who receive him in faith: "This is my body given for you."

There are two essentially different aspects to this growing awareness of Christ that is meant to occur through eucharist. The first deals with the Christian community's understanding of what Jesus was and did, and of the way Christians over the centuries have understood and related to Christ; that is, there is a growth in understanding what has been. The second deals with a clearer and deeper knowledge of what it means for Jesus to be the risen Christ now as experienced by today's Christians.

Regarding the first aspect, a growing understanding of who and what Jesus was and has been for Christians, we benefit from all the modern development of historical methods by which we are able to study historical happenings more accurately. So, recent work in biblical studies, research into the history of Christianity, applications of sociology, anthropology, and social psychology to the study of history—all give us resources for accurately understanding past events that previous generations did not possess. Consequently, a group of Christians participating in eucharist can, to some degree at least, have a more accurate knowledge of what occurred in the Christ event. To see that such new possibilities of Christian insight become part of today's eucharistic experience is one of the principal challenges facing liturgists.

Regarding the second aspect, the deepening knowledge of the risen Christ as he now is, we benefit from the insights that come with prayerful experience of shared faith and recent theological clarification of what we mean by "the resurrection and ascension" of Jesus. Eucharistic celebration is meant to be a privileged situation of Christians experiencing the continuing presence of the risen Christ in their lives. Like the disciples at Emmaus on Easter evening, we are meant to recognize the risen one "in the breaking of the bread." Central to such awareness of the still-with-us Christ is the commitment of Christians to discipleship, which allows them psychologically to accept the implications of Christ's presence to the world through the ministry of Christians. For this reason, initiation into knowledge of Christ must also be initiation into Christian decision making, a dimension of eucharist that we will examine in our next chapter.

Summary

While baptism and confirmation are more commonly thought of as "sacraments of initiation," eucharist is the sacrament that provides most of the liturgical contribution to the process of Christians being initiated into the Christian community and thus into the mystery of Christ. Through repeated participation in eucharistic liturgies, people share ever more deeply the community's faith, understand in deepening awareness the community's myth, and live with a growing Christian vision of human life. But because this faith they grow in is basically a personal relationship to the risen Christ, Christians are led in eucharistic liturgy toward an ever closer friendship with Christ.

Being such an intensely personal experience, this growing knowledge of Christ interacts with everything else in people's lives. Their relation with Christ gives a new meaning to all they are and do, and what they are and do as humans interprets for them the reality of their relation to Christ. This happens to Christians as individuals and to communities of Christians gathered together into church. In this way, the celebration of eucharist by Christian communities throughout the world and over the years provides the central thread of meaning that transforms time into human history.

Questions for Reflection and Discussion

1. How is eucharist meant to shape Christians' hermeneutic of experience?

2. How is celebration of eucharist the central thread in the unfolding of Christian history?

3. What is Christian discipleship? How is it expressed in eucharist?

4. Explain: In eucharist the meaning of the gospel and the meaning of Christians' lives interact.

5. How is eucharist meant to effect a deepening relationship of Christians to the risen Christ?

14   EUCHARIST: INITIATION INTO COVENANT DECISION

I f the Second Vatican Council was anything, it was an opening to the future. It pointed to a new epoch in Christian history, one that would be both in continuity with and quite different from Christianity as we have known it; but it also left to Catholics the carrying out of the new directions for Christian life. Among the many items on this post-Vatican II agenda, none is more basic than the formation of truly Christian conscience among the members of the church.

There had always been, of course, the need to help people develop their conscience. Christianity is a way of life, demanding of its faithful an outlook on life and a set of values that are morally idealistic. This means that Christian teaching, at least as far back as Paul's letters, has always contained directives to guide Christians' moral decisions. However, as masses of people became Christian and the level of popular education remained low for many centuries, the prevailing approach to moral formation was one of giving people a list of things to do and things to avoid, chiefly the latter. Morality—many equated it with religion—was a matter of keeping laws; and the purpose of moral education was to acquaint people with those laws.

Broader View of Conscience

Today, however, psychological studies and other considerations have made us more aware that moral decision goes far beyond keeping laws, and that moral formation is in no way supplied by mere acquaintance with laws. In Christian education something like a revolution has occurred in the understanding and formation of conscience. We have come to see that Christian conscience means the complex ability to make appropriate Christian decisions in the midst of changing life situations.

Conscience is, then, something other than a feeling of guilt experienced after one has done something sinful. It is something beyond a developed habit of performing some good action, such as children doing what parents or teachers tell them. Nor is it simply the detailed knowledge of which actions are acceptable and which sinful according to Christian teaching. Conscience rests on an accurate knowledge of moral behavior, but it goes beyond that and actually involves a person's entire psychological life, one's whole hermeneutic of experience.

To quite an extent conscience is the art of translating Christian understandings into practical life decisions. And like any art, it can be developed only by doing. One learns how to make appropriate Christian decisions by making Christian decisions, learning in the process which decisions are true and which untrue, coming to know one's weaknesses or strengths as a decision maker, discovering the knowledge or motivation that one must acquire in order to form correct moral judgments. Since conscience judgments always represent an appraisal of a particular situation, they flow from what we have been calling the "hermeneutic of experience," that is, that basic understanding of and attitude toward reality that conditions a person to interpret any given happening in a particular way.

The formation of Christian conscience is, then, a complex process that is somewhat different for each person. For practical purposes, it is identical with the process of acquiring genuine maturity, with the process of developing an accurate hermeneutic of experience, with the process of becoming authentically Christian. Each person must gradually form his or her own conscience, but each of us is able to do this only in a community. It is not enough to keep on making decisions; one needs guidance in evaluating such decisions, in learning from them, in discovering how decisions were inadequate or unfaithful, and in deciding how one can decide better in the future. More than that, one needs the support and comfort of a community of friends in order to admit failures in decision making and to go on to risk new decisions.

Actually, the formation of conscience is something a person is engaged in throughout a lifetime. New situations are always arising in which a person must discover somewhat new applications of Christian faith. Transitions from one stage of human life to another bring with them new self-discovery and therefore somewhat new self-identification and self-image, with a consequent shift in one's approach to moral decision making. Life often brings surprises; things do not work out exactly as one had anticipated; the decisions made in the past no longer fit. And if all this is true of us as individuals, it is also true of communities of people and specifically of the Christian community, the church, as it moves through history. The corporate conscience of the church is always in the process of formation. Today, for example, we are trying to find appropriate approaches to new areas of moral decisions such as genetic engineering, psychological manipulation, and the artificial prolongation of life.

Eucharist as Conscience Formation

If formation of Christian conscience, both individual and community, is so challenging, where are we to find the resources to undertake it? This is where eucharist as a continuing initiation into Christianity is meant to function. Not that eucharistic celebration, even when it is excellent liturgy, provides some kind of instant or magical solution. But if eucharistic liturgy is celebrated genuinely and humanly, it is a convergence of the meanings of our life experience and the meaning of the gospel, a meeting of the demands of life and the demands of faith. This means that it is an act of deciding to live, or not to live, according to the meanings and demands of the gospel. Eucharist should be the focal act of Christian decision making, from which we acquire the ability to make Christian choices. Eucharist should be the key to the formation of Christian conscience. Let us spell this out.

The earliest Christian evidences indicate that eucharist has been from its origins an act of prophetic proclamation. The Eucharistic Prayer, the Canon of the Mass, is, if one examines it closely, prophetic praise of the God revealed in Jesus' death and resurrection. This is why the *Didache*, one of the earliest Christian documents, says that the appropriate person to lead the eucharistic celebration is a prophet.

Prophetic proclamation is, however, always aimed at conversion. The prophet speaks for a God who invites humans to "leave their present home," the understandings and decisions and goals that now govern their lives, and to "go into a land that I will give you," the new level of human existence that will come to those who respond to the divine invitation. The word of God, especially in eucharist, demands of those who will accept it in freedom a *metanoia*, a change of mind. Concretely, this mind-change is the transformation that comes when one's hermeneutic of experience is "trans-signified" by the meaning of Christ's death and resurrection.

The basic structure of eucharistic celebration is that of "word and response." To that word eucharist speaks; the celebrating community is meant to respond by its genuine acceptance. Because it is an acceptance of a self-revealing God, eucharist is a profession of faith; indeed, it is the most basic creed in Christianity. It is an act of covenant commitment, which must always take slightly different form because the circumstances of life in which it is to find realization are always changing. As a covenant act, it should be the governing life decision for the Christians gathered for eucharist. And it can be that, because any given eucharist gathers up into itself all previous eucharists and anticipates future and even fuller eucharists as steps toward the eschatological fulfillment of liturgy in new and risen life.

Initiation Into Freedom

As we saw in an earlier chapter, growth into maturity is very largely a matter of being initiated into the process of making decisions. Both the pattern of experiences that makes up our daily lives and the identity we build for ourselves come about in large part because of the things we choose or do not choose. Making wise decisions is not something that is native to human beings; it is something we must learn from our experiences of success and failure and from the inherited wisdom our family and friends communicate to us as we grow up.

Making Christian decisions is a special aspect of this basic human need to grow into mature freedom. The gospels describe Jesus telling his disciples that it is the truth that will make humans free, but this is not just truth in some abstract form. It is the understanding that comes with honest acceptance of the word that God speaks to us in the course of our lives; it is the truth we realize as

we try to live out Christian faith with fidelity. Accepting the revelation that takes place in Jesus is liberating; it frees us from the
false viewpoints and values that prevent us from being what we
genuinely wish to be.

Eucharistic celebrations are meant to be a critical element in this
progressive growth in Christian decision making. Proposing the
challenge of the gospel to a Christian as he or she brings to eucharist
the ever-changing experiences of life, the liturgy demands a decisive,
personally free response to the word of God. What is true of individual Christians is also true of the community. It, too, must grow
toward greater freedom and strength of commitment as changing
historical circumstances bring new demands of discipleship.

What makes the eucharistic context of decision special, something more than just a growth in human decisiveness, is the action
of Christ's liberating Spirit in the consciousness of a celebrating
Christian community. The Spirit moves Christians, individually
and corporately, toward the freedom that comes through union
with God. Since this is the ultimate goal intended by any genuine
Christian choice, Christ's Spirit cooperates with Christian decision
making as its animating force. The Spirit, the very life force at the
source of his own risen human existence, Jesus shares with those
who believe in him. The Spirit moves in human history to invite
humans toward their eschatological fulfillment. Invoked in eucharist in the prayer we call the *epiklesis*, the Spirit brings into human
life the power of divine love that will ultimately unite us into full
community and bring us to full freedom.

Christians are meant to be guided by the Spirit, as was Jesus
himself in his early career, but not in some completely blind fashion. Humans are meant to work with God freely and knowingly in
creating history. This means that they must discern the movement
of God's Spirit in their lives and freely decide to move with this
Spirit. So, for each generation of Christians, there is the need to discern the presence of Christ's Spirit in the happenings of their lives.
Difficult and unclear as this discernment sometimes is, particularly
at those points in history when civilization is undergoing a major
shift, it is an indispensable element in the church's living out of its
prophetic character.

Not only is eucharist a privileged context for such discernment,
it is meant to set the pattern for discernment in all the other situations of Christians' lives. Clearly, a community of Christians gathered for eucharist should have a special awareness of God present

in their midst through Word and Spirit, an awareness conditioned by the degree of prayerfulness that marks a particular liturgy. Knowing God in shared prayer and knowing also the risen Christ who is always present when "two or three are gathered together" in his name, a group of Christians at eucharist develop a deepening sense of what in their lives is incompatible or compatible with this divine presence. They come to know, by a special sensitivity, where the Spirit of God is inviting them. They learn how to "read the signs of the times," how to discover in the happenings of the world the liberating actions of God, which their own ministries should further.

This pattern of decision making—exposing any given situation of choice to the word of God, prayerfully examining the manner in which this word and the experiences of life shed light on each other, listening to the enlightening and persuading movement of God's Spirit—is meant to mark any Christian deliberation. Such openness in prayer to the guidance of Christ's Spirit provides the final dimension to Christian conscience, to a Christian hermeneutic of experience. This inspiration of Christ's Spirit, followed throughout one's days and discerned with others in eucharistic gatherings, tells a Christian what life is ultimately all about.

Covenant Interpretation of Human Life

What eucharist is meant to provide for Christians is an opportunity to decide what interpretation they wish to give their lives, how they wish to understand themselves and their world, what values they wish to espouse as the genuine goals of life, what actions they wish to undertake as part of the process of creating human history. While the "word" elements of the eucharistic action proclaim that story about human life we call "the gospel," each of the people celebrating eucharist must determine whether and to what extent they wish to identify their own life story, their myth, with this shared Christian myth.

Because the Christian story is that of a covenant between God and humans, it cannot be accepted as one's own apart from a personal decision, because a covenant is a free relationship between two parties. One must genuinely wish to ally oneself in the battle against evil with Christ and the God who sends him, if one is to believe that this is the true interpretation of human experience. One must accept the divine offer of covenant friendship, if he or she is to root his or her personal identity in this friendship.

Because it is liturgy of covenant, eucharist provides the ideal context for Christians to reiterate their commitment to this covenant. This is the symbolism of Christians breaking bread together in the name of Christ. As they share the eucharistic body of Christ given for them, they respond by the gift of themselves to Christ and to one another, covenanting to live as a sacramental community committed to establishing the kingdom of God. As this symbolism finds effective translation into the consciousness and lives of these people, they are gradually initiated in ever greater identity with the risen Christ. Eucharist is the key sacrament of Christian initiation.

Summary

Since Christians are meant to live with free and mature decisiveness, it is imperative that there be effective formation of Christians' consciences. Such conscience formation requires accurate understanding of the moral dimension of human activity, but it requires more than that. It calls for a genuine conversion of the whole person, a total personal response to the challenge of God's revelation in Christ. This, in turn, rests upon discerning the movement of Christ's Spirit in the Christian community itself and in the world at large.

Celebration of eucharist is meant to be the key situation for such formation of conscience. Here the gospel is preached in living fashion; here the community gathers to invoke the gift of the prophetic Spirit; here the assembled Christians are to share their insights into the meaning of the gospel for today's world. In eucharist Christians are to accept with greater fidelity the new covenant offered them in Christ's death and resurrection.

Questions for Reflection and Discussion

1. Why is it important to realize that eucharist is a covenant meal?

2. What elements enter into the formation of Christian conscience?

3. How is the celebration of eucharist the key to formation of Christian conscience?

4. Eucharist is the key sacrament of Christian initiation. Explain.

5. How is eucharist a privileged situation for Christians to discern the movement of God's Spirit in their lives?

PART FIVE

MINISTRIES OF HEALING

15 JESUS' MINISTRY: TEACHING AND HEALING

Christians are initiated into the church not only for their own sakes, but in order to be part of a community that carries on with the risen Christ his work of bringing humanity to its destiny. This co-working with Christ in the various ministries Christians are involved in is the practical context in which we can come to understand what classically we have called the sacraments of holy orders, anointing, and reconciliation. Since any authentic Christian ministry must be a continuation of what Jesus began during his public ministry, our first step must be a careful look at what Jesus himself did to minister to people.

What basically did Jesus do in his public ministry? He acted for God in meeting people's needs. Simultaneously he served both his Father and his human brothers and sisters because his service of his fellow humans was precisely what the God who sent him wished him to do. Jesus' service to the people he encountered was a sacrament of God's own service to these people. God's saving power, God's Spirit, was present to Jesus' activity, creatively animating and empowering it. For this reason, Jesus' public ministry "gave glory to God," manifested God's saving intent.

Jesus' Servant Ministry

The New Testament description of Jesus' saving ministry reveals a basic conflict in people's notions of "salvation" and God's challenge to ordinary human views on this topic. The Jews of Jesus' day longed for God's expected "day of salvation," but most of them looked for this in terms of the arrival of a messiah who would be a powerful political and military leader, who could lead them in successful revolt against the oppressive power of Rome. Israel's God from earliest times had been called *Yahweh Sabaoth* (Lord of Armies), and it was to this divinity of avenging might that most Jews turned in their prayers for the sending of a messiah. Jesus, however, refused to be identified as such a messiah.

Early in Jesus' public career, the crowds who heard his teaching and witnessed his works of healing raised the question: Is this the messiah? Realizing what this term meant in popular understanding, Jesus apparently refused to acknowledge such public identification. Among his own disciples, however, he admitted to being the awaited messiah of Israel. In accepting the confession of Peter and then of the other disciples that he was indeed the messiah, Jesus made it very clear that his understanding was drastically different than their own, a difference of understanding that even Jesus' closest friends did not really grasp until after his death and resurrection.

This difference is made quite explicit early in the gospels, in the scene of Jesus' temptation in the desert, which we examined earlier when talking about the Christian values system. The tempter does not suggest that Jesus abandon his mission as messiah; rather, it is a question of "more effective" ways of fulfilling his messianic role. He bids Jesus work some magic (changing these stones into bread), do something sensational (jumping from the temple top), or using wealth and power to achieve his purposes. There is no doubting the meaning of this opening scene of Jesus' public ministry. The kingdom of God is not established by economic, political, or military power; God in his wisdom does not use such means to bring humans to their destiny.

As Luke's Gospel tells us, this temptation "left Jesus for a time" but it returned in various forms, particularly in the expectations and remarks of the closest disciples who could not yet rid themselves of the notion that the kingdom would come through force, prestige, and wealth. Replying to such misunderstandings of his messianic work, Jesus described himself and his ministry in terms of the so-called fourth Servant Song in Isaiah 52-53. As he tells his disciples (Matthew 20:25), civil rulers ("the lords of the gentiles") rule by domination, but that is not the way of his kingdom, for he has come "not to be served but to serve and to give my life." This is a direct allusion to the Isaian passage; Jesus proposes to his followers the strange strategy of achieving his mission through suffering and death. Jesus is not to be a political messiah but a prophetic messiah, according to the Isaian ideal. He is to be the servant who saves his people by the gift of himself even unto death.

We are not completely certain that Jesus explicitly identified himself as this servant, though it is quite likely that he did. But it is quite certain that the earliest Christian communities interpreted Jesus' mission in this way. The very early Christian hymn that Paul incorporates into the second chapter of his letter to the Philippians already speaks of Jesus "taking on the form of a servant, becoming obedient even unto death." All four gospels use this servant theology in explaining the meaning of Jesus' life, death, and resurrection.

Not only did Jesus refuse power as a means of accomplishing his mission of saving humans from evil; he refused as well to give any theoretical solution to the problem of evil. To put it in current sociological terms, Jesus did not provide any new ideology. It may well be that the reason was that no such explanation is possible, since evil ultimately is a mystery rooted in the unintelligibility of human sin—sin makes no sense! What Jesus did, as we will see in more detail, was to give a practical solution; he worked against evil in whatever form he encountered it. Whether it was physical disability or hunger or social oppression or psychological disorders or fear, Jesus worked to heal people.

However, beyond this straightforward attack on evil, Jesus went on to that mysterious confrontation with evil that occurred in his death and resurrection. Though we will never be able to probe fully the reality and implications of Jesus' suffering and death, there are a few things we can say. 1) It was not Jesus' suffering as such that overcame evil, nor his death, insofar as it was simply the loss of life, for these things are themselves evils. Rather, it was his experiencing suffering and death as realities chosen out of love for his fellow humans. 2) Jesus triumphed over suffering and death, because even these ultimate threats to existence and meaning diminished neither his faith-filled witness to God as his Abba nor his love for humans. 3) Indeed, in refusing to return hostility for the murderous hostility directed against him, Jesus broke that circle of vengeance that in human history has always led to wars and to human destruction. Jesus' love, itself sacramental of divine love, literally absorbed evil and thus robbed it of its power. Love is revealed as a creative power able to overcome the radical negativity of evil. 4) In this way, as Suffering Servant who is also risen Lord, giving himself lovingly to his human brothers and sisters, Jesus provides both the "secret" and power by which humans can cope with and overcome the forces of evil in their lives. This is the ultimate dimension of his ministry. This is what continues to work within and through the Christian community because of the creative presence of Jesus' own Spirit.

Jesus as Teacher

Granting the climaxing importance of his death and resurrection, Christian catechesis as contained in the New Testament concentrates on two aspects of Jesus' ministerial activity, his teaching and his healing. By reflection on these, later generations of Christians are to find guidelines for their own ministry.

There are several aspects of Jesus' teaching that have special relevance for Christians today, at a time when a plurality of ministries, among them teaching, has emerged spontaneously from the ranks of the laity. Jesus' teaching was itself that of a Jewish lay person. It was unofficial, having neither mandate nor validation nor approval from any official religious group of his day. Actually, his teaching activity was viewed with suspicion by much of Jewish religious officialdom. Jesus' teaching did not result from any structured education he had received. He belonged to none of the rabbinic schools of his day, followed none of the rabbinic masters (as, for example, did Paul), espoused no particular "party line." Rather, his teaching was prophetic, breaking suddenly on the scene and speaking immediately for and about God. Jesus' teaching had none of the "sacrality" that surrounded the pronouncements of the temple priesthood. Though he spoke constantly about God, it was about a God concerned with the ordinariness, the "secularity," and therefore the deeper sacredness, of people's lives and persons.

Christian teaching ministry can learn much from examining the themes that dominated Jesus' teaching. 1) Foremost and constantly, Jesus talked about God, whom he knew in intimacy as his Abba. 2) He talked about "the kingdom of God," the way his Abba had guided and was still guiding the history of Israel and of all humankind. 3) He talked about the purpose of life and the destiny of people and he did this with hope in the ultimate goodness and meaning of human existence. 4) He talked about a new set of values by which to judge the actions of people and the happenings of life, a set of values that constituted a paradoxical God-given wisdom. 5) He talked about the goodness of creation, the fundamental goodness of people, particularly the goodness of the marginated men and women with whom he so frequently and so easily associated, whom he loved and about whom he was so deeply concerned.

The manner of Jesus' teaching is also instructive. Though he was a superb teacher whose didactic skills are reflected in the gospel accounts, even through the filter of several decades of interpreting memory, Jesus dealt with his hearers in essentially prophetic fashion. He witnessed to that God he knew so intimately in his own religious experience; he proclaimed the wonder of God, rather than giving any educated theological explanations; he spoke in strong denunciation of hypocrisy and exploitation when that was demanded; he stated straight out and forcibly whatever he meant to say; and he clearly spoke for God, even to the point of going beyond the Mosaic Law. One never gets the impression that Jesus was sharing with people his opinions of how things might be. Instead, Jesus is described as telling his auditors how things really are from God's point of view.

Another aspect of Jesus' teaching that has a very modern ring was his exemplification of what he taught. His own lifestyle and dealings with others were marked by the simplicity and genuineness he advocated. His values and life decisions quite obviously flowed from his total acceptance of the God he proclaimed. But the issue cuts deeper. Jesus' message shifted somewhat in the light of his experience, which included rejection by the Jewish religious establishment, abandonment by the crowds that had followed him at the beginning, growing opposition and hostility from the high priesthood, lack of comprehension, even on the part of his closest followers. Pondering all this apparently led Jesus to alter his ministerial strategy and to shift the emphasis in his teaching. He still proclaimed the God of the covenant but he drew much more attention to its deeper levels, the mystery of passing through death into newness of life.

What took place in Jesus' teaching exemplifies what liberation theologians are saying today about *praxis*. One can only do theology in depth if one is reflecting upon actual experience of God's saving action. But on the other hand, one can only participate effectively in this saving action if one's activity is infused by accurate understanding of what this saving action truly is.

Still another element of Jesus' teaching activity, one that marked the second half of his public career and whose applicability is hard to assess, was the abandonment of large-scale preaching in favor of forming a very small circle of immediate disciples. No doubt there is need in Christian teaching ministry both to instruct the mass of people and also to form an inner core in greater depth. What priority to set on each of these is, however, something that will probably always remain a debatable strategic choice. Jesus' own approach remains a source of fruitful reflection, but it demands a certain faith that subordinating immediate gains to long-range objectives will ultimately prove wise.

Finally, there is the theological depth of Jesus' teaching. This has to do with the fact that Jesus the teacher is God's own embodied personal word. Other prophets, before and after him, bear God's word on their lips and speak it to their contemporaries. Jesus is that word. For this reason, Jesus' teaching has unique creative force. It is able to bring into being what it speaks of, provided only that those who hear him do not refuse to listen. This special power of Jesus' words is clearly reflected in the gospel description of his "signs," the striking works of healing he performed. With one or two exceptions, such as the woman cured of hemorrhaging by touching Jesus' garment, Jesus cured people simply by speaking.

Jesus as Healer

This creative, life-giving power of Jesus' words means that we should not separate too sharply his teaching and his healing ministries. Yet, the gospels themselves do parallel Jesus' words and his works, and those "works" can be described generically as healing. More than other humans, Jesus was sensitive to the disastrous impact on humans of the various forms of evil: sickness, ignorance, fear, abject poverty, social oppression, religious exploitation, and particularly sin. His concern took practical expressions. Wherever he encountered evil he worked against it; he taught in order to remove ignorance and error, he cured the handicapped, he condemned social injustices, he led people to conversion and forgiveness of their sins.

While such healing activity was in fulfillment of his saving mission, it is good to remember that the gospels depict Jesus as doing all this because of his own deep compassion for people. Jesus cared very deeply for people, especially for those in need; he could not stand by inactive while people suffered. At the same time, Jesus had a profound sense that his own loving concern for people was completely in line with his Father's creative compassion for humans. In going out to help those who needed him, Jesus was aware that this was what his Abba wished and what the Father was sending him to do. This was his mission: to be the expression in people's lives of his Father's love. This was what it meant for him to be about the business of establishing the kingdom of God. His own restless concern to heal men, women, and children was the experience through which Jesus himself came to understand the mystery of the transcendent God who was compassionate and personally involved with each and every human.

As the gospels describe Jesus' healing actions, it seems that he (and the early Christians who produced the New Testament) considered "evil" somewhat globally, as a reality with several levels. Sicknesses and other physical disabilities, suffering, psychological disorders, social inequalities, death, and sin were somehow all linked together, but sin was the root of all the other evils. So, Jesus' healing often occurred on different levels. His healing of physical blindness, for example, was joined to the cure of spiritual blindness; and on many occasions when he is described as healing some physical disorder, he says to the person, "Go and sin no more."

One of the most intriguing aspects of Jesus' healing is its link with people's faith; without such faith Jesus apparently was unable to heal. Besides, Jesus tells those who had just been healed, "Go in peace; your faith has made you whole." This seems to say that the person's own faith was the source of the healing. We have tended to water down these statements by considering the faith as a condition for Jesus causing the cure but the gospel wording seems unavoidable: The individual's faith is a cause of the healing. Although we still have little understanding of the manner in which psychosomatic healing occurs, how states of consciousness actually affect bodily processes for good or ill, and even less understanding of how deep faith affects this entire psychosomatic interaction, it seems quite clear that Jesus and his early disciples took for granted that there was such interaction.

Despite the obscurity of our understanding, there are a few insights we can gain from this, insights that provide valuable guidelines for Christian ministry. 1) Since healing people is always a matter of nourishing life, healing must come from within, whether within an individual or within a community. It is the person or the group that must heal; no one else, even God, can do that healing, though they may well provide the stimulus, the support, and the resources necessary for the healing. 2) The one in need of healing must be open to receiving help from outside. That person must wish truly to be healed, must be willing to admit dependence upon others in the process of healing, and must trust the concern and love of others. This is where faith in God's saving love is required but also faith in the concerned love of other humans. 3) Any lasting cure is tied to conversion; it involves a continuing nurture of the inner healing that has begun. Jesus frequently tells the cured person, "Go, and sin no more."

Much of Jesus' healing can be classified under the term "reconciliation," a classification the New Testament itself uses. Both Jesus and early Christianity had inherited, through the biblical texts, the Israelitic description of sin as "alienation." As described, for example, in the story of Adam and Eve's sin in Eden, sin involved an alienation of humans from Earth which no longer yielded its fruits without human toil. It involved an alienation of humans from God, an alienation of humans from the rest of life, as many animals now become "wild beasts"; it involved an alienation of humans from their own psychological integrity, as they now felt shame at their naked bodiliness; it involved alienation of one human from another, as Cain killed his brother.

Jesus' saving work is described in Paul's writings particularly as one of reconciliation, of overcoming these various alienations. Jesus has "broken down the walls of separation" that divided Jew from gentile, powerful from powerless, rich from poor, women and men from one another. More radically, Jesus has overcome the alienation of humans from God. He has shared his Abba with his brothers and sisters; he has joined these fellow humans to himself in love so that he can bring them with him to God who is their destiny. And this reconciliation touched the entire universe; the whole of creation is meant to share in Jesus' task of unifying all reality by the power of his Spirit.

Jesus' healing works, especially the reconciliations achieved through his death and resurrection, take on added depth when Christian faith sees him as God's incarnate Word. Whatever Jesus of Nazareth is or does embodies what God is "saying" to human beings; he embodies it creatively. Everything about Jesus "speaks for God," who is present personally to the consciousness of this Jesus and who works personally through this presence. Jesus is, as we saw earlier, the sacrament of God.

Sacramentality of Jesus' Healing

Ultimately, all Jesus' healing is rooted in his self-giving to others. This becomes most clear through Christian reflection on his death and resurrection. As the gospel theology is structured, the final supper of Jesus with his disciples interprets the meaning of the death and resurrection that follows. Itself the first stage in Jesus' passage through death into new life, because it is the solemn commitment to that passage and inseparable from what immediately follows, the supper conveys through its dense symbolism the inner meaning of Jesus' saving act. Without going into detail, we can simply remember that Jesus' words as he shared the bread with his friends—"This is my body given for you"—state unmistakably that his action is one of profound self-giving.

So, if Jesus' self-giving is sacramental, it means that God's dealings with humans is one of creative self-giving. When we probe further into the various kinds of healing, we can begin to see that it is precisely the divine self-gift that provides the most basic source of healing. To mention but one element of this, nothing in our human experience provides more assurance of our self-worth and dignity than being genuinely loved by another. This experience, which helps create our identity and heal our insecurities, is greatly intensified when the lover in question is the transcendent God. Human reasoning could never imagine, much less argue to, such personal love on the part of a transcendent God. Christian faith believes, however, that such divine self-giving is sacramentalized in the human Jesus.

Persons give themselves to one another through communication. By the use of symbols such as language, they share their personal reality as conscious beings; they reveal to one another their self-identity. Self-giving, then, is always self-revelation. So, when we use the term "revelation" to speak of God's word to humans, it means basically the divine self-revelation; it means the understanding communicated to humans of what it is for God to be self. Christians believe that in some unique fashion this kind of self-revelation comes to humans through the "Abba experience" of

Jesus, an experience in which Jesus is inescapably and immediately aware of the transcendent God as someone for him.

Jesus' teaching ministry takes on new significance when we now see it as sacramental, as a human activity that is at the same time God's own self-revelation. The viewpoints and attitudes, the values and wisdom, the prophetic invitations to a new future that mark Jesus' teaching can in some mysterious but true way be attributed to God because Jesus who is teaching is doing so as God's self-revealing Word.

This reality of God's self-gift being sacramentalized through Jesus' self-giving finds its fullest expression, of course, in the death and resurrection of Jesus. This is truly Jesus' redeeming action, his loving obedience even unto death, but it is also God's work. Earliest Christianity recognized this in saying that "God raised Jesus from the dead." For Jesus, this is an act of giving his very life to his friends, an act that takes on full and unending form with the Pentecost gift of the Spirit, from which his own risen life springs. But that Spirit is also God's Spirit; Christ and his Abba have but one Spirit together. Pentecost is at once Christ's self-gift and God's self-gift, the latter sacramentalized through the former.

What all this says is that the deepest level of Jesus' ministry is his very existing as sacrament of God's saving presence in human life. But such "existing" is not inactivity; it is not simply "being there." It is rather a state of consciousness completely open to hearing and responding to the divine self-revelation; it is that living faith that makes divine presence possible.

This leads us to one final question about Jesus' ministry that we can respond to only briefly. What was the source of Jesus' empowerment for ministry? Obviously, the question is closely linked with our present-day questions about the need for Christian ministers to be empowered through some form of ordination.

While we cannot forget that Jesus' case was unique, since he alone stands at the origin and continues at the center of Christianity, still it is theologically significant and practically important that he received no social commissioning for his ministry. The "call" to Jesus to minister did not come through any official agency; rather, it was a mission directly from God, a mission that consisted in the gift of God's own Spirit. Moved by this Spirit of creative compassion he shared with God, Jesus himself had this impelling desire to help his fellow humans in whatever way he could and particularly to bring them into contact with this Abba who alone could provide ultimate salvation from the evils that afflicted them. The Spirit he shares with his Father is Jesus' empowerment.

Being essentially a community endeavor, Christian ministry needs some social forms by which claims to ministerial charism can be validated. Not everyone who claims to have some special gift for ministry should be given recognition as such and be permitted to act in the name and on behalf of the community. However, it must always be remembered that the fundamental power to work effectively for the personal good of people comes from that Spirit one shares as member of a community which is body of Christ. Any empowerment to carry out a particular ministry comes by way of special "gift" from the same Spirit.

Summary

Jesus' dealings with the people who made up his world was one of simple and straightforward interest in them and living concern for their human needs. Because he encountered in these people so much pain, suffering, and damage, his outlook on human life was one of deep compassion; he truly suffered with his sisters and brothers. However, this compassion took a practical form: He fought against the evils that enslave humans whenever he encountered them. Basically, he taught and he healed; but even more basically, he gave himself to all he met in the offer of friendship. He himself was the ultimate teaching, God's parable; his self-giving was his ultimate healing.

This self-giving ministry of Jesus is sacramental of God's self-giving service to humans, for Jesus exists and acts as God's embodied Word. Whatever Jesus is or does "speaks for God," reveals the selfhood and the saving love of God who is made present to Jesus in this Abba-experience and through Jesus to all who share Christian faith. What is revealed in the sacrament of Jesus' ministry is God's service to the needs of humans.

Questions for Reflection and Discussion

1. In what sense does the title "messiah" apply to Jesus?
2. What was Jesus' "solution" to the problem of evil?
3. How would you characterize Jesus' teaching?
4. Explain the link between Jesus' healing and the faith of those he healed.
5. What does the sacramentality of Jesus' healing tell us about God?

16   SERVICE TO HUMAN BODILINESS

J esus told the crowds that followed him that they missed the deeper meaning of his physical cures. Then, after the multiplication of the loaves and fishes, when the people wished to make him king and followed him around the lake, he again told them that they had failed to grasp the deeper significance of what he had done: Beyond this bodily healing was his healing of their spirit; beyond this bodily feeding was the nourishing of their lives as persons. But he *did* heal and feed their bodies and this care of their bodiliness was sacramental of the inner spiritual effect and sacramental of God's saving action in these people's lives.

Christian ministry is an extension of this sacramentality. Christians, the body of Christ, are meant to embody and thereby implement the risen Christ's own healing activity. Christian healing has within it the life-giving power of risen life, which springs from Christ's Spirit. This healing ministry is meant to find expression, in the first instance, within the Christian community itself and within its members, but such healing of Christians is for the sake of their then going out to heal the world they live in.

The need for healing is universal. No person is free from the forms of evil that enslave and harm people at every level of society.

Even in the realm of physical healing, where more affluent groups have such disproportionate access to medical help, the evils of physical debility and suffering eventually touch even the rich. Thus, the need for ministration to people's bodily ills is immense, and our age, despite all the advances of medicine and medical technology, is still far from providing for people in this respect.

However, there are some exciting developments. There are, of course, the still expanding areas of professional medical care—by physicians, nurses, medical technicians, and paramedical personnel—that can truly be Christian ministries, if undertaken as response to the gospel and with genuine desire to serve one's fellow humans. Moreover, in some quarters there is a promising shift in attitude and in resulting practice. Although the bulk of medical activity is, quite understandably, directed still to the cure of people, much more attention is being given to caring for patients, especially those with terminal illnesses. This shift represents an increasing awareness that sickness is something that touches the entire person, and that physical healing should be directed toward care of the patient as a person. The applications of this to the Christian ministry of bodily healing are obvious.

Since most Christians are not themselves engaged as medical practitioners of one sort or another, they probably do not see themselves as likely to become involved in ministry to human bodily ills. Yet, careful study of the nature and causes of disease in our world suggests that no one is free from responsibility in this regard, especially if she or he belongs to one of the economically more privileged portions of the globe. We now know that by far the greatest causes of physical ailments are starvation and lack of decent drinking water. Technologically we are able to remedy most, if not all, of this disturbing situation. The question is whether people in the powerful nations of the world will decide to turn their attention and energies to the physical needs of the vast bulk of humankind. Christians in the First World can hardly claim that they carry on Christ's own healing ministry if they do not seriously respond to this unprecedented opportunity to heal much of the world's present physical suffering.

Besides the widespread effect that social sins of injustice, exploitation, and oppression can have in causing physical suffering for millions of people, there is also the effect that personal sin has on people's ailments. Many of the illnesses people suffer from are the outcome of their own actions or of some person's assault upon them, actions that at least objectively are sinful: sickness of one kind or another that springs from and is aggravated by excesses in drink or drug use, various forms of venereal disease, child abuse or wife beating. In these instances, what is required as the root solution is an act of conversion. Any effective ministry to people in these situations must lead them to decisions that will either reverse the damaging behavior or remove a victim from the context in which he or she is abused.

Psychological Healing

Healing extends beyond purely bodily ailments and deals also with humans' psychological illnesses. One of the important advances in modern consciousness has been the growing awareness that psychological disturbances are illnesses. People who formerly were characterized as "insane," as "crazy," are now seen to be suffering from one or other form of psychological illness, though we are only at the beginnings of understanding the nature and cure of such illnesses. Because such persons are sick, we no longer simply incarcerate them, but instead seek to cure them, or at least care for them more humanly. This is what we claim to do, and in many instances actually do, though there are still some shocking instances of barbarous handling of those who are seriously disturbed psychologically.

The needs and opportunities for dedicated ministry to those afflicted with psychological illness are almost unlimited. Because of the prejudices and fears still attached to mental illnesses, relatively few people are attracted to this form of service and even fewer are willing to obtain the professional formation required for competent psychological therapy. Yet, there is a particular aspect of this work that is linked with Christian faith and that suggests a specifically Christian contribution to psychological healing. This has to do with the link between sin and psychological disorder.

To mention this connection is not to suggest that sin and neurosis are the same thing, nor that psychological problems are always rooted in the person's own sinfulness. But deviant behavior, particularly deviant sexual behavior, that formerly was considered simply as sin, we now know to be frequently an expression of psychological disorder of one sort or another. Christian attempts to help people be healed of their sinfulness cannot ignore the psychological elements that may be present. Conversely, people's sin is quite often an element in their mental illness, and no effective therapy can ignore this fact. No one is completely in touch with reality; and in our more honest moments we know that this is to some extent our own fault. We deliberately refuse to accept ourselves or our world because we do not wish to accept the responsibilities this entails, and we take refuge in fantasy. If such unwillingness to face reality is severe enough we describe it as mental illness.

Although this does not mean that every Christian who ministers to human sinfulness—for example, an ordained minister of the sacrament of reconciliation—need be a professional psychologist, nor that every psychological therapist needs to accept Christian belief about sin, it does suggest that there should be some cooperation between these two areas of expertise, between these two kinds of ministry.

Again, there is a clear and important link between people's psychological disturbances and the economic, political, and cultural injustices in human society. One need not accept the theory that people are behaviorally determined by their environment, nor "go soft" on blatantly criminal behavior because of the deprived background of the offenders, but there is clear evidence that both psychological illness and criminal activity are rooted in social injustices. Ministries that deal with overcoming social injustice are a necessary ingredient in the human battle against psychological illness and crime.

Intrinsic to the Christian community's ministry of bettering people's life situations is the celebration of eucharist, detached as this action might seem from the practical effort to heal people. This action is meant to be a clear acknowledgment by all present that there is no place in Christianity, in human life for that matter, for the injustices due to economic or social stratification. There will be some richer people and some poorer, some more powerful and others less so, but these are very secondary to the basic equality and concerned friendship that should prevail in any group of Christians. Eucharist celebrates this equality and friendship.

The New Testament lets us know that at early eucharistic gatherings Christians took up collections to aid the poor in their midst or to send help to other communities that were struggling financially. This custom has never ceased to be part of Christian assemblies. But a still deeper commitment to providing for the health and the dignity of the poor is contained in that prayer that has always been part of Christian liturgy, the Our Father. The phrase "Give us this day our daily bread . . ." is not a petition for some miraculous provision of food. Daily bread is the normal sustenance that men and women provide with responsibility and dignity for themselves and their children. In praying for this daily bread, Christians are asking for the opportunity to take care of themselves in decent human fashion, but also pledging to help provide this opportunity for the "little ones" of Earth.

Christian Care for Persons

Certainly, Christians have no monopoly on the idea that in caring for either physical or psychological needs of people one must always keep in mind that one is dealing with a person. Yet, for any Christian who would become involved in healing ministry, this is a cardinal principle. The revelation that takes place through Jesus' public activity is quite explicit. The transcendent divinity Jesus knows as "Abba" is interested in the healing of the whole person, particularly in the healing of those levels of being that are most truly human: thought, affection, imagination, and freedom. So, Christian ministries should be motivated by a genuine personal concern for people and grow out of a keen sensitivity to people's real needs. Only ministry of this kind can most fully sacramentalize the divine concern for the ultimate well-being of every human.

What this says is that Christian ministry must learn increasingly to deal with the immense problem of human suffering in our world today. And it must do so with both intelligence and compassion. It will not be enough to feel sorry for those who suffer; we must learn to discover and eradicate, as far as is possible, the roots of people's suffering; and while we are working to remove the causes of suffering we must become as effective as we can in healing those who have been victimized by disease, social injustice, or economic oppression. At the same time, it is important that we keep in mind that there is an intrinsic and ultimately unavoidable link between suffering and the fact that we are part of the created universe. This does not mean that we cease working against human suffering as Jesus himself worked against it; it does mean, though, that we cannot remove from human experience such realities as death, but must instead settle for seeing that such limitations are kept from diminishing persons as persons.

People suffering from either physical or psychological illness need food, medicine, or therapy of one sort or another, but more than that they need the attention, love, and support of others. They need to know that there are friends who understand and care. They need to share with others the faith vision that can bring some meaning to their suffering, and the hope that can give them courage to bear it. Sickness and physical pain are evils because of the harm they do the human body, but more so because of the damage they do to the human spirit. Serious and prolonged illness tends to depress persons, to wear down their emotional stamina, to make them overly concerned about themselves and increasingly self-centered, to destroy optimism, hope, and self-esteem. Christian healing ministries must be directed particularly to prevent such damage to the human person.

Sacrament of Anointing

This is precisely where the sacramental liturgy of anointing is meant to function. Often in the past, the sacrament of anointing was limited to a last minute ceremony performed on a Christian at the point of death. The name used for centuries, "extreme unction," reflected this. As explained theologically, this sacrament was seen to have two effects: 1) It somehow fortified a Christian for passage through death. 2) If God so willed, it could occasionally work almost miraculously to restore the person to health. If the dying person was already unconscious and therefore unable to confess his or her sins and obtain sacramental absolution, the sacrament of anointing could supply for this if the person when last conscious had been basically contrite and open to God's forgiveness. Such anointing was performed very individualistically, with no apparent connection to a Christian community, apart from the ministering priest. In very many instances, the person being anointed in no way participated in the act.

Yet, both the origins of this sacramental action and the official liturgical rite itself indicate that this is intended to be a comforting and strengthening symbol of community support. Ideally, some people, at least of the Christian community the individual belongs to, should share in this ceremony. Perhaps the anointing could even be celebrated as part of a Sunday eucharist, if it is appropriate. If circumstances dictate that only the ordained minister can be present, the sick person should see the minister's presence as representative of the community. The person being anointed began Christian life by baptismal initiation into a Christian community. It is obviously incongruous for that person to be now entering the final and most critical stage of initiation into Christ without the support that the community had pledged in the baptism liturgy.

At times, the sacramental act can assist the person's physical recovery. However, the principal purpose of the sacrament of anointing is to help heal the person from those personhood-destroying influences of suffering we discussed earlier.

There is another purpose that is often overlooked: Anointing, like each of the sacramental liturgies, is basically a profession of faith, most importantly the sick person's faith. Faced with serious illness, even more so when faced with death, the anointed person has the opportunity, as in few other circumstances, to bear witness that the death and resurrection of Jesus is truly the key to understanding human existence.

It is relatively easy for a Christian to believe and hope in risen life beyond death when that person is not yet close to death, but when one is at death's door, the uncertainty intrinsic to faith and hope become manifest. The decision to believe and hope becomes a very real act of Christian faith, which clearly bears witness to God's fidelity. This final witness pledged to the Christian communities a person belongs to should not be given in solitary circumstances that prevent those communities from being enriched by it.

Even if death is not an immediate prospect, which is often the case now when the anointing is given for a non-terminal illness, the sick person bears witness that it is the death and resurrection of Christ and the supporting love of the Christian community that can give meaning to human suffering.

What the sacrament of anointing is intended to do is to alter people's hermeneutic of experience, their approach to interpreting life's experiences, specifically the experience of suffering. One of the worst aspects of suffering is its apparent meaninglessness.

Those who suffer in one way or another quite logically ask why. Christianity replies that there is no ultimate answer apart from the mysterious wisdom expressed through Jesus' life, death, and resurrection. The sacramental liturgy of anointing the sick celebrates Christian gratitude for the gift of this wisdom at the same time that it brings to the sick person the comforting love of the community.

Finally, it is appropriate here to mention an area of sacramental ritualizing that has been largely ignored: the process of bereavement. Recent liturgical revisions have provided an improved ritual for Christian burial, though this too needs to be further revised to take fuller account of the nature of risen life in union with Christ and more account of the traditional belief in "the communion of saints." But we still do not have liturgies that assist people to handle the various stages of grieving that follow upon the death of a loved one. This despite the fact that serious study of this process has given us considerable insight into the sequence of stages that generally make up people's sorrowing after a death. Developing such liturgies would seem a logical extension of the confrontation with suffering and death that occurs in the ritual of the anointing of the sick.

Summary

God's concern for the entire human person is sacramentalized in Christian ministries to people's bodily well-being. While such ministries provide for physical nurture and cure, their more ultimate objective is the spiritual and personal health of people. At the root of many of the ills that afflict men, women, and children lies the evil of human sin. It is to the eradication of this evil that the Christian ministry of reconciliation, which our next chapters will study, is directed. However, this should not obscure Christianity's concern for the whole person, body and spirit.

The sacramental liturgy of anointing the sick is a focal expression of this concern. Quite recently the understanding and practice of this rite have shifted. Not too long ago, the liturgy was called—and actually was—a sacrament of extreme unction, a rite performed when a Christian was on the point of death. Now the rite is used more broadly, for any serious situation of illness, as a help to the individual in dealing with the personally damaging effects of sickness and suffering. The name is appropriately changed to sacrament of anointing. The purpose of this liturgy is to sacramentalize both the support of the Christian community and the faith witness of the suffering person.

Questions for Reflection and Discussion

1. In what ways can Christians contribute to people's bodily healing?

2. Is there a distinctively Christian contribution to psychological healing?

3. What is the basis for Christian commitment to social justice?

4. How does the sacrament of anointing of the sick act symbolically to heal people?

5. Explain how the sacrament of anointing is a distinctive profession of faith.

17   RECONCILIATION
OF SINNERS

While the healing of the whole human person must, as we just saw, provide for people's bodily well-being, there is an even greater need to heal the consciousness, imagination, emotions, and desires of persons, that is, to heal people as people. This includes ordinary psychological healing as a most important element, but such personal healing must go still further and deal with the reality of *sin* in human life.

While biblical thought views all evil as alienation, it sees sin as the most drastic alienation and the source of all other evil. Or, to use another biblical category, evil is ultimately identifiable with chaos; and what underlies the worst and yet most common forms of chaos—hatred and vengeance, dissensions, destruction, wars, and death—is sin. Sin is the most chaotic and alienating force in human experience. Christian faith affirms this and a good deal of our human experience tells us the same thing.

If people are to be safeguarded from the influences that stand as barriers to their full human realization, or healed from the wounds already inflicted by those influences, sin must somehow be overcome. In Christian teaching, we have traditionally talked about "the forgiveness of sin," about the fact that only God can ultimately triumph over sin, and that God does this by mercifully forgiving our human sinfulness. At times, one almost gets the impression that there is practically nothing that people can do about their propensity to sin, except throw themselves helplessly on the divine mercy and hope for the best. There are certainly some elements of truth in this view—humans do need divine help to overcome sin, God is merciful and does not deal vindictively with sinners, etc.— but we know today that we must reconsider what we mean by "the forgiveness of sins."

Biblical studies, particularly in the New Testament, have made it quite clear that we can dismiss any notion that God needs to be persuaded to forgive us, that God sits over us in harsh judgment, or that humans and the society they create are essentially evil. Quite simply, God "so loved the world that he gave his only son, so that everyone who has faith in him may not die but have eternal life" (John 3:16). Jesus described God in the parable about the father of the prodigal son. It is clear that God seeks out the sinner, "forgives" the sinner before that person is even aware of the need to be forgiven, and that it is impossible for this God to be other than continuously loving toward creation.

"Forgiveness of sins" needs to be understood more accurately in terms of what God does; it also needs to be understood more accurately in terms of the human need for forgiveness. What is it that needs to be forgiven? What does "forgiveness" really mean? For one thing, we are increasingly aware that the question deals not so much with sins as with sin. Although individual actions can, obviously, be morally wrong, and humans do commit sinful acts, the more basic issue is the person's fundamental attitude toward oneself, and the world, and God. This is what we have sometimes called "the state of sin" or "the state of grace." There are some people who may do very little that is clearly sinful, perhaps because they do very little of anything, but who live with deep resentment against God and a basic rejection of themselves and their life situation. If such persons were to run down a list of sins before going to sacramental confession, they might find practically nothing to mention; yet, they would be fundamentally alienated from God. On the other hand, a person who regularly lived in basic openness to reality and God might, at times, perhaps because of human weakness, do something morally wrong, almost immediately regret it, and never really break the link of friendship with God.

Personal sin is an alienation within the self. One who lives in such a "state of sin" is living untrue to his or her selfhood. Such a person is refusing to recognize reality, refusing to go out to others in genuine love and concern. Often a person in this state has made the choice for comfort and safety at the expense of freedom, autonomy, and mature responsibility. Such an approach to life can find expression in sinful acts, but the fundamental evil is that person's alienation from his or her true self. Conversion must be a reconciliation with their genuine self, a grateful acceptance of who they truly are, and a willingness to live with this reality.

Sin is always a deviation from what one ought to do or ought to be. It means that one is turned aside from one's goal, is misdirected, and this by one's own foolish, deliberate choice. One is neither acting nor existing authentically, neither acting nor existing wisely. One is not being truly human, not really living, not really free. A sinner needs to be converted, "turned around," re-oriented, revitalized; a sinner always needs to be healed, for sin is like a wound or sickness. No one can do another's healing for them but we can minister to one another's healing. This has always been one of the church's most basic ministries, though for a long time we confined it too narrowly to the sacramental liturgy of confession and absolution of sins.

If there is to be a genuine healing from sin, one of the first requisites is that the person forgive herself or himself. This may sound strange but people cannot begin to recover from what sin does to them as persons unless they admit their need for recovery and wish to recover, that is, convert. It is difficult for all of us to recognize that we are less than we ought to be, that to some extent at least this deficiency is our own fault—to put it bluntly, that we are sinners. And if we have such an awareness, it becomes difficult to accept ourselves as good, difficult not to become overly upset by our humanness, and difficult to truly forgive ourselves for self-betrayal in the way we would forgive a dear friend who had betrayed us in a moment of weakness.

We can be of great help to one another in this situation. We can assure one another, in a variety of ways, that despite our faults we are still accepted in friendship and understanding. We can be for one another that kind of support community that makes it possible for a person to face himself or herself candidly without fear of social rejection, and makes it possible for a person to run the risk of genuine self-discovery. By honestly sharing experiences of human frailty we can help one another appreciate the strengths and the weaknesses of our common humanity. We can thereby help others to acknowledge with us our common need for moral healing. We can to some extent heal together, but there is a certain amount of healing that each of us must do as an individual and that no one else can do for us.

Sacramental liturgies of reconciliation are an important element in this healing of sin, but they are only part of a broader process and function effectively only as part of that broader process. Sin is itself a process, a process of growing self-destruction, of denying one's selfhood, of self-refusal, of continued indecision or deviant decision. This sinful development needs to be reversed by the person's own fundamental option to live more genuinely, to live according to the principles of the gospel. And then this option must flow into a continuing process of self-acceptance, authentic, free decision making, honest response to others, a process of positive growth as a person, which replaces the damaging effects of sin.

Ministering to one another in this healing process can take many forms, because sin, our own sin and other people's sins against us, leaves various kinds of wounds. Not all our neuroses are the result of sin, but many are at least indirectly that. Though we may have turned away from deliberate hatred of another and decided not to be vindictive, there will often be a residue of hostility deep in our emotional response. Our previous history of sin remains in our memory, and it can cause undue anguish, or it can attract us to some of the false values that led us into sinful courses of action in the first place. The knowledge of one's past failure in Christian decision making can undermine one's confidence and lead to indecision and apathy. Many who have been born and lived in blighted human situations have been deeply wounded by what is sometimes called "the sin of the world," that is, the disorder, injustice, and exploitation that pass into the structures of human life generation after generation because of humans' sinful activities. Each of these "woundings" calls for a particular kind of therapy. In many instances, effective ministry demands special expertise, such as training in psychological counseling, on the part of the minister. All such ministry is sacramental, an intrinsic part of the sacrament of reconciliation.

Forgiving One Another

Sin is always a matter of denying our true selfhood and such denials occur in terms of relating to others, since "existing in relation to others" is what it means to be a "self." When we sin, we refuse to be self for others. We refuse others what they have a right to expect from us: honesty in our use of language and other symbols, respect for their life and personhood (including the things they need to nurture), genuine concern and regard for them as equals. So, the healing of sin within persons requires also a healing of the damaged relationships between persons, the reconciliation of person to person. The ministry of reconciliation is one of helping to overcome the antagonisms that separate people; it is one of helping people to "forgive those who trespass against us." The human reconciliation that occurs here is the very heart of the sacrament of reconciliation.

While patching up the frequent quarrels that separate people is an important part of this reconciling ministry, there are often much deeper and long-lasting alienations that need to be overcome. People are opposed to one another, hostile to one another, for a variety of reasons. Sometimes it is a matter of ethnic or social prejudices rooted in ancient grievances that have practically nothing to do with people living today. Sometimes one is hostile to another, generally someone one does not know very well, because one fits that other person into a stereotype. For example, one intensely dislikes all motorcyclists who wear black leather jackets "because they are dangerous and disorderly types."

One of the most important aspects of the ministry of reconciliation is the work to counteract and ultimately eliminate such prejudices and stereotypes from our shared human consciousness. The difficulty and yet necessity of this task become clear if we only reflect for a moment on one instance: the centuries-old and inherited hostilities and tensions, grounded in prejudice and stereotype, of many men and women toward those of the opposite sex.

Teaching is ministry that can be most influential in overcoming such alienating prejudices and stereotypes. Not just religious education, but practically every area of teaching can help lead people to a truer and therefore prejudice-free understanding of what people and human life are all about. The same is true of modern communications media, a new situation of mass education where Christians must learn to minister imaginatively because of the enormous impact these media have on the attitudes people develop toward their fellow humans.

Nurturing Communication

Just as a good deal of the need for physical healing can be eliminated by preventive medicine, so also much of the division and hostility that separate people can be prevented by fostering positive relationships among people. To a large extent, this is a matter of nurturing lines of communication, helping persons to continue conversing with one another; in many instances, even shouting at one another is better than a total break in communication. Many a marriage could be saved and even grow if the couple could be helped toward genuine communication. If parents and children could learn to talk sincerely and openly to one another, many a family could become a community of caring persons rather than a group bickering daily and misunderstanding one another. Many a friendship could have continued if the two persons had talked to each other and discussed their differences, instead of remaining silent and imagining what the other person was thinking.

Within the broad ministry of reconciliation, there is, then, a "ministry of diplomacy" by which one helps bring people into genuine and productive conversation. More basically, Christians are meant to work toward ever more honest dealings with one another, speaking the truth—with love, of course, but still speaking the truth—for only the truth can make humans free to be themselves with one another, to communicate. Such open communication is often blocked by fears of rejections ("My friend will no longer love me if she knows what I really think"), by old hostilities ("There's no point in even trying to talk to that person"), or by desire to remain popular ("People don't like those who always speak their mind"). But if Christians can form communities in which they are free to deal candidly and honestly, where differences can continue to exist along with open lines of communication, where people do at times offend one another but are soon reconciled, such communities are sacraments of reconciliation.

Fostering Fidelity

If any ministry of reconciliation is to be effective, if a Christian community is to exemplify such reconciliation among its members, the problem of infidelity must be faced. Experience teaches us how difficult it is for humans to be consistently faithful, even to themselves, to say nothing of faithful to one another. Infidelity is at the very heart of sin. Perhaps the most accurate description of sin is that it is the denial of that love we should have toward ourselves, one another, and God. It is not accidental that in the Bible the attribute most characteristic of God is "faithful" and that all human sin is grouped under the term "infidelity."

The imagery used by the Scriptures to portray both God's fidelity to his people and the people's tragic infidelity toward God is marriage. Drawing from what we discussed in an earlier chapter about the sacramentality of human friendship and especially of Christian marriage, we can argue that Christian couples who are lovingly faithful to each other help nurture human fidelity in the church as a whole and in the world generally. They do this by being a sign that fidelity to each other is possible and that it is a "pearl of great price."

Since the key to people remaining faithful in friendship is their wanting to do so, ministering to such fidelity must be a matter of helping people evaluate fidelity as a great good. People must not only be told that possessions, power, or prestige cannot match the benefits of true friendships; they must themselves also experience the ultimate happiness that comes in truly loving and being truly loved. Christian communities, especially Christian families, can provide some of this experience for themselves and for others they invite to share their life by living out the discovery that mature loving does bring joy.

Most likely, this is why early Christianity placed so much emphasis on the virtue of hospitality. Christian homes were the welcoming centers of Christian assemblies where men, women, and children had a sense of being "at home," of genuinely belonging to one another, of being a community whose sharing of one another was sacramental of their sharing the presence of the risen Lord and his Spirit. When the pastoral epistles describe the qualifications for one who is to be publicly recognized as a presbyter, that is, a more responsible leader of the community, hospitality is one of the few virtues mentioned. Christian hospitality can provide the context in which people come to treasure one another as friends, where they learn to value friendships above the wealth or power that might tempt them to betray their friends, and where they learn to trust their own and others' ability to be faithful.

But even in such deeply Christian communities, human frailty often enough leads people to be unfaithful in some way to one another. This means that there is a constant need for people to be forgiving; the phrasing of the Our Father recognizes this need. Paul urges the early Christians not to harbor resentments: "Do not let the sun go down on your anger." Reconciliation must be part of any lasting and developing human friendship, and an acceptance of the need for reconciliation with one another must mark any maturely loving human group. The presence of such frank forgiveness of one another is what Christians should celebrate in their liturgies of reconciliation.

Summary

The deepest level of people's need for healing is that of human sinfulness. Although this certainly has to do with forgiveness of sinful actions, it touches more deeply the "state of sin," a person's basic alienation from self, others, and God. Such forgiveness of sin must start with the person's self-forgiveness. One must be healed from sin, and this can occur only within the sinner. But such healing is inseparable from the reconciliation of individuals to one another or to social groups. Moreover, there is great need in our society for social groups to be reconciled to one another.

Restoring and fostering communication among people is the key to such reconciliation, and much of the ministry of reconciliation consists in nurturing lines of communication. One of the more effective forms of such ministry is Christian hospitality, a service that is especially appropriate to the Christian family and part of the sacramentality of Christian marriage.

Questions for Reflection and Discussion

1. Explain how sin is appropriately described as "alienation."

2. Why is it important for people to forgive themselves?

3. Our reconciliation with one another is the heart of the sacrament of reconciliation. Explain.

4. Relate the notions of "reconciliation" and "forgiveness of sin."

5. Why is it so important to foster fidelity?

18 HEALING HUMAN SOCIETY

A mong the important shifts that have occurred recently in the Christian view of sin, none is more basic than the increased awareness of the social dimension of sin. Not only individual humans can be sinful; social groups and whole societies can be corporately sinful. One effect of this shift has been to lessen people's narrow concentration on the sinfulness of certain sexual behavior and to draw their attention to the relatively greater evil of much social injustice.

If one thinks of sin in terms of the biblical category of alienation, it is evident that very much of the alienation that afflicts human life is social. Ethnic or national imperialisms pit one populace against another, often in bitter and destructive wars. Social and racial prejudices divide one group of people from another. Class struggles dominate most of human life today: the poor and powerless fighting to free themselves from economic or military domination, women attempting to obtain full recognition as equals despite the forces in a patriarchal culture that resist such attempts, affluent and powerful groups struggling to retain and even increase their position of privilege in the face of attempts to create a more equitable distribution of goods and opportunity.

Clearly, our society needs healing; most radically it needs healing from its sin. Social groups of various kinds need to be converted corporately; they need to repent and to be healed. In a special way, the church, meant to be a paradigm of loving community, needs to face its corporate sinfulness and undertake to heal itself through the life-giving power of the Spirit. Human society as a whole, for the first time in history truly "a global village" where no group can exist in isolation, needs to convert and be saved from its sin. We are faced with the unspeakable alternative: humanity obliterating itself in nuclear holocaust.

Paralleling this new perspective on social sin, there has been in Catholic theological circles a "rediscovery" of the ecclesial character of the sacrament of reconciliation. Indeed, we have become more aware that all our sacramental liturgies bore a basic "church-meaning." The effect of sacrament that was other than "grace" and that we had called the "sacramental character" (or in the case of some of the sacraments, "the *res et sacramentum*") was somehow specially connected with one's role in the church.

Theologians had long found difficulty in explaining the *res et sacramentum* of the sacrament of reconciliation (or penance as it was until recently called). Actually, they had difficulty in general in explaining how this sacramental liturgy was effective. Did the absolution pronounced after the penitent's confession really cause the forgiveness of sins, or did it simply proclaim to the person the fact that God had forgiven them? Most puzzling was the relationship between the person's own conversion (one's repentance or contrition) and the sacramental action. If one had committed some grave offense but had, following the pastoral advice given, sometime later repented and turned contritely to God in prayer, that person (according to church teaching) was forgiven and back in "the state of grace." What, then, happened when that person went to confession and was "absolved"? Was that person simply fulfilling a church law that required such public confession? If the person did not go to confession, did the sin already forgiven by God somehow return? Or did the person incur a new sin because of not following through on a "promise" to comply with sacramental confession that was implicit in the original act of repentance?

As theologians puzzled over such questions in the light of our renewed insight into the ecclesial element of sacramental significance, a response emerged: The fundamental purpose (and therefore meaning) of the sacramental liturgy was to celebrate and cement the reconciliation of the sinner to the Christian community. Even if one's sin was quite "private" and involved no open offense to another or to the group, it was still a failure in fidelity to the community. In liturgies of initiation and in eucharist a person had pledged to be Christian for the others, to help support their faith by one's own fidelity to the gospel. In violating this pledge through sin, one became somewhat alienated from the community, and this alienation needed to be healed. Conscious that the healing of this rift between the sinner and the community was precisely what was meant to occur in this sacramental act, we are increasingly calling it "the sacrament of reconciliation."

Confronting the Sin of the World

Our deepened understanding of sin and of the sacrament of reconciliation has made clearer the need for ministries directed to healing the corporate sinfulness of our society. Such ministries must deal with "the sin of the world," that residue of people's sinful activity that has become institutionalized in the attitudes, values, and structures of society. One of the first steps in such ministry is the discovery, through both human expertise and spiritual discernment, of the ways this institutionalized sin diminishes people's opportunity to fulfill their human potential.

Such discovery is taking place today, aided by the tools of social analysis provided by the social and behavioral sciences. We know more clearly today that a great deal of evil is systemic evil. Granted that the systems in question came into being through human invention and decision, they tend to develop a life of their own, a tendency that is greatly accelerated by the rapid spread of computer technology. In many of the sinful decisions being made today in industry and business, it is difficult to pinpoint any particular individual or group as committing sin; yet, millions of men, women, and children are being damaged in body and spirit by massive corporation systems and processes that exploit and enslave them.

One can simply decry the presence of such systematized evil and place the blame on modern technology, but this is an immature and non-productive approach. What is needed is a creative ministry that will work to modify these systems and processes so that they serve humans rather than exploit them. If a particular system is clearly "unredeemable," we must discover a more suitable alternative. History cannot be reversed; we cannot wipe out advances in science and technology, even if that were a good thing to do, which it is not. Instead, we must learn to minister to the emergence of a future in which new systems and processes are created that will further the physical and psychological well-being of all.

This may seem far removed from Christian ministry, but if evil in the modern world has taken such large-scale systemic form, then large-scale systemic remedies must be used by Christians who wish to continue Christ's work of healing. Actually, there already exist a number of agencies that are directed, or could be directed, to this need. There are the so-called think tanks, specialized planning centers in which experts try to analyze present trends in social development and to suggest ways of building a more human future. There has been considerable expansion of urban planning, a cooperative effort of public officials, social scientists, and architects to give some guidance to the growth of urban regions, so that life in these population concentrations can be more human. There has been increased public involvement in providing housing for lower-income groups, even some beginnings of provision for the rapidly increasing numbers of indigent old people. These are only a few of the concerned attempts to build a more human future. Many more are needed. All need to be guided by the values espoused by Christianity.

Granted that such attempts are still in their infancy and are still far from providing adequate response to our problems, they do indicate new avenues for effective Christian ministry. Many of the old avenues of ministry also offer exciting new possibilities for overcoming the systemic evils of life today. To take education as one example, since it is specially linked with Jesus' ministry of teaching, there is today widespread discontent with our educational systems. Complaints range all the way from schools' lack of discipline to their lack of creativity in providing the kinds of learning needed for today's world. Clearly, there are many needs. More public appreciation and support of education is a critical need; teacher education needs to be thoroughly updated and intensified; curricula and course materials often bear little relation to the real interests and needs of the students, etc.

But the most basic need is that people consider education, in whatever form it takes, as a genuine service to society. For Christians this means that education undertaken within the perspective of faith is a most important area of ministry. Precisely because of scientific and technological advances, the ministry of teaching has new tools to make instruction stimulating and effective. It has the possibility, within the very near future, of extending educational opportunities to the entire human race. Whatever changes occur in the patterns of human life, they will come about because of changed ways of thinking. To influence future thinking, so that it is accurate, honest, imaginative, and humanistic, is the purpose of education. Without genuine education of people, there can be no healing of human society.

Curing Social Insanity

It may sound strange to talk about society's insanity and the need to cure our corporate mental instability. Yet, there are numerous indications that humans as groups have shared mental illnesses. Professional psychology has not only recognized this situation, it has already initiated some response, if for no other reason than that individuals cannot be healed if their context of experience is psychologically disruptive. Often, families as a group need therapy; neighborhoods have shared anxieties; groups such as the Ku Klux Klan are founded on the basis of people sharing irrational fears and hatreds; whole nations have a paranoid view of other nations.

To state it mildly, there is little hope for genuine human community unless such insanity is healed. A more accurate statement would be that this is an explosive situation that could lead to massive harm to human life. There have always been such insane hatreds and fears among groups of people, but modern communications have made it possible that such insanity might be shared, even fostered through propaganda, on a massive scale. But such communications have also opened up the possibility of healing society's insanities. Good attitudes as well as perverted ones can be fostered; people can be led to a healthy hermeneutic of experience as well as to a sick one.

But why link all this to Christian ministry of healing? What distinctive contribution can Christians make to curing society's mental illness? There seem to be several areas in which Christianity can provide part of the cure to this social illness, some indispensable elements in the broader human effort to build a safer and better world. For one thing, Christianity proclaims a gospel of hope. When so much of the disturbed mental state of social groups is rooted in a distrust of others, it is obvious that there is need for well-grounded hope that God is faithful, that God has created all humans fundamentally good and therefore basically trustworthy, and that Jesus' death and resurrection represent a triumph of human goodness over hatred and fear that will carry on through history.

But there is a more radical contribution that Christianity is meant to make: its proclamation of the true God, its most basic ministry of evangelization. This can sound like a trite "just what we expected" and therefore an unrealistic response to a very real problem, but it is quite realistic, if one looks carefully at the context and the character of the evangelization in question.

In the history of religions, people's view of God has often been a projection of their fears and anxieties, a justification for their aggressions, a legitimation of their cruelty and oppression of others. In one way or other, humans believe that their God (or gods) should set the example of personal behavior; humans should become better by following this example. So, if a people's divinities are capricious and cruel, suspicious of one another and craftily trying to outwit one another, unforgiving and vindictive and violent, one can scarcely expect the people to cherish gentleness, forgiveness, and openness in their dealings with one another.

For the most part, Christianity's God has not been preached in such dark tones, though some of the "fire and brimstone" sermons of the past do not seem to be describing the God Jesus knew as Abba. But in more than one context the God of Christianity is still being proclaimed as the ultimate authoritative power that stands behind human domination and justifies it. This domination has frequently been quite violent and oppressive. It has created in both oppressed and oppressor a mixture of fears and hostilities that is not psychologically sound.

Portraying the centuries-long and painfully slow process of Israel's spiritual growth, the Bible itself bears witness to the long struggle of leading Israel from a view of God as the powerful war-god, "Lord of Armies," to a view of God as a tender lover. And the struggle was far from successful. The gospel scene of the Jewish crowd choosing Barabbas before Jesus makes clear that very many rejected Jesus' nonviolent approach as revealing God's way of saving people.

One of the mysterious and disturbing aspects of Christianity's history is the prominence of violence and war in Christian portions of the world. Starting out with a markedly nonviolent stance, founded by one described as "the prince of peace," Christianity was not too long in absorbing a military model for the church: the church militant, its members soldiers of Christ. One can insist that such words were used only metaphorically, but it was a metaphor misapplied to many "holy wars," wars among Christian peoples themselves or "crusades" against people judged to be evil. And God was invoked in support of such cruel adventures. What this seems to say is that Christians in our day must be careful not to continue this misrepresentation of the God revealed in Jesus. Instead, their ministry of healing human society must be grounded in the proclamation of a God who, to put it in human terms, is gracious and understanding and gentle, who rules by love and care, who cherishes the worth and dignity and freedom of every person. Human society would be much saner if people's values and activity were measured against such a view of the transcendent one.

Healing Family Life

Christian concern about healing social groups must certainly embrace concern for healing family life in today's world. So severe are the strains on families in today's world and so fundamental the social impact on changing family structures that many serious thinkers have forecast the demise of the family as we have known it. Such negative predictions are probably excessive, but there is little question about the gravity of the challenge now facing the family. Fortunately, the challenge is not going unanswered. A number of effective movements have come into being in recent decades to support and deepen Christian family life. A healthy ministry to the family is already in place.

These very movements, however, have helped us discover how deep is the change now going on in familial structures. Until very recently, and even now to a large extent, the family has been thought of as a community held together by an interplay of roles: the father as head and basic breadwinner, the mother taking care of the home and children, the children relating to parents in obedience and sharing in the tasks of the home; the husband protecting and loving but also making decisions for his wife, the wife cherishing and supporting and complying with her husband. Clearly this is rapidly changing. What is replacing it is a view of the family as a community of persons who may perform different and complementary functions, but who do so as a result of shared decisions and therefore with greater personal choice.

Not everything about these new developments is, obviously, good. But for one thing, they have made us more sharply aware of the forces of destructiveness that can work in family groupings, forces destructive of the family and of the individuals in it. Added to this is our more accurate understanding of the psychological dynamics that operate in groups of people who must associate with one another in close quarters and over extended periods of time. We are, in other words, more keenly and concretely aware of families' need of healing. To help accomplish such healing by maturely fostering the emergence of more person-respecting structures of family life is one of the more delicate but also more important ministries in Christianity today.

Another part of the challenge to Christian marriage and family life comes from outside the family, from the attitudes and values of society. Increased social acceptance of premarital and extramarital sexuality, open admission of homosexuality, and much more display of subtle or not so subtle erotica in movies and magazines (even in those not thought of as "adult entertainment") have marked the past few decades; but the greatest effect of the so-called sexual revolution may well be on marriage and the family.

Attitudes of spouses to each other cannot but be deeply affected by the views of their society toward human sexuality. Such views inevitably touch what a man and woman think about fidelity to their marital relationship, what they think about the role their sexual lovemaking plays in the broader reality of their friendship, what they consider "successful" sexual intercourse, what they expect from each other and hope to give in their sexual intimacy. There has been a very worthwhile growth in positive acceptance and appreciation of sexual lovemaking in many marriages, but there has also been a great deal of anxiety and tension among couples who felt they should adopt all the avant-garde views and practices, even when their common sense and loving reverence for each other told them that much of this was nonsense.

Again, the deepening debate about gender roles, about society's images of "male" and "female," about the distinctiveness and yet full equality of women and men, is upsetting and in some instances disrupting marriages that seemed quite stable and happy. Fundamentally, this debate is fruitful, for it draws attention to the injustices inflicted on women in patriarchal culture. Yet, in some quarters there is a narrow focus on the personal rights of the two parties in the marriage, and little mention of the profound responsibilities to each other that are intrinsic to any such intimate friendship. Certainly, neither person is to be "sacrificed" to the other, nor for that matter are parents to be subordinated to their children any more than the children are to be subordinated as persons to them. But any real personal love involves the freely and joyously chosen sacrifice of giving oneself for the beloved. Christianity insists that this is a basic element in the meaning of Jesus' death and resurrection.

Invitations to choose individual comfort and personal satisfaction as life's goals are being proposed as truly mature, "modern" wisdom. Some married persons are attracted by what appears to be a new freedom; many others are simply confused. Both groups need to be supported in the judgment that authentic personal love, the kind that brings people lasting happiness, is simultaneously self-giving and self-fulfilling. It is self-fulfilling in proportion as it is mature self-gift. Christianity, particularly through the sacramentality of Christian married couples, is to minister to this need.

Healing Society's Symbols

Symbols and myths, images and stories, are the deepest "motors" of any society. They are at once the flower and root of that society's culture. If the symbols and myths are sick, obscene in the most radical meaning of the term, the society is sick and its culture decadent. If the symbols and myths are honest and beautiful, a society's culture enriches and dignifies people's experience. What happens to people in any society is inseparable from the symbol systems that permeate that society's culture. This means that effective Christian ministry to people's human development must include the effort to create or to sustain those symbols and myths that will in turn create and sustain people.

What is at stake here is the role traditionally played by the arts, a role debated for millennia. Much of this debate has been, and still is, a rather shallow discussion about "art and morality" that concentrates on the "obscenity" of nudity or of portraying sexual lovemaking. Unquestionably, there is something about titillating, vulgar, and perverted depiction of sexual activity that is potentially harmful to people. It can help destroy the sense of beauty, the reverence for persons, and the loving joy that are part of mature sexual experience; it can upset the delicate integration of personal love and sexual passion, of *eros* and *agape*. But the more important question deals with the function of the arts in shaping a culture's most basic symbols, which are used to express its vision of goodness, beauty, and truth, and which embody its judgment about the meaning of human existence.

More influential than abstract studies about the present condition of humans are the movies, plays, and television shows that portray that human condition in a way that immediately resonates with people's experiences, and in a way that either reinforces or questions people's attitudes, values, and lifestyles. Somewhat less obviously, painting, sculpture, music, and dance formulate much of the aspiration, discontent, and revolutionary ferment that are still deep and hidden in society's psyche. These art forms are often, like authentic prophecy, an anticipation of the future, and like the word of the prophet, they help create the future to which they point.

In today's world, any discussion about the social impact of the arts must include an appraisal of modern communications and advertising. Not only do communications media offer an unprecedented exposure of the arts to masses of people, they have their own power to affect society's symbols, a power we still understand only imperfectly. Perhaps those who understand best what this power is and how to harness it are the experts in the advertising industry; its use of the arts and communications media needs careful examination. Honest and imaginative advertising can help people make intelligent choices, and it can alert people to the very real advantages of certain products. Advertising can also be manipulative, deceptive, and vulgar. What most demands examination, however, is the way advertising presents certain values and the symbols embodying those values as the taken-for-granted value system of society, and then appeals to this presumed value system to sell its goods. How much, for example, of the sales pitch used to sell cosmetics is grounded in the presupposition that showing one's age is an evil to be avoided at considerable cost.

At least two areas of involvement in the arts seem appropriate to Christian ministry: professional art criticism and artistic creation. We need artistic criticism as a guide for public appreciation of and enrichment by the arts: knowledge of art history, educated sensitivity to art forms, some understanding of the psychological sources and impact of art, informed insight into the social functions of artistic media. Artistic creation is needed to provide society with instances of authentic beauty, with artifacts that can more deeply humanize people's responses to one another and to the world, with experiences of the beautiful that can give an aesthetic glimpse of that ultimate beauty that Christianity identifies with God revealed in Jesus the Christ.

There is a long-standing Christian tradition, perhaps more honored in the Orthodox approach to creating ikons than in Western religious art, that artistic creation is a sublime form of prayer. The obverse is also true, that Christian liturgical prayer, particularly eucharistic liturgy, is an art form that should lead a Christian community to experience the transforming beauty of God present in the liturgical creativity of the assembled Christians.

One could continue to suggest other areas of human life today in which Christian ministry could and should be a healing influence, but one last area cannot be omitted. It is the ministry of making peace. As never before, the absolute need for concerted effort to avoid further war is apparent, though we do not yet seem able to implement what is so apparent. Yet, avoidance of war is far from sufficient as a goal. There is a positive making of peace that is much more than avoiding conflict; it is itself the only solid hope for avoiding such conflict.

Unquestionably, we are faced with a task of great complexity and immense proportions. Moreover, Christian faith tells us that without divine help we are incapable of overcoming the evils that culminate in war. However, this same faith assures us of this divine help as the correlate to Jesus' teaching, "Blessed are the peacemakers, for they will be called the children of God." Peacemaking is quite clearly, then, one of the ministries that Christianity today cannot responsibly shirk.

Christian Communities: Sacrament of Healing

As sacrament of the risen Christ's saving presence in history, the church is a sacramental cause of society's healing. This it is by being itself a community in which Christians live in honest reconciliation with one another, in which the values Jesus taught and exemplified counter the person-denying values embodied in modern systemic evil, and in which commitment to a covenant relationship is translated into justice and beyond that into loving concern for each person in the community.

To the extent that it is faithful to its own nature and destiny, the Christian community is a paradigm of all that human life should be; it is an example of what will come to be on a larger scale. More than that, the community's acceptance of the risen Christ and his

Spirit as the guiding and animating force of its corporate life means that God's Word and Spirit are present to this community as sources of healing. Christianity proclaims God's saving and healing intent by itself being a healed and healing agent in human life.

What this requires of Christian communities is that they become increasingly healed groups of people. Divisions of one sort or another need to be discovered and admitted and then overcome—whether between old and young, progressive and reactionary, affluent and needy, one racial group and another, women and men, clergy and laity. All these alienations still exist within the church, often within a local community. The most important task of Christians in ministering to humanity's need for social reconciliation is to respond to the gospel's demand that peace, that is, true reconciliation, be established within Christianity itself. Whenever Christians gather for eucharist, they express their gratitude for the peace that exists in their community. This statement needs to be made more honestly.

Summary

The Christian ministry of reconciliation must extend beyond reconciling persons to themselves and to one another; there is grave need to heal human society. For one thing, the evils afflicting people today have become increasingly systemic. Massive structures and processes exploit and destroy people, and to the extent that they are evil, such systems need to be converted or replaced. One can speak even of the need to heal the insanity of human society; there are any number of situations in which there is shared mental illness.

Basic to all such healing is a correction of the view that people have of God as vindictive, dominating, or supportive of unjust human institutions. Evangelization is intrinsic to the ministry of social reconciliation.

One of the most important areas of social reconciliation is that of healing family life in today's world. Severe tensions arising from a new understanding of the family as a society of persons threaten family unity. Shifting societal attitudes toward sexuality also impact strongly on married life.

Another ministry of great importance has to do with the creation of art forms that can bring people to a sense of beauty and a desire for goodness and truth. Societies live out of their symbol systems at the same time that they create them; what those symbols are is a key to the humanity of any society. There is a special Christian aspect to this ministry, since the very purpose of Christian sacraments is to challenge, infiltrate, and transform all the other symbols that are present in human experience.

Perhaps no ministry is more pressing today than that of making peace. Because war can lead now to utter destruction of humanity, it is imperative that Christians draw from their own deepest traditions to assist in eliminating war from human history.

Questions for Reflection and Discussion

1. What is meant by "the social dimension of sin"?

2. What is the "ecclesial character" of sacramental liturgies? How is this applicable to the sacrament of reconciliation?

3. How would you describe "the sin of the world"?

4. How can preaching of the gospel help heal human society?

5. Why is it important to create and foster appropriate symbols for human society?

6. How are Christian communities meant to be a sacramental force for the healing of society?

LITURGIES OF RECONCILIATION

I t is difficult to think of anything in Catholic life that has changed more rapidly and more drastically in recent years than the sacrament of reconciliation. Just a few years ago, it was a common scene on a Saturday afternoon and evening to have numbers of people coming to the church to go to confession, and these numbers were greatly increased just before key religious holidays, such as Christmas and Easter. Hearing confessions was one of the principal activities of parish pastors, and not infrequently there was need to bring in an extra priest to help with these confessions.

Today, one recalls this as something out of an almost-forgotten past. Saturday afternoons and evenings are now relatively quiet times around most parishes. The parish billboard lists an hour when the pastor will be available for confessions, but scarcely anyone comes. Large numbers of people who previously would have gone to confession at least twice a month now go once or twice a year, if that often. On the other hand, when there are well-planned parish liturgies of reconciliation, they are often well attended, particularly by young people.

This change has happened very rapidly, with no obvious causes.

No one is quite certain what is happening, except that something new is coming into existence. Already, official modifications of the penitential rite have, in some local areas, led to changing the title from Sacrament of Penance to Sacrament of Reconciliation (although the Vatican's title is still the former), have introduced a more personal mode of confession that emphasizes the spiritual counseling aspects of the relationship between confessor and penitent, and have moved in the direction of community celebrations of reconciliation, even toward general absolution. This new ritual, with its multiple suggestions for celebrating reconciliation, recognizes that liturgies in this area must be flexible and must take account of people's actual needs, because different people are at much different stages. Perhaps the most profitable thing we can do in this situation is to clarify, as far as we can, the goals that effective reconciliation liturgies should seek. If we can do this, we will have some criteria for creating suitable liturgy.

Liturgy as Part of the Sacrament

1. Liturgies of reconciliation must be seen as only one element in the sacrament of reconciliation; they must be situated in the broader context of the actual human reconciliation going on within a Christian community. The reconciliation of Christian to Christian, of group to group within the community, and the community's ministry of healing the various alienations that splinter human society—these are what sacramentalize the reconciliation of humans with God. A liturgy that is not grounded in and giving expression to such actual reconciling is without meaning and therefore sacramentally ineffective.

This is by no means to suggest that liturgies of reconciliation are incidental or unnecessary; their role in the process of reconciliation shares in the indispensable role that language plays in human relationships. We humans need to tell one another of our wish to be reconciled; we need to say that we are once more united in friendship; we need to voice our happiness in being no longer estranged. A reconciliation liturgy should accomplish all this.

2. Each Christian needs to admit, as part of a mature, realistic approach to life, that he or she has failed somewhat in living out Christian faith. One has not been a completely faithful disciple of the risen Lord; one has not been, to that extent, completely faithful in bearing witness to one's fellow Christians; one has betrayed the trust that Christians owe one another. To say this to one another,

even specifying, when appropriate, the particular form of in-fidelity, is part of each one of us coming to greater self-knowledge. It is also an important bond that links us to one another; there is nothing we more universally share than the need to be forgiven.

One important advantage that comes with such open admission of our human infidelity is the correcting of our basic notion of sin. We come to understand sin as violation of persons, as infidelity to ourselves and to one another. We begin to experience our sin-fulness as undesirable alienation rather than as oppressive anxiety or failure to comply with laws. We cannot turn away from and be healed of our sin unless we know what this sin really is. When, during a liturgy of reconciliation, the proclamation and explana-tion of the gospel challenges our infidelities we can come to know better and admit to ourselves the real needs we have for conver-sion.

3. Liturgies of reconciliation should foster Christian formation of conscience. Even if our general notion of sin becomes more ac-curate, as personal infidelity, we still need to develop the ability to appraise actual situations of moral choice and decide which cours-es of action would be authentically Christian and which would be unfaithful. Another way of expressing this is to say that we need to form a genuinely Christian conscience, something we must do as individuals but drawing from the shared moral wisdom of the Christian community. Community liturgies of reconciliation should provide important occasions for people to reflect prayer-fully on the real decisions they face. They should be a major in-strument for the formation of Christian conscience.

This is intimately linked with what we have been calling a per-son's hermeneutic of experience, the basic attitude with which one confronts and interprets experience. Reconciliation liturgies in which people really share their Christian moral judgments about common elements of experience can be a powerful influence in shaping people's interpretation of their experience. A liturgy of reconciliation should guarantee the prophetic proclamation of the meaning of Jesus' death and resurrection, so that this meaning can be a norm for the community's moral evaluations.

There is another advantage that comes with public statement of conversion. We tend to follow through more consistently on prom-ises made in public; the public statement of repentance itself acts to crystallize our decision. And if this public commitment to living the Christian faith is shared with others, as it is in a liturgy of reconciliation, there is an element of community support that gives individual conversion greater force. This supposes, of course, that the liturgical celebration is such that people can actually have such an experience of conversion in response to the word of God.

Celebrating Reconciliation

Like other sacramental ceremonies, the liturgy of reconciliation is meant to be a celebration, and be experienced as celebration. This clearly takes the focus off sin and healthfully places it on reconciliation. Obviously, no one would be celebrating human sinfulness, which only a truly malicious person would do, but reconciliation is truly something to celebrate.

Even if reconciliation dealt only with the relationships of Christians one to another, or with individuals' reconciliation with themselves, it would be something for people to treasure and rejoice in together. How many humans can assure themselves that they will receive understanding and support from a genuinely compassionate community? But what Christians celebrate in addition is the personal loving forgiveness of a compassionate God. And what assures them of divine forgiveness is the human reconciliation they are experiencing, for that reconciliation is sacrament.

There are any number of situations in which liturgies of reconciliation can occur. Often they can be quite short, even informal: before a family meal, among a group of friends, as an element in other liturgies such as anointing or eucharist. They can also be appropriate after some negotiations, to help heal wounds after some particularly aggressive competition in business, or in professional or public life, to welcome a person back into a group he or she had defected from because of some misunderstanding or conflict. It is important to keep in mind that eucharist is and always has been the principal liturgy of reconciliation.

Corporate Repentance

Part of our growth in understanding sin has been the increased awareness of corporate guilt. As we saw in the last chapter, there are many sinful actions we do as *groups*. As groups we oppress other groups, undertake unjust wars and destroy other people's lives, refuse to shoulder the responsibilities that are really ours. As groups we are in certain respects "in a state of sin." Nations can exist arrogantly, and even glory in their arrogance and presumed superiority. Christian churches have lived with pious hatred of one another and refused to believe anything good of the others.

If such corporate guilt and need for conversion exist, and they do, some liturgies of reconciliation must be directed toward the recognition of this guilt and communities must be converted, as communities, to more authentic discipleship. Without this frank evaluation by a Christian community of its actual status before God, it is impossible to have honest discernment of the Spirit at the heart of that community's decision making; it is impossible for that community to hear the word of God for it. What is called for is not some agonized worry about possible faults, nor a pessimistic self-evaluation, but an honest and peaceful facing of the situation. This can be greatly assisted by liturgies in which the gospel is proclaimed as both challenge and consolation, and the response of the community is that of grateful conversion.

Again, there is a continuing need for liturgies that can be part of the effort to foster reconciliation within a given Christian community. No human group, no Christian community is without some friction and some alienation of individuals from individuals or groups from groups. One of the most common mistakes we make in communities is to hide such differences, to carry on as if they do not exist, to avoid admitting them lest they openly divide the community. Yet, these divisions can be healed only if they are recognized and dealt with. There could be a form of reconciliation liturgy that would deal quite explicitly with this problem. Its goal would be to help the community discover and confess the inequities, injustices, prejudices, and hostilities that mar its existence, and then undertake—perhaps with pain but also with hope—a shared ministry of healing itself. As the process of reconciliation advanced, such liturgy could serve as continuing stimulus and thanksgiving for the unity already achieved.

To reiterate a point made before, any discussion of liturgical ceremonies of reconciliation should include the fact that eucharist is preeminently the liturgy of reconciliation precisely because in unique fashion it is the sharing of Christ himself, the ultimate source of reconciliation. In Paul's words, "He is our peace." It is not accidental that "peace" is a recurrent theme in eucharistic liturgy, nor accidental that the liturgy draws attention to the distinctiveness of the peace in question. It is "the peace of Christ," the reconciliation of persons to one another that comes when Christians recommit themselves to the new covenant. It is that peace "which the world cannot give," because it flows from the life-giving and unifying power of the Spirit.

Eucharist makes clear that reconciliation within a Christian community is most deeply a matter of that group becoming truly the "body of Christ." What most awakens Christians to their infidelities and motivates them to love one another with greater fidelity is their relationship as individuals and as a group to the risen Lord. Christians' faith and discipleship go hand and hand with their acceptance of one another. In eucharist, Christians share the bread made body of Christ as the sacrament of their being reconciled to one another in a truly compassionate community of persons.

Summary

In the rapidly changing context of the sacrament of reconciliation, it is difficult to determine exactly what shape or shapes the liturgy should take in this sacramental area. For one thing, the liturgical celebration is but one element in a much broader sacramental reality, namely, the actual reconciling that goes on in human life and especially in the Christian community. At least for the moment we can describe some of the needs that reconciliation liturgies should meet if they are to be sacramentally effective.

There should be a liturgical situation in which Christians can publicly declare their infidelity to one another and, more importantly, their determination to live more faithfully and more lovingly. This must, of course, be coupled with a declared willingness on everyone's part to forgive those who have injured them. At the same time, there are corporate elements of sinfulness that Christian groups need to discover and disown together: divisions, animosities, and prejudices within a community, or shared neglect of Christian responsibility for the needs of the world.

Reconciliation liturgies should develop within the community an authentic sense of human sinfulness and the need of salvation, a peaceful awareness of a shared need for forgiveness, a hope in God's compassion, and a concerned support for people as they struggle to overcome evil.

Questions for Reflection and Discussion

1. Why is the liturgy of reconciliation only part of the sacrament?

2. What is the distinctive role of reconciliation liturgies?

3. How should liturgies of reconciliation be professions of faith?

4. What is meant by "corporate repentance"? How can it be celebrated liturgically?

5. Explain how eucharist is pre-eminently the liturgy of reconciliation.

20 SACRAMENT OF MINISTRY

S o far, we have seen the broad scope of Christian sacrament, one that carries considerably beyond the distinct liturgical actions we have long called "Christian sacraments." We have seen that Christian sacramentality actually touches the entirety of human experience, transforming the most basic meanings of our life.

The fundamental significance of human relationships, and especially those positive relationships we call "friendship," have their meaning deepened by Christian marriage, which witnesses to the depth and fidelity that is possible in love between people. The universal experience of socialization, of growing into adulthood within the context and responsibilities of human community, of being initiated into full personal experience takes on new meaning through people's initiation into Christian community and into the mystery of Christ. Coping with the problem of evil and suffering is understood in a new and hopeful way because of Christians who work to heal their fellow humans, striving to overcome the alienations that plague individuals and societies, ministering to reconcile hostile elements in human society—and thereby sacramentalizing the saving activity of a compassionate God.

In each of these areas of sacramental activity, sacramental liturgies play a special role that depends upon the wider sacramentality of Christians' lives, but is itself essential to that sacramentality being realized. So, liturgies of baptism and confirmation make explicit in symbol the significance of entry into the death and resurrection of Jesus. Liturgies of reconciliation and anointing reveal the insight into sin and suffering that can come with faith in Christ's resurrection; they reveal also the presence in life of the saving compassion of God who works through the mystery of Jesus.

The marriage liturgy draws attention to the link in meaning between human friendship and God's love for humans, the entwined significance of Christ and the Christian community as one body, and husband and wife as one body. In constant interaction with the meanings expressed in these rituals, eucharistic liturgies draw attention to the continuing presence of the risen Jesus who shared our life and death so that he might give them radically new meaning in resurrection.

Apparently, we have not yet dealt with one of the traditional "seven sacraments," holy orders. At least at first glance, this sacrament seems to be more limited in its application; it does not deal directly with the experience common to all Christians but only to the activity and experience of a special group within the church, the ordained clergy. However, the Christian sacramentality connected with orders extends far beyond the liturgical ceremony of ordination, just as was the case with the other sacramental liturgies. Actually, we have been talking about this broader-based sacramentality throughout the past few chapters; the broader reality in question is that of Christian ministry.

Historical Emergence of Holy Orders

It might help us understand the connection between holy orders and ministry if we recall very quickly the historical process by which orders came to be seen as a sacrament. At the very beginning of the church there was no specially consecrated group of persons to whom ministry within the church was entrusted.

There were special roles—teaching, prophecy, healing, etc.—that individuals exercised because of special gifts (charisms) of the Spirit, and there was a very special role of witness exercised by those, particularly the twelve, who had been immediate disciples of Jesus himself, but these roles were in no way limited to "officials" within the community. Very quickly, because the order and stability of the communities required it, some Christians came to occupy positions of permanent leadership. For more than a hundred years the pattern of each community having a bishop along with presbyters and deacons was not yet universal, but it became so by the third century.

As this "official" group became more prominent, three things happened. 1) They gradually took over the various ministries that had been relatively autonomous in earlier decades, absorbing them all into "the pastoral office," which was possessed fully only by the bishops. 2) The roles of "witnessing" and "governing" coalesced, because it was the bishops governing the church who were recognized as successors to the witness of the twelve. 3) These bishops, and to a lesser extent other ordained individuals like presbyters and deacons, came to be viewed as "sacred." Contrary to the practice and outlook of earliest Christianity, the bishops were now called "priest."

Quite rapidly, this official and consecrated leadership became distinct from the rest of the Christian people; they soon developed into a group with special responsibility for the church, and with special prestige, power, and privilege within the church. As "clergy" they became distinguished from "laity." Within this group itself there was a certain hierarchical arrangement of power and authority. The highest level or "order" was that of the bishops, next was the order of presbyters, next the order of deacons, etc. Together they formed the sacred orders whose existence and activity signified to the rest of the church the ministering presence of God; they were the sacrament of holy orders. As sacrament they not only signified, they signified effectively. They were the mediators through whom God worked to "give grace" to the rest of the faithful.

From very early times, this leadership of the church was recognized and set apart, that is, ordained, in a special liturgy. The early third-century *Apostolic Tradition* of Hippolytus contains a detailed description of such a liturgy, but we know that some form of public designation existed long before that. And for centuries the approval of two groups was required for this ordination: 1) The ordained was approved by the community involved, for example, the Christians of Rome or Corinth, and 2) he was approved by the pastoral group he was joining—a new presbyter by the local presbyterate, a bishop by the bishops of the region. Gradually, the communities of lay people lost a voice in the selection of their pastors.

Somewhere around the beginning of the second Christian millennium, a major shift occurred in the understanding of this liturgy and of its effect. Earlier centuries had seen the sacramental liturgy as an empowering for effective leadership of the community. This implied, of course, the power to do what the community required, eucharistic celebration, baptizings, preaching, etc. In the medieval period there developed a new approach to empowerment. Ordination was now seen to give the ordained the power to transubstantiate the bread and wine in eucharist and the power to absolve sins, though, as we saw, there was some question about the meaning of the second power. From that time until the present, such liturgical empowerment has been seen as the principal sacramental effect of ordination.

At just about the same time as this shift, theologians began to reflect on the church's sacramental activity. What was a sacrament? How many sacraments were there? What did sacraments effect and how was this effect brought about? How were faith and sacrament related to each other? What was the role of the church, of God, of the ordained celebrant in sacramental acts? The very wording of their questions indicated that the term "sacrament" was being applied ever more narrowly to a certain number of liturgical ceremonies. Before long, "sacrament" was reserved for seven of these. The basic sacramentality of Christian life we have been describing in this book was no longer considered intrinsic to the sacraments. Rather, this broader reality was described as the *preparation* for and in some cases the *condition* of "fruitful" sacramental actions. The "giving of grace" occurred only through the sacramental action itself in which God used the activity of the ordained sacramental minister to confer grace on the faithful. Ordained ministers administered sacraments; the faithful received sacraments. Providing sacraments for people was the principal responsibility of the ordained, particularly ordained presbyters.

Re-Emergence of the Laity

Although the viewpoint and practice we have just described are still prominent in many portions of the church, they are being rapidly replaced by a broader understanding of Christian ministry and leadership and by an expanded view of Christian sacrament. Ministry is no longer being restricted to an official group of ordained clerics; it is no longer seen as belonging exclusively to the episcopacy and to those delegated by the episcopacy. Sacraments are now being seen as something Christians do rather than occasions when something is done to them.

Central to this development is the increasing prominence of the laity in the life of the church. Much of this re-emergence of the laity can be traced in successive Catholic movements in the twentieth century: the growth of the Catholic Action movement between the two world wars; the rapid expansion of the Jocist movement (Young Christian Workers) in Europe and North America; the shift after World War II from "Catholic Action" to "Apostolate of the Laity," with implications of greater lay initiative; and most recently the "base communities," prominent in but not limited to Latin America and Africa. Very significantly, the last of these, the "base communities, " are not just a manifestation of increased lay involvement in the church; they no longer honor the lay/cleric distinction; they are a new and promising form of church order.

There has been a parallel and less easily documented happening. Especially in the period after World War II, a number of relatively autonomous ministries have emerged among Christians. Without official mandate, often without much official notice, Christian men and women have been helping one another within the church and others outside by their teaching, healing, reconciling, counseling, and shared prayer. They have, by and large, not thought of themselves as performing Christian ministries because they were neither clerical nor ordained, but what they were doing was ministering as Christians. Much as in earliest Christianity, such activity has been a response to the needs of people, a response rooted in the impulse of Christ's Spirit.

As a result, we now see Christian ministry as a range of activities, all of them springing from Christian faith and concern for people, all of them contributing to the establishment of the kingdom of God, some of them but by no means all contributing to the internal betterment of the Christian community itself, some of them carried out in an "official" context but more and more of them undertaken by men and women, regardless of status, because they recognize their responsibility as Christians to work for a better church and a better world. All such ministry is sacrament; it is the broader reality of sacrament of which the service of ordained officials is a part.

Impact of Vatican II

Much of the movement toward greater lay participation in the life of the church found support and validation at the Second Vatican Council. Perhaps most critical was the "new" emphasis on the church as being the entire people. (For centuries "the church" tended to designate the higher clergy.) Moreover, the entire community was described by the council as prophetic and priestly. One of the chapters of the *Dogmatic Constitution on the Church* spoke of the "universal call to holiness," reversing the previous view that only those with a special vocation were called to holiness. While the council did little to diminish the prerogatives of the clergy or the distinction between clergy and laity, it did open the door to fuller participation of lay women and men in the activity of the church's life.

No previous council of the church had produced a document comparable to Vatican II's *Pastoral Constitution on the Church in the Modern World,* an outline for Catholic involvement in all the various dimensions of contemporary life. Economic development, political activity, marriage and family life, medical-moral issues, war and peace, cultural evolution—all were described as important fields of Christian ministry to the modern world. And most of them obviously concerned the Christian activity of non-clerics. Such ministries were to be undertaken not in fulfillment of some mandate from church leaders, but as the normal response of mature Christian faith to the promise and problems of the age.

Much of this could support the contention that there are two realms of ministry in which Christians can and should devote themselves: the "secular world" of ordinary human life and experience in which the laity should be active, and the "sphere of the sacred or spiritual" in which the clergy should minister. Lay people should leave to the ordained clergy the care, or at the very least the direction of the care, of the internal well-being of the Christian community—such things as liturgy, religious education, governance of parish or diocesan life, ecumenical relations. On the other hand, the ordained should confine their activities to this spiritual realm; they should not take active part in politics of any of the other sectors of life in which laity more properly represent the church. The council does not support such a dichotomy of ministry.

While Vatican II certainly envisages lay people as the ones who would minister ordinarily to the needs of people "in the world," it does not see such needs as purely "secular," nor does it deny the cleric's responsibilities of citizenship and membership in a given social and cultural community. More importantly, as the *Constitution on the Sacred Liturgy* indicates, lay persons have both the right and responsibility to participate in the most spiritual and "sacred" of ministries, the creation of relevant liturgy, even eucharistic liturgy. What the council seems to hint at, and more recent events have indicated even more clearly, is that we are moving beyond cooperation of clergy and laity toward a true community ministry in which distinctive and complementary functions will be exercised on no other basis than people's ability to do what is needed.

With the Second Vatican Council, the Catholic church has definitely moved beyond official mandate as the ground for lay ministry. Though not using the language of "charism addressed to need," the council documents are grounded in theological insights that lead to a justification for any Christian, cleric or lay, undertaking a given ministry. Since (as the council more than once states) the Spirit of Christ, the source of Jesus' own ministry and therefore of the ministry of any of his disciples, abides in the Christian people as source of its life and activity, both the motivation and the empowerment to minister must be the gift of the Spirit.

After the council, and even more so after the post-conciliar expansion of lay involvement in various ministries, we are faced with new questions about a liturgy (or liturgies) of ordination. As we continue our present ordination practice, what are we ordaining these young men for? What precise ministry is envisaged by the liturgy and by the celebrant bishops and ordinands who participate in it? Should we devise other ordination rituals to provide some community recognition of and validation for the other ministries that people are exercising? It is too early to answer such questions, and the response will have to be a combination of learning from experience and from historical and theological study.

Christian Ministry as Sacrament

If we reflect on the manner ordained ministers actually functioned for centuries as a sacrament within the life of the church, apart from any theological recognition of that fact, we discover that this group was a continuing revelation of God's saving work in human life. Their service to the Christian people was a sign of the divine saving activity that worked through them. Moreover, the service performed by any given pastor was also sacramental of the saving intent and concern of the larger church. Even though the language of theology and doctrine narrowed the meaning of the word "sacrament" to the ordination liturgy, the existence and activity of the ordained continued to function sacramentally as a symbol of salvation.

Today, this is true also of the expanded phenomenon of Christians ministering to people in various ways. The concern and ministration of these people, whether lay or clerical, proclaims and makes present in human lives the saving power of God's Word and Spirit. Such ministries declare that this God, who continues to send his own Son into the world with the transforming power of resurrection, wishes humans to live, and to live more fully. This declaration is made practically, by human lives actually coming to greater fulfillment through Christian ministry; it is therefore a credible witness to God.

Most important and most significant in Christians' ministry is their gift of themselves to others. As we saw earlier in greater detail, this gift is what we humans most need from one another; this is what can help us gain dignity and positive self-identity, and nurture our growth as persons. In being for others in this way, Christians sacramentalize the mystery of God's own self-giving in love. This self-gift is God's action of creation and salvation. The most profound level of Christian ministry is its sacramental giving of God to people.

Summary

One of the most basic shifts occurring in Christian sacraments today is the emergence of lay involvement in a number of ministries previously thought to be reserved to the ordained clergy. Through most of Christian history, ministry was identified with the clergy's pastoral concern for the faithful. Because the empowerment for such "sacred tasks" as the consecration of the elements in eucharist and the absolution of sins came with the liturgy of ordination, this ritual has long been identified as "the sacrament of holy orders."

Although the need for some specially designated ministers remains, there is today a widespread activity of lay people that is truly Christian ministry, a ministry that functions at its deepest levels in sacramental fashion. This has forced us to broaden our view of that area of Christian sacramentality that we called "holy orders."

Questions for Reflection and Discussion

1. How is the distinctiveness of Christian ministry linked with its sacramentality?

2. What kind of empowerment has been associated with the sacramental liturgy of ordination?

3. Describe Vatican II's impact on the re-emergence of lay people in the life of the church.

4. Is it realistic to say that Christians' self-gift to people is their most important ministry? Explain.

5. How are holy orders and ministry related?

21

CONCLUSION: SACRAMENTAL GRACE

Any discussion of sacrament is automatically a discussion of human salvation; any discussion of Christian sacrament deals with the manner salvation is accomplished through the life, death, and resurrection of Jesus. When we use the term "salvation" we think, of course, of that ultimate destiny which is the final goal of human life, the goal we sometimes call "heaven," or to use Jesus' term, "unending life." We are referring, or should be referring, to God's influence upon our personal growth toward that final goal; God is saving us in the midst of our saving ourselves, which is our becoming mature persons capable of unending personal life. The divine saving action makes possible our personal maturing.

A word we often use to refer to this special divine influence is "grace," although it has had many meanings and is often used ambiguously. As we have already indicated and will explain more fully in a moment, the reality of grace deals with God's self-gift to humans. This unexpected and undeserved gift of divine friendship transforms and heals the experience and the lives of people, and invites them toward new life. Clearly, such transformation and healing by grace is related to what we have been saying about sacraments; Catholic teaching has expressed this relation by saying that "sacraments give grace." It has also talked about the transformation effected in sacraments as "sacramental grace."

By way of conclusion, then, to our study of Christian sacraments, we might see how sacramental grace results from the sacramental activity of Christians. Our first step, however, must be some preliminary clarification of the term "grace." Traditionally, "grace" was described as either "sanctifying grace" or "actual grace," the former being the re-orientation and elevation of our basic human nature and the latter being the special assistance given our moral actions. Clearly, if there is some transformation of our human life, it must affect both our being and our activity; but the way we thought about this transformation, and therefore the way we used the terms "sanctifying grace" and "actual grace" was controlled by our model for thinking about God's influence on human life.

Models for Grace

For many centuries the dominant model for thinking about the world and about God's impact on it was hierarchical. Reality was arranged like a ladder, with God at the top and acting through intermediate rungs on lower portions of the ladder. In the "giving of grace," God worked through the intermediate agency of ordained ministers and especially through their "administration of sacraments" in giving grace to the faithful. Since in such a model God is imagined as working upon people from outside, as sending down help from above, the emphasis was placed on "actual grace." This was the added "illumination" of the mind and the added "impetus" to the will that were available to people in situations of moral choice. With such added help, a person was capable of meeting temptation and of making morally good choices; without such help one could not over an extended period avoid sinning.

There were difficulties with this view of grace, difficulties that led to centuries of bitter dispute about "predestined grace," "grace and free will," "efficacious and non-efficacious grace." Such disputes need not delay us here, since they have been outdated by more recent theology. What concerns us here is the way "sacramental grace" was understood in that context. Theologians and religious teachers continued to say that sanctifying grace was somehow increased on the occasion of sacramental celebration and that this additional sanctifying grace was the more important effect of the liturgical act. Yet, emphasis tended to be placed on the gift or the promise of actual graces. For example, a married couple on the occasion of their wedding were thought to receive "in escrow" the actual graces they would need to handle the temptations that would assail them in the years of their life together; a young man on the day of his ordination would likewise receive the promise of those graces needed to carry out faithfully his role in the church. God either acted upon Christians "from outside" by giving them grace through the sacramental actions of the ordained celebrants, or later on gave such grace "from outside" because of what had been promised in sacramental liturgy.

Today we are questioning the accuracy of such a hierarchical model. Instead, we are returning to the model of life that dominated the imagination of the biblical authors and, as reflected in his parables, the imagination of Jesus himself. Though we may use instances of biological life as metaphors to describe the life of grace, for example, a mustard seed that grows into a large bush, the life we are dealing with is human life, the life of thought, love, and freedom we have as persons.

While God in creative power sustains the existence of human life, the influence that helps this personal life to grow comes by the divine self-gift. And while God is distinct from us, the reality of divine self-giving happens within our consciousness through God's presence to each of us. God does not stand outside us and send graces to us; God dwells within us personally as a lover in the awareness of the beloved. God is "grace," the great grace, uncreated grace.

If one uses this model to think about God's saving action, there is no need to think of God giving "actual graces" from time to time as we need them; nor is "sanctifying grace" something that we increasingly accumulate through faithful reception of sacraments. God, rather, given for us and dwelling with us, brings forth depths of personal growth that would not otherwise be possible. This divine friend's loving presence provides ultimate hope and support as we encounter the difficulties, decisions, and sufferings of life. The reality of this relationship, as we increasingly accept it, provides a wisdom to guide us in the important decisions that shape our personhood and destiny.

In such a model of thought and imagination it is truly appropriate to speak of "growth in grace." This is the growth of life that coincides with our growth into human maturity. Growing in grace means growing in insight, freedom, self-assurance, love, and joy; it means growing more vital as a person, often despite the debilitation of sickness or old age. Growth in grace, however, is more than just ordinary human development; Christians believe that it is a growth "into Christ," a deepening friendship with the risen Lord that itself leads to increasing personal relatedness to God and increasing personal transformation, that is, growth in the life of grace.

Transformed Experience

But where and how does such meeting with God, such growth in grace, happen? We saw that this occurs in and through human experience. The concrete reality of existing humanly is the sequence of experiences that makes up the lifetime of each of us. Although we are not exactly our experience, for us to exist as human means to experience. Central to our experience are the meanings that various happenings have for us. Occurrences can be more or less significant, and can be significant in many different ways. Awareness of the presence of a loving God gives a new and transforming meaning to all these occurrences; they become graced happenings.

To a greater or lesser degree, we humans "impose" a meaning on happenings; we interpret a happening according to our expectations, desires, or cultural formation, and we experience it according to that interpretation, even if it is a false interpretation. For that reason, it is essential, as we have insisted, that people develop an accurate hermeneutic of experience, an attitude to life, an approach to reality, a set of understandings, values, and convictions that leads a person to interpret what happens to him or her in a relatively objective way. Nothing so radically modifies one's hermeneutic of experience, so basically changes the way one views and reacts to life, as does the presence of God as revealed in Jesus. This is the grace that transforms our experience and our being as persons.

Jesus, the Basic Sacrament

Awareness of such divine transforming presence can come, however, only through God's "intrusion" into human history. Human thought and imagination, no matter how profound or creative, could never by themselves conceive the possibility of a truly transcendent God relating to humans in friendship. Christians believe that such a personal "intrusion" has happened and that it came to full expression in Jesus of Nazareth, who in death and resurrection becomes Messiah and Lord and is revealed as God's own Son and Word. As such, Jesus is the privileged instance of divine presence to a human; his is the completely graced experience that is the paradigm for our own. He is God's "parable"; he is the sacrament of God's saving presence in human history.

It is not just a matter of divine power working in and through Jesus. Jesus' own experience of God as his Abba reveals to us who this ultimate reality is. The impact of this intimate experience of this Abba on his entire life experience, including his death and resurrection, reveals to us how life's meaning is transformed by God's loving self-gift. Through this revelation that occurs in Jesus as Word and sacrament of his Abba, the divine personal presence can come to us. Through Jesus as Word and sacrament, God shares with us the creative grace of his own Spirit. God acts sacramentally to transform human life, to make it a "graced" reality. In this mysterious self-giving, God is "uncreated grace"; the resultant transformation of humans as persons "created grace." Since this transformation comes about sacramentally, we can also call it "sacramental grace."

Christians as Sacrament

Having passed beyond our sensible space-time context in his resurrection, Jesus is no longer able to function immediately as sacrament. Instead, he continues to act through the mediation of the Christian community, the church, which as his body is the sacrament in history of both the risen Christ and his Father. Through being a community of faith in the resurrection and through the various activities by which it expresses its discipleship, this community of people signifies the continuing saving presence of God in Word and Spirit.

By injecting the "Christ meaning" into the different spheres of human experience and involvement, Christian communities and individuals help change the significance of human life. They are a transforming influence; they are creative of a distinctive dimension of human history. Essentially, what they do is to unleash in human awareness a knowledge of Jesus' Abba, a knowledge that has power to revolutionize the meaning and the reality of human life, individual and social. To put it another way, these Christians introduce "uncreated grace" (that is, God in self-giving) into the lives of people, so that those lives can become increasingly transformed, increasingly "graced."

The Christian community proclaims this "Father of our Lord Jesus Christ" in many ways, but most basically by its own existence as a sacrament. By the intensity of its faith, this group of believers makes possible an intense presence of the transcendent God, a presence that can then manifestly transform the lives of these Christians as a sign to all the world of the loving power of God. Thus, by freely being "graced," the Christian people brings "grace," the personal transformation that results from the impact of God's saving presence, to the rest of humankind.

Sacramental Grace of Friendship

Because the years-long experience of a person is to a large extent interpreted by a relatively few key experiences, Christianizing the meaning of these key experiences changes the significance of our entire life. As we saw, this is precisely where Christian sacraments function "to give grace." But in explaining this, we found it necessary to expand our understanding of "sacrament" to include the traditional liturgies of sacrament, but to include also a broad range of Christian activity that is "sacrament" in the strict sense and without which the liturgical actions are irrelevant and ineffective.

Probably the most basic of these sacraments is human friendship. All human love is sacramental of the divine love, although Christian revelation, building on the prophetic insights of Israel, attaches a paradigmatic sacramentality to the love between husband and wife. The married couple are sacrament of the saving presence of God's love; they reveal the strangely paradoxical power of personal love to create individuality and community interdependently. They make credible the gospel that humans are truly loved by the transcendent.

Wife and husband are clearly "grace" for one another; their existence and their persons as individuals are transformed by becoming a new corporate person, a new co-existence, by becoming human and Christian and "graced" together. They are also "grace" to their children, with whom they share their faith in the loving presence of the risen Christ, "grace" to their fellow Christians as they witness to the possibility and desirability of true human community, "grace" to a world that needs its cynicism about human relationships transformed into real hope in personal fidelity.

"Grace" ultimately is a shared reality. Humans are meant to reach their destiny by becoming increasingly a community of persons; the full achievement of such community will be the eschatological kingdom of God. Christian marriages sacramentalize this communion. Christians are meant to experience this in their communities and to celebrate this in the sacramental liturgy of eucharist. In the eucharistic sharing of the body and blood of Christ, Christians are meant to be "graced" by Christ's self-gift, to be transformed as individuals and as a community, becoming increasingly body of Christ so that they can more effectively sacramentalize for others the grace of God's saving presence in their midst. By being a community of persons who love and care for one another, the church is meant to be a grace-causing sacrament for the transformation of the world.

Grace as Initiation

Entry into such a community is not something to be accomplished in one or two initiatory rituals, indispensable as such rituals may be. We saw that Christian initiation is a life-long process of growth: growth in knowledge of the gospel, growth in depth of conversion, growth in Christian self-identity, growth in discipleship, growth in commitment to Christian ministry, growth, above all, in personal relatedness to the risen Christ. Nothing less is involved than a process of developing into human maturity as a Christian.

Liturgically, this initiation includes the rituals of baptism, confirmation, and eucharist, but these are only the key experiences, the ritual moments, in the broader sacramental reality of being initiated into the mystery of Christ. Such liturgical actions are certainly intended to be specially transformative of people's outlook, attitudes, values, and self-understanding, that is, to be especially grace-giving, but the continuing lifelong experience of becoming Christian is grace-life growing toward its eschatological flowering.

Grace as Mission

Grace is the transformation of individuals and communities at the deepest levels of their being and meaning; it is also the transformation of their finality, their basic destiny. The creative power of the Spirit, by which God vitalizes people into new and risen life, directs and impels these persons to co-create that future. Grace is not just for the sake of the graced individual or community; it is given so that it can be communicated to others. Christians have no monopoly on the God they worship as Abba. Knowledge of that God is a privilege, but it is also a responsibility. The call to evangelization is intrinsic to Christian discipleship.

Grace as a life force expresses itself in service to others, in one or other form of ministry. Special gifts are given by Christ's Spirit to enable certain individuals to meet special needs; however, the more basic call to ministry flows from the life of grace itself. For a Christian to live in grace implies living in personal relationship with the risen Christ, which in turn implies identification with Christ in his continuing historical task of bringing human history to its destiny. This can include all the tasks of physical and psychological healing, all the teaching and preaching, all the reconciliation of people with themselves and others, all the social healing, all the confrontation with the forces of evil and sin we discussed in relation to Christian ministry. All this is most profoundly effective as it is sacramental, insofar as it signifies to people the healing presence of God in the risen Christ. Such Christian ministry transforms human life, that is, it causes grace, but it does so sacramentally.

Christian life is sacramental. It is an experience that is thoroughly different because it has been transformed in its significance by the life, death, and resurrection of Jesus, the Christ. But it expresses that transformed meaning so that it can be communicated to others. Christians as individuals and in community bear witness to the "grace" of God's self-gift, profess their faith in the saving presence of this gracious God, and embody as sacrament this grace-giving revelation.

Grace is the transformation of human persons under the impact of God's loving self-gift in Christ. This transformation comes about through the reinterpretation of life's experiences in the light of Jesus' life, death, and resurrection. Christian sacraments are those elements of Christians' life experience that mediate this reinterpretation and thereby transform human existence into new and unending life. Sacraments give grace.

Questions for Reflection and Discussion

1. Explain: The sacraments of Christianity deepen the human aspects of our lives.

2. How do sacraments "give grace"?

3. How is eucharist meant to contribute to Christians' growth in grace?

4. Explain how "transformation" is an appropriate way of describing grace. How do sacraments contribute to this transformation?

5. What is the sacramental role of Christ, of Christians, in this transformation of human experience?

BIBLIOGRAPHY

General Works

Worship magazine, published by Liturgical Press, is probably the best means of remaining in contact with current theological and pastoral writing on Christian sacraments.

Alternative Futures for Worship (B. Lee, ed.). Collegeville, Liturgical Press, 1987. Multi-volume treatment of the sacramental liturgies from sociological and theological perspectives, with suggestions for revision of present rituals.

Bausch. W. *A New Look at the Sacraments*, rev. ed. Mystic, Conn.: Twenty-Third Publications, 1983. Popular and helpful explanation, historical and theological, of the various sacraments.

Cooke, B., *Christian Sacraments and Christian Personality*. New York: Holt, Rinehart, Winston, 1965. Chapters on Christian initiation and on the eucharist are still up to date.

Fiorenza F. and J. Galvin, *Systematic Theology*. Minneapolis: Fortress Press, 1991. The latter half of vol. 2 is devoted to treatment of sacraments.

Guzie, Tad. *The Book of Sacramental Basics*. Mahwah, N.J.: Paulist Press, 1982. A very readable explanation that situates sacraments in the context of people's lives.

Hellwig, M., ed. "Message of the Sacraments." Series of volumes published by M. Glazier Publishing in the 1970s and 1980s. Non-technical, but thorough and up-to-date explanations of Christian sacramental life.

Huebsch, W. *Rethinking Sacraments: Holy Moments in Daily Living*. Mystic, Conn.: Twenty-Third Publications, 1989. A practical look at sacramentality in daily life.

Martos, J. *Doors to the Sacred*. New York: Doubleday, 1981. Still one of the few historical studies of Christian sacraments.

Chapter 1

Fowler, J. *Stages of Faith: The Psychology of Human Development and the Quest for Meaning*. New York: Harper & Row, 1981. Building on recent developments in developmental psychology, Fowler describes the growth of faith.

Groome, T., *Sharing Faith*. San Francisco: Harper & Row, 1991. Creative method to prepare people for religious education or pastoral ministry.

Johann, R. *Building the Human*. New York: Seabury Press, 1968. Still one of the clearest explanations of what "human" means and how human development can be achieved.

May, R. *Love and Will*. New York: Dell, 1973. A "golden oldie." Provides psychological underpinnings for a theological anthropology.

Miller, J. Baker. *Towards a New Psychology of Women*. Boston: Beacon Press, 1986 (2nd ed.). A basic challenge to Freudian models of personal development; stresses the reinforcement of relational activity.

Chapter 2

Frankl, V. *Man's Search for Meaning*. New York: Simon and Schuster, 1970. A personal witness to human need for meaning, written out of his concentration camp experience.

Leonard E. "Experience as a Source for Theology," *CTSA Proceedings* 43 (1988),

233

pp. 44-61. Good introduction to the shift in theological method.

Maslow, A. *Religion, Values and Peak Experience*. New York: Penguin Books, 1976. Classic study on the role of "peak experience."

Chapter 3

Barbour, I. *Myths, Models, and Paradigms*. New York: Harper & Row, 1976 and *Religion in an Age of Science*. San Francisco: Harper & Row, 1990. Both a scientist and theologian, Barbour has unusual ability to explain the use of myths and images in human knowing.

Dulles, A. *Models of the Church*. New York: Doubleday, 1978. Classic book on application of "models" to understanding of the church.

McFague, S. *Models of God*. Philadelphia: Fortress Press, 1987. Feminist application of "models" to the understanding of God.

Shea, J. *Stories of God: An Unauthorized Biography*. Chicago: Thomas More Assoc., 1978. Himself a master storyteller, Shea explains how story (myth) functions to interpret religious reality.

Chapter 4

Duncan H. *Symbols in Society*. New York: Oxford University Press, 1968. One of the pioneering studies of the social function of symbols.

Firth, R. *Symbols, Public and Private*. Ithaca, N.Y.: Cornell University Press, 1973. Systematic analysis of symbols' social and individual effectiveness.

Schoonenberg, P. "Presence of the Eucharistic Presence." *Cross Currents* 17 (1967), pp. 39-54. Deals specifically with eucharistic presence, but discusses also the basic reality of personal presence.

Terrien. S. *The Elusive Presence*. New York: Harper & Row, 1973. A synthesis of biblical thought from the point of view of God's presence to humans.

Chapter 5

Cooke, B. *God's Beloved*. Philadelphia: Trinity Press International, 1993. Study of Jesus' religious consciousness with a focus on the "Abba experience" as root of Jesus sacramentality.

Jeremias, J. *New Testament Theology*. New York: Charles Scribner's Sons, 1971. Drawing from his earlier studies of Jesus' "Abba experience," Jeremias focuses his treatment of New Testament theology on Jesus' prophetic activity.

Schillebeeckx, E. His two volumes *Jesus* (1979) and *Christ* (1980), New York: Crossroad, probe at length Jesus' historical role in Christianity's origins. His earlier *Christ, the Sacrament of the Encounter with God* is generally recognized as one of the seminal books in recent christology.

Senior, D., K. Osborne (F. Eigo, ed.). *The Sacraments: God's Love and Mercy Actualized*. Philadelphia, Villanova University Press, 1979. Essays dealing with Jesus' relation to the Christian sacraments.

Chapter 6

Brown, R. *The Community of the Beloved Disciple*. Mahwah, N.J.: Paulist Press, 1979. A clear, imaginative presentation of the manner in which one section of early Christianity actually developed in the earliest decades.

Fahey, M. "The Contemporary Context of Ecclesiology," *Systematic Theology* (eds. F. Fiorenza and J. Galvin). Minneapolis: Fortress Press, vol. 2, pp. 4-74. An approach to ecclesiology that honors the principle of starting from the actual experience of today's church. Notre Dame, Ind.: University of Notre Dame Press, 1963. A collection of essays studying various aspects of the church as Christ's body.

Rahner, K. *The Church and the Sacraments.* New York: Herder and Herder, 1963. Classic explanation of the church's role of sacramentalizing God's saving presence in history.

Chapter 7

Hart, T. *Living Happily Ever After: Towards a Theology of Christian Marriage.* Mahwah, N.J.: Paulist Press, 1979. Combines theological and psychological insights into a balanced study of marriage as a human and Christian reality.

Mackin, T. *What Is Marriage? Marriage in the Catholic Church.* Mahwah, N.J.: Paulist Press, 1982. Historical and theological study of Catholic marriage, probably the most comprehensive to date.

Roberts, W. *Marriage: The Hope and the Challenge.* Cincinnati: St. Anthony Messinger Press, 1983. Practical and probing reflection on the nurture of Christian marriage and family life.

Thomas D. *Christian Marriage, A Journey Together.* Wilmington: Glazier, 1983. Popular treatment of marriage as an evolving process.

Chapter 8

Emminghaus, J. *The Eucharist.* Collegeville, Minn.: Liturgical Press, 1978. Representative of post-Vatican II Catholic systematic theology of eucharist.

The Jurist 36:1/2 (1976). A special issue containing several essays on the topic of the church as *communio.*

Tillard, J. *The Eucharist.* Staten Island, N.Y.: Alba House, 1966. Detailed theological study of eucharist's role in building up the church in history.

Chapter 9

Cooke, B. *Christian Sacraments and Christian Personality.* New York: Holt, Rinehart, Winston, 1965. A lengthier explanation of eucharist as "sacrifice" is contained in Chapter 8.

Durrwell, F.X. *The Resurrection.* New York: Sheed and Ward, 1960. Pioneered the understanding of Christ's death and resurrection that underpins more recent insights into eucharistic action.

Power, D. "Words That Crack: The Use of 'Sacrifice' in Eucharistic Discourse," *Worship* 53 (1979), pp. 386-404. Studies the relation between the offering of Christ and that of the community. Power provides a more detailed and technical study of "sacrifice" in his 1987 book, *The Sacrifice We Offer.* New York: Crossroad.

Chapter 10

Ganoczy, A. *Becoming Christian: A Theology of Baptism as the Sacrament of Human History.* Mahwah, N.J.: Paulist Press, 1976. Situates Christian baptism in the process of developing human freedom and maturity.

National Council of Catholic Bishops. *Rite of Christian Initiation of Adults.* Washington, D.C.: 1988. Official U.S. text of the new ritual, with brief but helpful commentary.

Searle, M. *Christening: The Making of Christians.* Collegeville, Minn.: Liturgical Press, 1980. Excellent pastoral guide to catechesis on the process of initiation.

Wagner, J. Baptism and the Catechumenate (Concilium Series, 22). New York: Paulist Press, 1967. Contains several essays on the revised rite of initiation.

Chapter 11

The Jurist 39:1/2 (1979). A special issue containing the papers from the Canon Law Society's continuing seminar on the church as mission.

Küng, H. *On Being a Christian.* New York: Doubleday, 1976. Widely influential explanation of what it means to be a Christian; lengthy but worth the effort.

Schelkie, D. *Discipleship and Priesthood.* New York: Herder and Herder, 1965. Study of the biblical understanding of Christian discipleship; a good scholarly complement to Bonhoeffer's *The Cost of Discipleship* (New York: Macmillan, 1949).

Chapter 12

Kavanagh, A. *The Shape of Baptism.* New York: Pueblo, 1978. Excellent guide to understanding the recent revision of Catholic initiation rites.

Osborne, K. *The Christian Sacraments of Initiation.* New York: Paulist Press, 1987. Situates the liturgies of baptism and confirmation within the process of Christian initiation.

"The Holy Spirit and Confirmation," a special issue of *Lumen Vitae* (1973), containing a wide range of articles on confirmation.

Chapter 13

Cooke, B. "Sacraments as Continuing Acts of Christ," Proceedings of the Catholic Theological Society of America (1961), pp. 43-68.

New Catholic World, January/February 1982. Devoted to several articles on Christian discipleship that stress Christian involvement in society.

Seasoltz, K., ed. *Living Bread, Saving Cup.* Collegeville, Minn.: Liturgical Press, rev. ed. 1987. Collection of essays originally appearing in Worship that discuss a range of topics regarding Eucharist.

Chapter 14

Benoit, P. and R. Murphy, eds. *The Breaking of Bread.* 1969 volume of Concilium reviewing current contribution of scriptural studies to eucharistic theology.

Conn, W. *Christian Conversion.* New York: Paulist Press, 1986. Building on his earlier volumes Conscience (1981) and Conversion (1978), the author draws from developmental psychology, the theology of Bernard Lonergan and the spiritual career of Thomas Merton to illumine the phenomenon of Christian conversion.

Cooke, B. "Synoptic Presentation of the Eucharist as Covenant Sacrifice," *Theological Studies* 21 (1960), pp. 1-44. Study of the gospel description of the supper as covenant action.

Chapter 15

Cooke, M. *The Jesus of Faith.* New York: Paulist Press, 1982. Presentation of Jesus' life and work, examined in comparison with several present-day studies of Jesus' ministry.

Dunn, J. *Jesus and the Spirit.* Philadelphia: Westminster Press, 1979. Study of N.T. theology of the Spirit's role in Jesus' ministry.

Sobrino, J. *Christology at the Crossroads.* Maryknoll, N.Y.: Orbis Books, 1978. Study of the life and ministry of Jesus from the perspective of Latin American liberation theology.

Chapter 16

Knauber, A. *Pastoral Theology of the Anointing of the Sick.* Collegeville, Minn.:

Liturgical Press, 1975. A theological commentary on the new rite of anointing.

Laurentin, R. *Liberation, Development and Salvation*. Maryknoll, N.Y.: Orbis Books, 1972. Exploration of the link between social development and human salvation, drawn from the experience of Latin American Christianity.

Paul VI. *Progress of Peoples* (Populorum Progressio, 1967). This encyclical is an excellent summary of the international social justice issues that affect human development.

Chapter 17

Cooke, B. *Reconciled Sinners*. Mystic, Conn.: Twenty-Third Publications, 1986. Popular presentation of current re-appraisal of sin and forgiveness of sin.

Curran, C. and R. McCormick, eds. *Moral Norms and Catholic Tradition*. New York: Paulist Press, 1979. Collection of essays that situate current moral reflection in the mainstream of Catholic ethical teaching.

Durken, D., ed. *Sin, Salvation, and the Spirit*. Collegeville, Minn.: Liturgical Press, 1979. Contemporary essays on biblical understandings of human sin and redemption.

Taylor, M., ed. *The Mystery of Sin and Forgiveness*. Staten Island, N.Y.: Alba House, 1971. Collection of essays on changing view of sin and reconciliation.

Chapter 18

Haring, B. *Free and Faithful in Christ*, 3 vols. New York: Crossroad, 1978-81. Compendious discussion of Catholic position on current moral issues.

Hellwig, M. *Sign of Reconciliation and Conversion*. Wilmington: Glazier, 1982. Excellent presentation of current Catholic theology about sin and reconciliation.

Orsy, L. *The Evolving Church and the Sacrament of Penance*. Denville, N.J.: Dimension Books, 1978. Studies briefly the historical evolution of penance and the modern shifts in understanding linked with the new rite.

Chapter 19

The Rite of Penance, Commentaries, 3 vols. Washington, D.C.: Liturgical Conference, 1975-78. Excellent explanation of the new rite, its content and background, by leading liturgical scholars.

Dallen, J. *The Reconciling Community*. New York: Pueblo, 1986. The most complete discussion of the ritual of reconciliation, its history, present shape, and theological explanation.

Osborne, K., et al. *The Renewal of the Sacrament of Penance*. New York: Catholic Theological Society of America, 1975. A committee report of the CTSA that studies present challenges and makes recommendations for future development.

Schillebeeckx, E. ed. *Sacramental Reconciliation*. 1971 volume of Concilium. Theological and historical essays on penance and reconciliation.

Chapter 20

Bausch, W. *Traditions, Tensions, Transitions in Ministry*. Mystic, Conn.: Twenty-Third Publications, 1982. Stimulating and practical reflections by a pastor engaged in cooperative ministry with his parishioners.

Bernier, P. *Ministry in the Church*. Mystic, Conn.: Twenty-Third Publications, 1993. Careful survey of the history of Christian ministry, with a special concentration on Vatican II's approach to the presbyterate.

Osborne, K. *Ministry: Non-Ordained Ministry in the Catholic Church*. Mahwah,

N.J.: Paulist Press, 1993. A history of lay ministry that complements his earlier (1989) *Priesthood: A History of Ordained Ministry in the Roman Catholic Church.*

Rademacher, W. *Lay Ministry.* New York: Crossroad, 1991. Studies the theological, spiritual, and pastoral aspects of lay ministry.

Whitehead, E., ed. *The Parish in Community and Ministry.* New York: Paulist Press, 1978. Examines the new role of the parish in the changing pattern of ministry.

INDEX

anointing, sacrament of, 184-186

baptism
   entry into Christ, 143-145
   entry into community, 123, 138-139
   infant, 121-122, 141-143
   initiation into Christian vision, 124-127
   profession of faith, 141
   rituals of, 138-145
   sharing Christian identity, 130-132
   sharing Christian mission, 127-128, 137
   sharing Christian myth, 125-128
   sharing Christ's Spirit, 132-133
   sharing Christian values, 129-130, 139-141
body, symbolism of, 54
body of Christ (*see* church)

celebration
   as hermeneutic, 39-41
   role of, 39-43
Christian community, sacrament of healing, 205-206
church
   body of Christ, 71-73, 106-107
   institution of, 69-71
   sacrament of Christ, 71-76
communio
   eucharist as, 100-107
   initiation as, 124
confirmation, 145-148
conscience
   discernment of Spirit, 163-165
   eucharist as formation of, 162-163
   formation of, 120, 160-162
   nature of, 161-162
conversion, 135-136

death, experience of, 23-24

discipleship, 68
   discovery of, 152-154
   initiation into, 130-132
   sacrament of Christ's presence, 68-69, 94-100

eucharist
   as storytelling, 151-152
   covenant sacrifice, 108-113
   growth into Christ, 156-158
   homily as sharing, 104-105
   human action, 102-103
   initiation into freedom, 163-165
   meeting of gospel and life, 154-156
   origins of, 101-102
eucharistic prayer, 105-106
evil, 14
ex opere operato, 8
experience, 15-17
   interpretation of, 16-17

faith, 68
forgiveness of sin, 187-194 (*see also* reconciliation)
   forgiving one another, 190-192
   forgiving oneself, 189-190
freedom, 13-14
friendship
   revelation of God, 80-85
   sacramentality of, 84-85
   significance of, 25-27

grace, 79-80
   as mission, 230-231
   as transformation, 79-80, 227, 230-231
   created, uncreated, 79-80
   initiation into, 230
   models for, 225-227
   sacramental, 224-231

healing (*see also* reconciliation)
   as Christian ministry, 180-184

239